Company Law in Ireland
Second Edition

GW00645367

Company Law in Ireland
Second Edition

By
Anthony Thuillier

Published by
Clarus Press Ltd,
Griffith Campus,
South Circular Road,
Dublin 8.

Typeset by
Deanta Global Publishing Services

Printed by
Sprint Print, Dublin

ISBN
978-1-905536-75-7

PREFACE

The Companies Act 2014 was commenced on 1 June 2015. It is a consolidation—with some amendments—of all existing company law in Ireland, the largest Act ever passed in the State, the outcome of years of analysis and planning by the Company Law Review Group. You might think: well that's company law settled, for a while at least. But the law never sits still and barely a month had gone by before the Supreme Court decided in *Re JD Brian* (9 July 2015) that the section which deals with the order of priorities in liquidations—s 621(7)—needed to be amended.

This book deals with the law as it now is for private companies limited by shares, which make up approximately 85% of Irish registered companies. There are some references in the footnotes to section numbers in previous Acts, but not too many. Practitioners will recognise the familiar sections and students coming to company law for the first time will want to know what the law is, not what it was. For that reason, when quoting extracts of judgments, all of which deal with the old Acts, I have inserted relevant Companies Act 2014 section into the quotation, where it is no different to its previous incarnation. Innovations and amendments are always noted.

All previous Companies Acts are now replaced. Existing private limited companies are for the time being—until the end of the transition period, on 30 November 2016—governed by the rules that apply to the Designated Activity Company, as set out in Companies Act 2014. If an existing private company makes no move to convert to the new model LTD before then, it will be automatically converted to a new model LTD on 1 December 2016. Directors may wish to avail of the new, leaner LTD model before then (discussed in Chapter 1) and if so they can convert, free of charge, by sending the relevant forms to the CRO in Carlow (the N1 and G1 forms, the company's new constitution, a copy of the list of the original subscribers).

How much has changed? In large part, the Companies Act 2014 is a consolidation. In many respects the law is the same, but you have to learn anew where to find it. There are things that look new, but aren't really: directors' duties haven't changed, for example, but now they are set out in statute. The same can be said about the powers of receivers. There are things that are almost identical, so you have to know the bit that has changed: for example, in the protection of minorities only one thing has changed, but it is important—the court can now award compensation to oppressed parties. Practitioners should be particularly aware of the following changes, however: there is now a new system for registering charges (dealt with in Chapter 14) and that the rules in windings-up have been shaken up considerably, with the court's role being pared back in favour of greater creditor involvement. Also, the minimum threshold for indebtedness increased from €1,269.74 to €10,000.

I would like to thank Joanne Williams BL for her very valuable input into the part of Chapter 13 which discusses the criminal prosecution of company law offences. I would like to thank David McCartney for all his work in bringing this edition to publication and to repeat my thanks to all those whose help and influence I acknowledged in the preface to the first edition.

Anthony Thuillier BL
1 October 2015

PREFACE TO FIRST EDITION

When Ireland first began to feel some self-confidence in the 1960s, the legal spirit of the times was embodied by a Supreme Court which broke new ground in constitutional law; today the sprit of our times is captured by company law writ large. For someone trying to understand a large part of the daily news, no other subject is more crucial. The Ireland of the Companies Act 1963 — the last great reform and consolidation in the area — was a different place. Mr Justice Niall McCarthy, writing in 1990 from the Supreme Court bench, remembered what things were like a few years before that Act came into force:

> "In my early days of practice commercial litigation was a fairly rare bird in the High Court. The then President, Mr Justice Cahir Davitt, regularly sat in the morning merely to preside over adjournments or, indeed, the adjournment of the one case listed for that day or that week."

Company law is a rare bird no more. Since Mr Justice McCarthy's early years at the Bar, Ireland transformed from an agricultural republic to a republic of investment drives and an economy of "knowledge." When I started at the Bar the zeitgeist was bankruptcies, insolvencies, summary judgments and defective house cases. Flamboyant restaurateurs were being disqualified from acting as directors, property empires, as well as the State's largest telecommunications company, sought court protection and there was an exodus of Irish businesspeople to the UK, in search of a gentler bankruptcy regime. These kinds of stories, as well as many others, have been the news stories of the last five years. They all touch on some aspect of company law.

The subject doesn't have a reputation for being easy. As Ms Justice Finlay Geoghegan noted in her foreword, it has a reputation for being dry and technical. This doesn't have to be the case and what is different about the approach in this book is that it brings the people and situations involved in the cases to the fore, to make it easier to understand why the law is what it is. This is the method I use when lecturing and I have tried to keep the book as close to this style as possible. To give a few examples, you will find a family of Cork butchers who couldn't recover €26,719 from a bar and restaurant business in Waterford (separate legal personality); architects struggling to recover fees after they carried out work for a would-be property developer who did a runner on them (ostensible authority); directors who carried on trading, hoping for the best, but incurred trading losses of €2,810,675 and defrauded the Revenue in the process (directors' personal liability on insolvency); a woman and her children who refused to register a share transfer in favour of her ex-husband, who cheated on her with two women and had children with both (share transfer); a South African who came to Meath to run a Spar shop during the Celtic Tiger, but failed (fraudulent preferences); Donegal brothers who fell out, spiraled into "allegations and counter-allegations" and sought the assistance of the court in bringing the matter to an end (minority protection); and a liquidator who was "determined to screw the Revenue, no matter what it took" and to "blow up anyone who got in my way" (restriction and disqualification). So, I hope that if you are coming to the subject for the first time, or returning to it, this book will make your time with the subject not only a lot easier, but enjoyable too.

Finally, I should note that the largest reform of company law in the last five decades is on the way. The new Act, which merges all existing legislation, may be coming into force in 2015. It will have almost no impact on students until then, and for this reason the law dealt with in this book is the law as it is in the Companies Acts 1963 – 2012. The law is stated as at 31 July 2013 and the usual caveat — that any mistakes are mine, and no liability is accepted — applies.

I would like to thank Ms Justice Finlay Geoghegan for taking the time to read this book during the sunniest weeks of summer and for kindly agreeing to write the foreword. I would also like to thank Bernard Dunleavy BL, who started me off in company law, Ray Ryan BL, who generously gave me the time I needed to write the book, to David McCartney who gave me the opportunity to write it, and Val Corbett for getting the ball rolling. Thanks to my parents and my brothers, to all in Garryduff, and to Cathy, who stuck with me when I started to find company law provisions in the numbers of passing buses.

Anthony Thuillier BL
1 September 2013

CONTENTS

TABLE OF CASES

Table of Legislation

Constitutional Provisions

Bunreacht na hÉireann/Constitution of Ireland

Acts of the Oireachtas

Secondary Legislation

UK Legislation

EU Legislation

CHAPTER ONE

INTRODUCTION TO PRIVATE COMPANIES IN IRELAND

Different Ways of Doing Business

The most popular way of doing business in Ireland is through the medium of a private company limited by shares. To the non-practitioner, the best known kind of company is probably the Public Limited Company ("PLC"), a company which trades its shares on the stock market. Aer Lingus, AIB, Bank of Ireland, Diageo, Fyffes, Glanbia, Independent News and Media, Paddy Power, Ryanair: these are some of the well-known companies listed on the Irish Stock Exchange. But the PLC is not at all the most popular means of doing business in Ireland. In fact, PLCs account for no more than 1% of all registered companies in this country. One reason for this is that it is far easier to set up and run a *private* limited company than it is to set up and run a public limited company. To give four examples: a PLC must have an allotted share capital of at least €25,000 — with 25% of that fully paid up — before it can commence trading; a PLC must have a minimum of seven members; the transfer of shares in PLCs is heavily regulated to prevent market abuse; and a prospectus must be prepared in order to sell shares to members of the public.

A private limited company can commence trading with only €1 paid up share capital; it needs only one or two directors (depending on which kind of private company it is); it is very easy to transfer shares; there is no prospectus requirement. We shall see further reasons over the course of this book, and it will come as no surprise that more than 85% of companies registered with the Companies Registration Office ("CRO") are private limited companies.[1]

It should be noted that a registered company is not the only way of doing business. A person can trade as a sole trader and people can come together to form partnerships. A sole trader is a "natural person" (as opposed to a corporate person) who is "engaged in a trade, profession or business on his or her own account".[2] To give a few examples, barristers, farmers, GPs, vets, dentists may choose to conduct their business as sole traders. It is very easy to operate as a sole trader. There is very little "red tape" (some areas driving a taxi, running a pub, selling insurance — may require the trader to obtain a licence and others — doctor, barrister, etc — require

---

[1] There are over 185,000 companies registered in Ireland.
[2] Courtney, *Law of Companies* (3rd ed, (Bloomsbury, 2012) p 2.

qualifications). There is no obligation to file annual returns with any office. The profits of the business are yours. You are your own boss. But there are disadvantages: the debts of the business are yours; if you want to transfer property your stamp duty will be higher than if you were a company; and you might not be able to obtain as much finance as if you were a company.

A second way of doing business which does not involve incorporation is partnership. The Partnership Act 1890 defines a partnership as "the relation which subsists between persons carrying on business in common with a view to profit".[3] Partnerships are easy to start: each partner has an equal role in the management of the partnership; the profits can be kept confidential because there are no filing requirements. But again, there is the personal exposure: if you are in a partnership, the debts of the partnership belong to you personally. Where a registered company will continue to exist if a director leaves or dies, a partnership dissolves if one partner dies, or simply gives notice of his intention to dissolve it. Private companies can have up to 149 members; partnerships are limited to twenty partners.

Private limited companies are the most popular form of doing business for good reasons. The first is that if you become a member, you will never be liable for all of the debts of the company — the most you will have to pay in the event of a liquidation is the value of your shareholding. This might be as little as one or two euro. If you are a butcher or a farmer or a seller of trampolines — whatever your line of work — you can incorporate your business for a small fee (€50 if you send the documents to the CRO on-line). You can become a director and shareholder of your business. You will only need to pay for one share, and never any more than that if you don't want, and that one share can be worth a mere euro. You will need another person to act as company secretary (certain documents might require both the signature of the director and the secretary). You will have to pay for your accountant's fee each year, because you will need him or her to audit your books and file your annual returns. For these relatively small outlays you will be protected from the threat of personal liability for the debts of the company, as long as you act honestly and responsibly in your capacity as a director. The company has a *separate* legal personality to you. It may be easier to raise finance because you can offer a lending institute a kind of security which is open only to companies

---

[3] Partnership Act 1890, s 1.

(the "floating charge", dealt with in chapter 14). Your business will be subject to a lower tax regime. It will be easy to allocate shares, if you wish to involve family members in the business. The company can continue to exist after you resign as director and sell your shares: it has the certainty of continuity. This is an overview of the advantages. This book is not concerned with PLCs, sole traders, partnerships or unincorporated associations.[4] Its subject is the private limited company in Ireland.

LTD Versus DAC

The Companies Act 2014 was commenced on 1 June 2015. In 2015, around 85% of companies in Ireland were registered as "private companies limited by shares". The Act does something new in Irish company law. It splits the private limited company into two kinds. First, it provides for a reformed private company limited by shares (which will continue to be known by the shorthand "LTD"[5]). Reforms include endowing the LTD with the contractual capacity of a private person, giving it the ability to dispense with AGMs, providing that only one director is necessary, and providing for a simplified single-document "constitution" to replace the traditional memorandum of association and the articles of association. All existing private limited companies are automatically converted into the new model private limited company on 30 November 2016 unless they wish to remain as they are, in which case they must convert to a "Designated Activity Company" ("DAC").[6]

The key features of the new model private limited company are:

1. Only one director is required (but if it has only one director, someone else must be the secretary; if there are two directors, one director can be both director and secretary);
2. It has the same contractual capacity as a natural person;
3. AGMs can be dispensed with if all the shareholders agree to do so;
4. It has a simple, one document constitution;
5. It can pass ordinary and special resolutions using a written procedure (i.e. it does not need to hold a shareholders' meeting to do so).

---

[4] With regard to this latter, see *Dunne v Mahon* [2014] IESC 24 (Clarke J, 8 April 2014).
[5] It seems that at one stage the proposed shorthand was to be "the CLS", the private company limited by shares.
[6] The CRO is charging no fee for conversions. Companies Act 2014 provides for a 18 month transition period.

The Designated Activity Company: Introduction

There are two kinds of DAC: a private company limited by shares and a private company limited by guarantee.[7] Charities, management companies, companies incorporated for a specific purpose, companies limited by guarantee: these kinds of companies are the likely candidates for DAC status. Unlike the private new model private limited company, a DAC continues to have an objects clause, must have at least two directors, and cannot dispense with AGMs. A DAC is therefore referred to as a private company limited by shares or by guarantee which only has the capacity to do the acts or things set out in its constitution (i.e. memorandum and articles).[8] If a company is a DAC its name must end with "Designated Activity Company"[9] unless it qualifies for an exemption (for example, if it is a charity).[10] Existing private companies which wish to convert to DAC status should do so by 1 September 2015.[11] Until 1 December 2016 all existing private limited companies will be governed by the rules relating to DACs,[12] unless they choose to convert before then, in which case they will be governed by Parts 2 to 14 of Companies Act 2014.[13]

A DAC's memorandum of association and articles of association are together referred to as its "constitution".[14] A DAC's memorandum of association must state: (a) its name; (b) which type of DAC it is (a private

---

[7] Companies Act 2014, s 963. Practitioners should note that a DAC limited by guarantee is different from a company limited by guarantee, which is dealt with in Part 18 of the Act.

[8] Existing Private Guarantee companies are deemed to be DACs.

[9] Or "Cuideachta Ghníomhaíochta Ainmnithe", s 969.

[10] If the DAC's objects are the promotion of commerce, art, science, education, religion, and charity; if its constitution requires its profits (if any) or other income to be applied to the promotion of its objects and prohibits the making of distributions to its members — then the DAC will tend towards the exemption; see ss 971 and 1180.

[11] The CRO Form N2 should be used; if the transition period is missed, see s 57 of Companies Act 2014.

[12] Set out in Part 16 of Companies Act 2014.

[13] Companies Act 2014, s 59 provides that a company can submit a special resolution, a new model constitution and the Form N1 to the CRO and the Registrar will issue a new certificate of incorporation; s 60 of Companies Act 2014 allows the directors to submit the Form N1 with the new constitution to the CRO, as long as in advance of submission to the CRO the directors have sent a copy of a constitution to all members; s 61 of Companies Act 2014 says that where a private company has not converted to the new model LTD by 30 November 2016 the deeming provisions of the Act apply and the company becomes a new model LTD, the CRO issuing a new certificate of incorporation.

[14] Companies Act 2014, s 967.

company limited by shares, or a private company limited by guarantee, and having a share capital); (c) its objects; (d) that the liability of its members is limited; (e) in the case of a DAC limited by shares, the amount of share capital with which the DAC proposes to be registered and the division thereof into shares of a fixed amount; (f) in the case of a DAC limited by guarantee a statement of how much the members will contribute to the assets of the company if it is wound-up.[15]

Which Rules Govern DACs?

The provisions of Parts 1 to 14 of CA 2014 apply to DACs except to the extent that those provisions are disapplied or modified by Part 16 of CA 2014, which specifically deals with DACs. Notable provisions which are disapplied in relation to DACs are the one director minimum and the unlimited contractual capacity.[16]

Key DAC Provisions

1. If a DAC wishes to alter its objects the company may do so by special resolution[17];
2. If a DAC wishes to alter or add to its articles, it may do so, also by special resolution[18];
3. A DAC must have at least 2 directors[19];
4. Unless its constitution says otherwise, a DAC can use the unanimous written resolution procedure to pass special resolutions without holding actual meetings[20];
5. Unless its constitution says otherwise, a DAC can use the majority written resolution procedure to pass ordinary resolutions[21];
6. In the case of a DAC limited by shares being wound-up, members' liability is limited to the amount unpaid on the shares; in the case of a DAC limited by guarantee the contribution is limited to the

---

[15] For a full list of requirements see Companies Act 2014 ss 967-8 and see Schedules 7 and 8 of the Act for guidance on writing the core documents of the DAC.
[16] For a helpful table of provisions disapplied see s 946; this list is not exhaustive.
[17] Companies Act 2014, s 974.
[18] *ibid*, s 977.
[19] *ibid*, s 985.
[20] *ibid*, s 193 read with s 989.
[21] *ibid*, s 194 read with s 990.

guarantee set out in the constitution, and an obligation on each member to pay any sums unpaid on any shares[22];

7. The same examinership rules which apply to LTDs apply to DACs.[23]

Guarantee Companies

The second most popular form of company in Ireland is the company limited by guarantee ("CLGs"). They are usually used where the company in question is not trading for profit. Traditionally, this has meant that three kinds of operations incorporate as CLGs: charities, management companies (of apartment blocks, for example) and sports clubs. CLGs will continue to have a memorandum and articles of association; they may opt to have just one member; they may opt to avail of the audit exemption, which was not previously been available to them; they must have a minimum of two directors; and they must have CLG at the end of their name.

CLGs are also the most popular corporate form for management companies in multi-development units. There is no special body of company law which applies only to management companies. The Multi-Unit Development Act 2011 ("the MUD Act") states that owners' management companies ("OMCs") are to be companies which are registered under the Companies Acts.[24] Incorporating OMCs became common for solicitors because there are so many multi-development units in Ireland, and every multi-unit development is obliged to establish an OMC. Ownership of the common areas of the multi-development unit must be transferred to the OMC.[25] When a person purchases a unit in the development, that person because a member of the OMC. Clarke J stated, in simple language, what the purpose of OMCs was in *Palaceanne Management Ltd v AIB Plc*[26]:

> "Under the typical scheme (and again the case here) what was contemplated was that the common areas together with the freehold reversion of the leases would be transferred to the management company when all of the apartments had been

---

[22] Companies Act 2014, s 997.
[23] Part 10 of Companies Act 2014 (particularly s 510) read with s 998.
[24] MUD Act, s 1(1).
[25] Multi-Unit Development Act 2011, s 3.
[26] [2012] IEHC 182 (at para 2.4).

sold so that the obligations formerly resting on the developer then passed to the management company. To that extent it was typical (and the case here) that the management company joined in each lease. Thereafter it was for the owners, in their capacity as shareholders in the management company, to make decisions as to the level of upkeep and expenditure consistent with the mutual obligations to which they had committed under the respective leases by virtue of which they held their individual apartments and the constitutional documents of the management company itself."

Most OMCs are incorporated as public companies limited by guarantee not having a share capital (CLGs). Only a minority have been incorporated as private companies limited by shares. If prior to 1 June 2015 a Guarantee Company has had a share capital, it will now be considered a private company, and will be considered to be a DAC at the end of the transition period (30 November 2016). The CA 2014 states that, in general, Parts 1 to 14 of CA 2014 — which apply to the new model private limited company — apply to CLGs. Certain provisions in Parts 1 to 14 are disapplied — for example, the doctrine of *ultra vires* is not abolished for CLGs because they retain their objects clause.[27]

A "company limited by guarantee" or "CLG" means a company which does *not* have a share capital, and one in which the liability of its members is limited by the constitution to such amount as the members may undertake to contribute in the event of the company being wound- up.[28] CLGs are *public*, not private, companies (which means, amongst other things, that they must have at least seven members, and must hold an AGM). The law in relation to CLGs is set out in Part 18 of CA 2014.

Categories of Offences

The Companies Act 2014 sets out four categories of offence. Reference is made to them throughout the Act. At the upper end of the scale, the penalties available for breaches of the Act extend to maximum fine of €500,000 and/or a prison sentence of ten years. At the lowest end of the scale a maximum fine of €5,000 may be meted out. It is tempting to

---

[27] See table at s 1173.
[28] Companies Act 2014, s 1172; the form of a CLG's constitution is set out in s 1176.

assume that, given our culture, the toughest penalties will not be imposed because they are too tough and the smallest fines not imposed because they're so small. Anyone who would dispute this need only look at the website of the Director of Corporate Enforcement. In 2015, there are three prosecutions for company law offences (as of September). In the first, the charges were struck out when the defendant agreed to pay €1,000 to the Simon Community and to pay the prosecution's costs (€1,250).[29] In the second, an auditor who produced false audit reports relating to a company and pleaded guilty was given a suspended prison sentence.[30] In the third, the accused pleaded guilty to five charges of (a) improperly acting as statutory auditor and (b) producing audit reports which he tried to pass off as having come from properly registered audit firms, and was fined a total of €8,500 and a made to contribute to the Prosecutor's cost.[31] There are only four reported prosecutions for 2014 on the DCE website. One of them in particular shows an outlandish leniency: the accused was charged with fifty offences arising out of having acted as auditor to thirteen companies and producing false reports relating to eleven of them. He acted as auditor when disqualified. He pleaded guilty to thirteen counts in all. He was convicted on one count and fined €1,000 and the other counts were "taken into consideration".[32] That is the kind of result a corporate delinquent can expect at first instance. This case was appealed and the Court of Criminal Appeal agreed with the DPP that the sentence had been too lenient: it increased the fine by €2,000 and imposed 200 hours Community Service on Mr Forde.[33] It is extremely difficult to avoid concluding that there is tremendous judicial reluctance to impose jail sentences for corporate crime. For breaches of company law that involved tens of millions of euro, the former director of lending and the former director of finance at Anglo Irish Bank received 240 hours of community

---

[29] *DCE v John O'Connell* (23 February 2015), Dublin Metropolitan District Court, Judge John O' Neill. The accused failed to provide the DCE with the prescribed Reports in relation to three companies of which he was acting as liquidator.

[30] *DCE v Thomas (Tom) Colton* (22 April 2015), Dublin Metropolitan District Court, Judge John O' Neill.

[31] *DCE v Brian Scannell of Brian Scannell & Co* (20 May 2015), Cork District Court, Judge Kelleher.

[32] *DPP v Ignatius Forde* (15 May 2015), Carlow Circuit Court, Judge O'Sullivan. The DPP has appealed on grounds of undue leniency.

[33] The Court of Criminal Appeal (Birmingham, Sheehan, and Mahon JJJ).

service.[34] Given these facts, the presence of possible jail time in the offences section of the Companies Act 2014 must be there only as window-dressing.

With that in mind, the new categories of offences are as follows:

- A person guilty of a category 4 offence shall be liable, on summary conviction, to a class A fine (a maximum of €5,000). This category is to cover technical and filing offences.
- A person guilty of a category 3 offence shall be liable, on summary conviction, to a class A fine (a maximum of €5,000) or imprisonment for a term not exceeding six months or both.

There are a number of category 3 offences. For example, failure by directors in their duty to notify of disclosable interests in the company[35]; the selling of non-cash assets by the company to a restricted director (until a number of rules are satisfied)[36]; the obligation on restricted directors to notify a company which they are about to join of their restricted status. Failure to observe these rules are category 3 offences. There is a strong possibility that category 3 and 4 offences will come before the courts, but from there, we leave the realm of reality and enter the realm of make-believe: the two most serious categories.[37] It should be noted that the number of offences which were indictable offences under the previous legislation has been reduced by Companies Act 2014.

- A person guilty of a category 2 offence shall be liable—(a) on summary conviction, to a maximum fine of €5,000 or imprisonment for a term not exceeding 12 months or both, or (b) on conviction on indictment, to a fine not exceeding €50,000 or imprisonment for a term not exceeding five years or both.[38]

---

[34] Patrick Whelan and William McAteer, guilty of breaches of s 60 of Companies Act 1963 (now s 82 of Companies Act 2014, sentenced by Judge Martin Nolan on 31 July 2014.
[35] See ss 261 to 266.
[36] Companies Act 2014, s 828.
[37] There are also a number of offences where massive fines may be imposed, fines of €1m (for a serious prospectus or transparency offence) to €10m (for a market abuse offence). These relate to PLCs only. See s 1356, s 1382 and s 1368 of Companies Act 2014.
[38] Failure to make full disclosure to a liquidator in a winding up is a category 2 offence; It is a category 2 offence—for any officer of the company—to enter into an arrangement that breaches the prohibition on loans (etc) to directors set out in s 239. It is a category 2 offence for a person to sign a satisfaction or release with regard to a charge knowing it to be false. It is a category 2 offence to contravene the rules on financial assistance for acquisition of own shares. If any person falsely and deceitfully personates any owner of any share or interest

- A person guilty of a category 1 offence shall be liable—(a) on summary conviction, to a maximum fine of €5,000 or imprisonment for a term not exceeding 12 months or both, or (b) on conviction on indictment, to a fine not exceeding €500,000 or imprisonment for a term not exceeding 10 years or both.[39]

---

in the company and tries to obtain the share, receives money due to the owner, or votes at a meeting as if he were the lawful owner, then that person is guilty of a category 2 offence.
[39] Knowingly being a party to the carrying on of the business with intent to defraud creditors is a category 1 offence.

CHAPTER TWO

SEPARATE LEGAL PERSONALITY

The Principle of Separate Legal Personality

One of the fundamental doctrines of company law is the idea that a company, which is a corporate entity, has a separate legal personality from the people who are its shareholders and its directors. The indispensable separate legal personality case is *Salomon v Salomon & Co Ltd*,[1] "which has stood unimpeached for over a century".[2] The point of controversy was whether an individual who had been a sole trader, and who had incorporated his business in accordance with the Companies Acts, should be allowed to strike a bargain with his company. The bargain in question was the granting of security by the company to Mr Salomon. The result of this would mean that, in the event of a winding-up, Mr Salomon would be a secured creditor and entitled to repayment ahead of the unsecured creditors.

In the Court of Appeal, Lord Justice Lindley, one of the most eminent commercial judges of his day, said that if you asked a jury whether the business belonged to Aron Salomon or to Salomon & Co Ltd, "they would say it was Aron Salomon's, and they would be right if they meant that the beneficial interest in the business was his". Lindley LJ believed that Salomon's "scheme" was a "device to defraud creditors", adding "I regard the so-called sale of the business to the company as a mere sham". The other judges on the Court of Appeal were equally disapproving.[3] But the Court of Appeal made one great mistake. The judges asked themselves the question "whose was this business *in fact* after the formation of the company?"[4] The point that the House of Lords made, in finding in Mr Salomon's favour, was that in law the business was the business of Salomon & Co Ltd. Where a person decides to incorporate a business, and that person becomes the director of the new company, though the assets, clients, premises, etc, are the same, the transfer is not "an utter fiction"; a new entity *in law* comes in to being.

The fundamental point was that

> "the company is at law a different person altogether from the subscribers to the memorandum; and, though it may be that

---

[1] [1897] AC 22.
[2] *Per* Lord Neuberger P [2014] 1 BCLC 30 at 61.
[3] [1895] 2 Ch 323 at 340–341.
[4] *Per* Kay LJ, [1895] 2 Ch 323 at 345.

after incorporation the business is precisely the same as it was before, and the same persons are managers, and the same hands receive the profits, the company is not in law the agent of the subscribers or a trustee for them."[5]

In the words of Lord Halsbury LC, a legally incorporated company

"must be treated like any other independent person with its rights and liabilities appropriate to itself ... whatever may have been the ideas or schemes of those who brought it into existence."[6]

The House of Lords recognised two reasons for incorporating a company, to avoid bankruptcy and to make borrowing money easier. Both were entirely legitimate wishes. Lord Macnaughten did not like the fact that, in a winding-up, the debenture-holders "generally sweep off everything", but, he said, that was the nature of the law, and until Parliament changed it, there was nothing judges could do (and the legislatures in England or Ireland have never changed it). "Every creditor is entitled to get and to hold the best security the law allows him to take".[7] Mr Salomon was simply another creditor. In cases where the Court is asked to take "a realistic view" and consider what "any person in the street would say", judges have clearly stated that this is "a dangerous doctrine" because it ignores the whole rationale of incorporating a limited liability company.[8]

Directors Can Contract with their Companies and be Considered Employees

One result of this doctrine is that it is accepted that a person who incorporates a business can act as director of that business and still be considered an employee. Two cases illustrate this. In *Lee v Lee's Air Farming Ltd*[9] a pilot in New Zealand incorporated the defendant company to carry

---

[5] [1897] AC 22 at 52.
[6] *ibid* at 30–31.
[7] Lord Macnaughten remains a highly respected judge, who, going on the comments of Harman J, almost never got it wrong. Speaking of Lord Macnaughten's judgment in *Poole v National Bank of China Ltd* [1907] AC 229, Harman J said "[i]n my view this speech is one of those very few by Lord Macnaughten where...even Homer may be seen to nod." (*Re Jupiter House Investments (Cambridge) Ltd* [1985] BCLC 222 at 225).
[8] *Per* Ormerod LJ *Tunstall v Steigman* [1962] 2 QB 593 at 600.
[9] [1961] AC 12.

on an aerial top-dressing business. Two years later, while spraying a field, his airplane crashed and he was killed. His wife, Catherine, sought compensation from the defendant company for her and their four young children. A technical point was made to prevent the widow obtaining compensation: Mr Lee couldn't be a worker *and* a governing director, he was clearly a director and not a "worker". Lord Morris stated:

> "On this view it is difficult to know what his status and position was when he was performing the arduous and skilful duties of piloting an aeroplane which belonged to the company and when he was carrying out the operation of top-dressing farm lands from the air. He was paid wages for so doing. The company kept a wages book in which these were recorded. The work that was being done was being done at the request of farmers whose contractual rights and obligations were with the company alone. It cannot be suggested that hen engaged in the activities above referred to the deceased was discharging his duties as governing director."[10]

The Court said that it was never suggested that the company had been a sham, and found it "impossible to resist" the conclusion that the pilot was in a contractual relationship with the company, which was a separate legal entity. In *Secretary of State for Trade and Industry v Bottrill*[11] the Court held that a director who held the only share in the company could be considered an employee, and was therefore not prevented from receiving redundancy pay. This was in circumstances where "Mr. Bottrill's status as sole shareholder was only temporary and any control which he had of the company was only theoretical"[12] because the actual control was held by the American group.

The Principle of Limited Liability

The principle of limited liability flows from the principle of separate legal personality. A person who becomes a shareholder in a company is only liable to pay however much of their shareholding remains unpaid. You might buy one hundred shares in a company at €1 each and only pay for twenty-five of them. The most the directors can ever ask you to pay will

---

[10] *ibid* at 24–25.
[11] [2000] 2 BCLC 448.
[12] [2000] 2 BCLC 448 at 451.

be the remaining €75. If the company is wound-up, with the company in debt for in excess of €300,000, the most a liquidator can ask you to pay is the €75. You are protected: your liability is limited to the amount you have still to pay for the shares you have purchased.

As a director, you are protected by the shield of limited liability, as long as you act honestly and responsibly in the conduct of the company's affairs. If the company goes into liquidation owing €1m, you cannot be made to repay any or even part of that money, as long as you acted honestly and responsibly (if, on the other hand, it can be proven that you acted recklessly or fraudulently, or that you failed to maintain proper books of account, the court might impose liability on your personally: this is rare).

The Impact of Personal Guarantees and the Principle of Limited Liability

What has been troublesome for Irish directors in the wake of the financial crash which began in 2008 has been the ability of lending institutions to pursue them on foot of personal guarantees (a "Deed of Guarantee and Indemnity"). During the boom years, it was normal for banks to seek the personal guarantees of directors for the loans their companies were obtaining. This was not a breach of the principle of separate legal personality: it was a way of bypassing it and, as far as those who had given the guarantees were concerned, making it somewhat irrelevant. Could a company director have refused to give a personal guarantee? Yes, of course, but then the lending institution would have refused to advance the loan. As we noted in *Salomon v Salomon & Co Ltd*[13] the House of Lords recognised two reasons for incorporating a company: to avoid bankruptcy and to make borrowing money easier (because companies can offer floating charges, something sole traders and partnerships cannot do). Given that over 85% of companies in Ireland are private companies limited by shares, and that most of these are small ventures where the shareholders and the directors are the same people, the giving of personal guarantees deprived these parties of one of the two core benefits of trading through the medium of a limited liability company: the protection from bankruptcy.

---

[13] [1897] AC 22.

Separate Legal Personality: Case Law

Because the concept of separate legal personality was so clearly enunciated by the House of Lords in 1897 it quickly became a cornerstone principle of company law. For this reason, the concept itself is uncontroversial and provokes little litigation. What does provoke litigation is the more difficult question of when the court should disregard the concept, and unveil the directors who stand behind the separate entity with a view to making them personally liable for some or all of their company's debt.

Before we turn to that issue, we will look at two cases which illustrate the principle of separate legal personality.

Quigley Meats Ltd v Hurley[14] is an object lesson in suing the correct defendant, and in order to do this, it was crucial that the plaintiffs understood whether the party they were trading with was a natural person or a corporate person. The plaintiff company was a butcher's in Cork, operated by Mr Quigley and his three sons. One of its mainstays was supplying meat to hotels and restaurants. There were two defendants, John and Margaret Hurley. They ran a bar and restaurant in Waterford called "An Seanachie Bar". When the defendants went into arrears in their meat payments the plaintiffs' forbearance eventually ended and they issued proceedings. But they sued the "Seanachie Bar and Restaurant". When they succeeded, there was no legal person to recover from. They issued a second set of proceedings, by which time "The Seanachie Cottages Ltd" — the corporate entity they had in fact been trading with — had gone into liquidation so they sued that company's directors personally, John and Margaret Hurley. The plaintiff butchers succeeded in the Circuit Court, but the Hurleys appealed and their appeal was allowed: the butchers could not sue the directors personally because they had been dealing with a private company limited by shares, whose legal personality was separate to that of its directors.

In *The Roundabout Ltd v Beirne*[15] the principle was invoked to put an end to the picketing of a pub. In essence, the directors of a company which ran a pub fired a number of their barmen because they became unionized. This led to the union picketing the pub, seeking the reinstatement of their

---

[14] [2011] IEHC 192.
[15] [1959] IR 423.

members. To circumvent this, the directors of the company which ran the pub ("Marian Park Inn Ltd") formed a new entity ("The Roundabout Ltd"), the new company taking a yearly tenancy of the premises from the old, and the old transferring the licence that attached to it to the new. The Roundabout Ltd reopened the pub and sought an injunction restraining the picket, on the basis that it was a stranger to the activity which provoked it. The Court accepted that there was an element of "legal subterfuge" in what had happened, but importantly — this consideration may have tipped the balance in favour of the applicant — the judge felt that the new company had not been incorporated *solely* to defeat the picket, but that "there was a genuine idea of getting new blood into the business and a genuine idea of the business eventually being taken over" by the three barmen who had joined the directors on the board.[16] The most important point was that, in the words of Dixon J,

> "I have to regard the two companies as distinct in the same way I would regard two distinct individuals...The question then is whether a picket can be placed on the premises of the new owner by reason of a trade dispute with the previous owner."[17]

The two companies were separate legal entities and could not be conflated simply because the parties behind the incorporated names were similar. Dixon J granted a perpetual injunction and costs to the plaintiff.

Disregarding the Principle of Separate Legal Personality

In certain circumstances the courts will disregard the "corporate veil", as it is sometimes called. They will "lift the veil" of incorporation (or "pierce the veil"). What this means is that the court will disregard the separate legal personality of the company. This is done to obtain a remedy against a person, who will usually say that the remedy lies against the company alone.

In civil law jurisdictions, as a general proposition, it may be stated that the courts will pierce the corporate veil: where the corporate form is being misused; where it is being used to commit a fraud ("fraud unravels

---

[16] [1959] IR 423 at 427.
[17] *ibid* at 427–428. The net technical point was that the new company was not an employer for the purposes of the Trade Disputes Act 1906, and so it could not be validly picketed.

everything"[18]); where it is being used to evade legal obligations.[19] English company law has no such general doctrine in relation to piercing the veil: instead, it has a "variety of specific principles which achieve the same result in some cases".[20] Irish company law has in almost every respect adopted English company law, therefore the commanding review of the topic carried out by the UK Supreme Court in *Petrodel Resources Ltd v Prest*[21] is an essential aid to understanding this tangled area: prior to this case the law in this area was "unsatisfactory and confused."[22]

The doctrine of piercing the veil came about as a result of two Court of Appeal cases. The first was *Gilford Motor Co Ltd v Horne*.[23] In that case, the plaintiffs sought an injunction restraining the defendant from breaching a non-competition clause he had signed when he was their managing director. The clause stipulated that Horne would not compete with his former employers for a certain period, in the event that his employment was determined. Horne set up a rival company, but placed his wife and son at the head of it, and argued that he had nothing to do with it, hence he was not in breach of the restrictive covenant. The Court looked behind the rival company Horne had set up (J M Horne & Co Ltd) and found that it was a "device" and a "sham"[24] to evade his legal obligations. The second case was *Jones v Lipman*,[25] where the defendant sought to renege on an agreement to sell a property. He formed a company, of which he and an employee of his solicitors were the sole shareholders and directors, and transferred the property in question to this new company. The Court ordered that Lipman specifically perform the agreement to transfer the property to Jones. Both of these decisions rested on the piercing of the veil doctrine "if you take the language of the judgments at face value".[26] The UK Supreme Court stated in *Prest* that if you submit these two cases to a "closer analysis" the facts and outcomes don't provide "much direct

---

[18] Denning LJ, *Lazarus Estates Ltd v Beasley* [1956] 1 All ER 341 at 345.
[19] For a civil law analysis of this point (which is governed by the principle of abuse of rights), see *Barcelona Traction Light and Power Co Ltd Case (Second Phase)* [1970] ICJ 3 (International Court of Justice).
[20] [2014] 1 BCLC 30 at 41.
[21] [2014] 1 BCLC 30.
[22] *Per* Lord Neuberger P [2014] 1 BCLC 30 at 60.
[23] [1933] Ch 935, [1933] All ER Rep 109.
[24] [1933] Ch 935 at 956.
[25] [1962] 1 All ER 442, [1962] 1 WLR 832.
[26] *Per* Lord Neuberger P, [2014] 1 BCLC 30 at 62.

support for the doctrine".[27] The Court found that there was an underlying assumption in the judgments: that where a judge thought there was no other method of achieving justice the doctrine provided a valuable means of doing so.

In *Gilford Motor Co* counsel for the company conceded that if the business was being carried on by Horne in breach of the non-competition clause then Horne's company should also be restrained. It also could have been found that the company was Horne's agent, thus justifying an injunction against Horne and his company. In *Jones v Lipman* there was no need to invoke the doctrine because an order for specific performance would have required Lipman to do everything which was reasonably within his power to ensure that the property was so conveyed.[28]

Not only did the UK Supreme Court conclude that the doctrine was unnecessarily invoked in these cases, it stated all decisions over the past eighty years which involved the doctrine could be put into three categories:

(a) decisions in which it was assumed that the doctrine existed, but it was rightly concluded that it did not apply on the facts;

(b) decisions in which it was assumed that the doctrine existed, and it was wrongly concluded that it applied on the facts;

(c) decisions in which it was assumed that the doctrine existed and it was applied to the facts, but where the result could have been arrived at on some other, conventional, legal basis, and therefore it was wrongly concluded that it applied.[29]

So does the doctrine of piercing the veil exist at all? Should it be done away with? These were the questions the UK Supreme Court considered in *Petrodel Resources Ltd v Prest*.[30] From that judgment, the following principles can be distilled:

1. "The principle has been recognised far more often than it has been applied."[31]

---

[27] *ibid.*
[28] [2014] 1 BCLC 30 at 63; see also *Wroth v Tyler* [1973] 1 All ER 897 at 910–913.
[29] *Per* Lord Neuberger [2014] 1 BCLC 30 at 63.
[30] [2014] 1 BCLC 30.
[31] *Per* Lord Sumption [2014] 1 BCLC 30 at 50.

2. "Piercing the corporate veil" is not a doctrine at all, in the sense of a coherent principle or rule of law. It is simply a label — often used indiscriminately — to describe the disparate occasions when some rule of law produces apparent exceptions to the principle in *Salomon*.[32] This is the view in the UK and in Australia,[33] New Zealand[34] and South Africa.[35] Examples of such disparate occasions include statutory provisions which disregard the veil, joint liability in tort, the law of unjust enrichment, and the principles of equity.

3. The use of a metaphor — "piercing the veil" — may have been helpful in the early days, but has tended to cloud and confuse the issue over time.[36] Sometimes expressions can mask the absence of rational analysis.[37]

4. Despite the above criticisms, the doctrine should be retained because (1) "it has generally assumed to exist in all common law jurisdictions, and (2) it represents a potentially valuable judicial tool to undo wrongdoing in some cases, where no other principle is available."[38] Crucially, the Court agreed on a limited definition of when the doctrine could be invoked, that is, only where "a person is under an existing legal obligation or liability or subject to an existing legal restriction which he deliberately evades or whose enforcement he deliberately frustrates by interposing a company under his control."[39] Put another way, "if piercing the corporate veil has any role to play, it is in connection with evasion."[40]

---

[32] *Per* Lord Walker, [2014] 1 BCLC 30 at 71.

[33] *Briggs v James Hardie & Co Pty Ltd* (1989) 16 NSWLR 549 at 567 (New South Wales Court of Appeal)

[34] *A-G v Equiticorp Industries Group Ltd (in Statutory Management)* [1996] 1 NZLR 528 at 541 (New Zealand Court of Appeal).

[35] *Cape Pacific Ltd v Lubner Controlling Investments (Pty) Ltd* 1995 (4) SA 790 at 802, Smalberger JA (Supreme Court of South Africa).

[36] Cardozo J's reference to the 'mists of metaphor' in company law, which, "starting as devices to liberate thought … end often by enslaving it", in *Berkey v Third Avenue Railway* (1926) 155 NE 58 at 61.

[37] See *VTB Capital plc v Nutritek International Corp* [2013] 1 BCLC 179 at [124].

[38] [2014] 1 BCLC 30 at 65.

[39] *Per* Lord Sumption [2014] 1 BCLC 30 at 50, and Lord Neuberger P [2014] 1 BCLC 30 at 65.

[40] *Per* Lord Neuberger P [2014] 1 BCLC 30 at 60; see also *Atlas Maritime Co SA v Avalon Maritime Ltd, The Coral Rose* [1991] 4 All ER 769 at 779.

5. "If the court has power to pierce the corporate veil, it can only do so in favour of a party when all other, more conventional, remedies have proved to be of no assistance."[41]

6. This is a limited principle, because "in almost every case where the test is satisfied, the facts will in practice disclose a legal relationship between the company and its controller which will make it unnecessary to pierce the corporate veil."[42]

Prest arose out of divorce proceedings where the husband was making use of the opacity of the Petrodel Group's corporate structure. The husband owned and controlled this group of oil companies, two of which legally owned seven properties in London. The wife sought a declaration that the properties were held by the companies on trust for the husband, or failing that, that he was beneficially entitled to them. The husband lived outside the jurisdiction, ignored orders to disclose his assets, and asserted that the London properties belonged to the companies and were protected, therefore, by the veil of incorporation. The UK Supreme Court found that the husband was deliberately attempting to evade or frustrate his legal obligations—the enforcement of the divorce award—by interposing his companies between him and his wife. In such circumstances the Court could deprive the person controlling the company of the advantage he would have otherwise obtained by the use of the company's separate legal personality.

Disregarding the Veil: The Statutory Basis

Various provisions of the Companies Act 2014 permit the courts to disregard the corporate veil and impose personal liability on company directors. If directors are found to have traded fraudulently or recklessly, or if they have failed to ensure that the company keeps proper accounting records, the court can impose personal liability on them for some or all of the company's debts (these issues are discussed in Chapter 8). If the directors make the statutory declaration of solvency before a members' voluntary winding-up and it later emerges that the company was insolvent and the directors had no reasonable basis for swearing the declaration, liability may be imposed on them for any or all of the company's debts.

---

[41] *Per* Lord Neubreger P [2014] 1 BCLC 30 at 60, approving Munby J in *Ben Hashem v Al Shayif* [2008] EWHC 2380 (Fam) [2009] 1 FLR 115.

[42] *Per* Lord Sumption [2014] 1 BCLC 30 at 50.

The principle may also be disregarded by virtue of provisions of the Tax Acts. The Safety, Health and Welfare at Work Act 1989 allows the court to impose a fine on a company and its directors where there has been a failure to prepare a safety statement. In *DPP v Roseberry Construction Ltd*[43] a Mr McIntyre and his company were fined on this basis, and Mr McIntyre sought to argue that he was being fined twice since he and his company were "basically the same thing".[44] The Court observed that there had been no obligation on Mr McIntyre to incorporate his business and that he did so for the purpose of interposing the company between himself and various liabilities which might arise in the course of business. You can't have it both ways:

> "If someone sued the director in respect of the liabilities of the accused, one can assume the director or his lawyers would be quick to point out that these are two completely different entities."

Finally, if an officer signs a cheque on behalf of the company where the name is illegible or does not appear at all he may be fined and will be personally liable to the person the cheque was made out to.[45]

Disregarding the Veil: Single Economic Entity

A case in the 1970s, *DHN Food Distributors Ltd v Tower Hamlets London Borough Council*,[46] introduced the concept that the courts could disregard the separate legal personality of a group of companies, treating them as one, if the justice of the case required. In *DHN* the Court of Appeal allowed a parent company to claim compensation for a loss that only its subsidiary should have been entitled, at law, to claim. The three companies were treated as one because the group was "virtually the same as a partnership in which all the three companies are partners".[47] The case made by the group was a sympathetic one and the judges on the Court of Appeal felt that they should be treated as a single entity so as not to be defeated on a "technical point". This idea flew in the face of *Salomon*, which was doubted

---

[43] [2003] 4 IR 338.
[44] *ibid* at 339.
[45] Companies Act 2014, s 49 (a category 4 offence).
[46] [1976] 3 All ER 462.
[47] *ibid* at 467.

at the earliest opportunity[48] and has since been abandoned in England[49] and Ireland.[50] It did gain currency in Ireland for a brief period,[51] even being apparently adopted by the Supreme Court,[52] but given the strong view of a later Supreme Court in *Allied Irish Coal Supplies v Powell Duffryn International Fuels Ltd*[53] the doctrine should be of historical interest only.

It is not possible, however, to say this with total confidence in an Irish context, given the comments of Laffoy J in *Fyffes plc v DCC plc*.[54] Laffoy J found that two companies were *capable* of being found to have been a single entity with regard to two things: the sale of shares in Fyffes and the generation of profit from that sale. Laffoy J did not actually make that finding, and stated that a finding that the two companies were a single economic entity would not be made unless: (1) it could be shown that there was "a factual identification" of the acts between the two companies; and (2) if in the absence of such a finding the holding group would be able to "evade its obligations" under the relevant part of the Companies Acts.[55] The judge also spoke of "preventing an injustice to parties".[56] *Fyffes* was appealed to the Supreme Court, but these issues were not part of the appeal. Thus, the terrain in Ireland is unclear. The single economic entity theory seemed to have been laid to rest by the Supreme Court in *Allied Irish Coal*, but its resurrection, in light of what was said in *Fyffes*, is not impossible. It might be argued, however, that Laffoy J's comments chime with the UK Supreme Court in *Prest*, if one concentrates on her point about companies seeking to evade legal obligations or liabilities: this is the quintessential ground for disregarding a company's separate legal personality, according to *Prest*. If this interpretation is accepted, there is no need to speak of single economic entity or of "preventing an injustice".

---

[48] *Woolfson v Strathclyde Regional Council* [1978] SLT 159 *per* Lord Keith of Kinkel.

[49] *Adams v Cape Industries plc* [1990] Ch 433.

[50] *Allied Irish Coal Supplies v Powell Duffryn International Fuels Ltd* [1998] 2 IR 519.

[51] *Power Supermarkets Ltd v Crumlin Investments Ltd* (Unreported, High Court, 22 June 1981); *The State (McInerney) v Dublin County Council* [1985] IR 1; *Lac Minerals Ltd v Chevron Minerals* [1995] 1 ILRM 161.

[52] *Re Bray Travel Limited*, Unreported, Supreme Court, 13 July 1981, which Laffoy J has said is "of somewhat doubtful value as an authority" because the decision was on an interlocutory application and no written judgments were handed down.

[53] [1998] 2 IR 519.

[54] [2009] 2 IR 417.

[55] *ibid* at 496.

[56] *ibid*.

Disregarding the Veil: Agency

The courts have, from time-to-time, accepted that the separate legal personalities of two companies can be disregarded where it can be shown that an agency relationship exists between the two. This is not a matter that arises often in litigation. Establishing an agency relationship is easy where the terms have been reduced to writing,[57] but a thorny question when the terms have not, and the court is asked to make the inference that an agency relationship exists. Usually judges can turn to a legal test, expounded in a founding case, for guidance. The problem with inferring agency is that the seminal case where a six-point test was expounded, *Smith, Stone and Knight v Birmingham Corporation*,[58] is problematic.

Atkinson J stated that if the following six questions are answered positively then the court may say that an agency relationship existed:

(a) Were the profits treated as the profits of the (parent) company?
(b) Were the persons conducting the business appointed by the parent company?
(c) Was the company the head and the brain of the trading venture?
(d) Did the company govern the adventure, decide what should be done, and what capital should be embarked on the venture?
(e) Did the company make the profits by its skill and direction?
(f) Was the company in effectual and constant control?

This test has been criticized as being too broad. Courtney says that most of Atkinson J's test concentrates the issue of control and that this is too broad a test — if may even be said it is an incorrect test — because

> "if such a criterion is to be applied to every case in which the day-to-day affairs of a company are controlled by a member, then a significant number of companies may be regarded as agents of their members, and the principle of separate legal personality would be the exception rather than the rule."[59]

---

[57] The company and its shareholders may agree to make the relationship an agency one. See *Rainham Chemical Works Ltd v Belvedere* [1982] 2 AC 465 or *Southern v Watson* [1940] All ER 439 (In the first case the company was acting as agent for the members; in the second case for the incorporators)

[58] [1939] 4 All ER 116.

[59] Courtney, *The Law of Companies* (3rd ed, Bloomsbury, 2012) at 226.

Laffoy J, in *Fyffes plc v DCC plc*,[60] did not endorse it for this reason, agreeing with Keane[61] that the six-point test was not helpful because if they were all applied the test would be too broad: unfortunately Laffoy J did not say which of Atkinson's points were useful, or propose a test of her own. This is frustrating from a student's point of view. It means, simply, that there is no way of saying with certainty: "this is the answer". If you are invited to consider an agency problem, you need to know the Atkinson test, be able to apply it to the facts, but advise on the reservations just outlined.

In *Fyffes* Laffoy J was prepared to find that one company had acted as the agent of another in relation to the holding and disposal of shares in Fyffes "if to do otherwise would lead to an injustice. Whether it should be, depends on whether the inference is factually justified".[62] This would appear to be a radically pared down test, invoking the sometimes criticized "justice of the case" concept. Other cases which involve agency are no more helpful.[63]

Factors when Considering Whether to Pierce

In conclusion, the courts have set no clear test for disregarding separate legal personality where they are invited to infer an agency relationship. The courts have thoroughly rejected the concept of single economic entity in England, and the concept may be no longer necessary in Ireland. Certain statutory provisions allow the courts to disregard the separate legal personality of companies, and there is no controversy about this. With regard to a general rule, the English Supreme Court has clearly stated that the courts should only pierce the veil where there is deliberate evasion of legal obligations or liabilities. The Irish courts, if they get the chance, may follow *Prest*. If they do, it is most likely that the following four points of

---

[60] [2009] 2 IR 417.

[61] Citing Keane's *Company Law* (3rd ed, Bloomsbury, 2000,) (para.11–38); see [2009] 2 IR 417 at 489.

[62] *Fyffes* [2009] 2 IR, at 496.

[63] Courtney says of *Munton Bros Ltd v Secretary of State* [1983] NI 369 that it is "less than convincing" (*The Law of Companies* (3rd ed, Bloomsbury, 2012), at p 226, para 5.025). Laffoy J in *Fyffes*, cited *Munton Bros* but did not pass any approving remarks on it ([2009] 2 IR 417 at 490). There are two 1950s cases which may be classed as "agency and tax", but neither is very convincing in their reasoning. *Re FG (Films) Ltd* [1953] 1 AER 615 is a two page judgment that never mentions *Salomon* and simply purports to take a common sense approach. *Firestone Tyre and Public Co v Llwellin* [1957] 1 AER 561 is also a short judgment where *Salomon* makes no appearance and the law of agency is not discussed at any length.

guidance will be adopted. First, the court will not pierce the veil simply because of who owns or controls the company. It will be necessary to show control, but that proof will not be enough in itself to justify a piercing. Second, the court cannot pierce the corporate veil merely because to do so would be necessary in the interests of justice. To argue that nothing more than a technicality stands in your way will not find favour. Third, the court may pierce the veil only if there is some element of impropriety involved.[64] Finally, it is essential to note that impropriety alone is not enough, but must be connected to the use of the corporate structure for some improper purpose, for example to avoid some liability. Sir Andrew Morritt VC explained this in *Trustor AB v Smallbone*:

> "Companies are often involved in improprieties. Indeed there was some suggestion to that effect in *Salomon*. But it would make undue inroads into the principle of Salomon's case if an impropriety not linked to the use of the company structure to avoid or conceal liability for that impropriety was enough."[65]

Holding Companies, Subsidiaries and the Principle of Separate Legal Personality

Holding companies are separate entities from their subsidiaries. The assets and liabilities of the subsidiaries belong to each of the subsidiaries. They are not intermixed. The holding company is not the legal owner of the subsidiaries' assets or liabilities (unless the court finds that an agency or trustee relationship existed between them). There is no such thing as "group liability". The distinction between parent and subsidiary is not a merely technical one.[66] Every company in a group must keep its own proper accounting records. The activities of subsidiaries may be reflected in the accounts of the group. This is because the legislature recognises

> "how companies trading in this way may require to be viewed as an economic entity, but there is no question of that legislation making the assets of one company within the group, liable for the debts of another."[67]

---

[64] In *Ord v Belhaven Pubs Ltd* Hobhouse LJ said "it is clear ... that there must be some impropriety before the corporate veil can be pierced." [1998] 2 BCLC 447 at 457.
[65] [2001] 2 BCLC 436 at 445.
[66] *Bank of Tokyo Ltd Karoon* [1987] AC 45 at 64; also reported at [1986] 3 All ER 468.
[67] Per Murphy J, *Allied Irish Coal Supplies v Powell Duffryn Intl Fuels Ltd* [1998] 2 IR 519 at 536.

Creditors and suppliers are entitled to deal with every member of the group as a separate legal entity. The Irish courts have acknowledged that there might be some circumstances in which the members of the group could conduct the business of the company in such a way as to render their assets liable to meet claims in respect of the business nominally carried on by the company, but that this "would be an altogether exceptional state of affairs" and, if litigated, there could be an "inherent difficulty in sustaining the case".[68] In addition, companies within a group of companies may have different shareholders. The debts of one company cannot be visited on the shareholders of another. Where the promoters of a corporate enterprise choose to run their business through a series of companies the courts assume they have done so for a good reason (for example, they may have created some form of interlocking shareholding arrangements).[69]

---

[68] *ibid* at 537.
[69] *IBB Internet Services Ltd & Ors v Motorola* [2011] IEHC 504, *per* Clarke J.

CHAPTER THREE

CORPORATE AUTHORITY AND CORPORATE CAPACITY

PART I

The LTD: Capacity of a Natural Person

Section 38 of Companies Act 2014 states that the new model private limited company shall have "full and unlimited capacity to carry on and undertake any business or activity, do any act or enter into any transaction". It has "full rights, powers and privileges" in this regard. This rule applies notwithstanding anything contained in the company's constitution. It applies whether the company is acting inside or outside of the State. In other words, the Companies Act 2014 abolished the *ultra vires* rule for the new model private limited company (the doctrine is retained for DACs and PLCs).

Registered Person

The provisions of a company's constitution with regard to a person's office or powers — for example, calling someone "CEO" of "managing director" — are not, in themselves, to be taken as an allocation by the board of directors to that person of the power to bind the company.[1]

The board of a private limited company may authorise any person to be entitled to bind the company in transactions. The entitlement to bind the company carries in it the authority to exercise any power of the company *and to authorise others to do so.*[2] "Power of the company" in the foregoing sentence does not, however, include any power of management of the company exercisable by its board of directors (as distinct from any power of the board to enter into transactions with third parties), or a power of the company which this Act requires to be exercised otherwise than by its board of directors.[3]

If the company chooses to do this it may notify the CRO and the Registrar registers the authorisation. This person is then known as the "registered person". If a company revokes the authorisation the registered person continues to be regarded as a registered person "unless and until the company notifies the Registrar (in the prescribed form) of that revocation".[4]

---

[1] Companies Act 2014, s 39(6).
[2] *ibid*, s 39(4).
[3] *ibid*, s 39(5).
[4] *ibid*, s 39(3).

Powers of Attorney

A private limited company may empower a person to be its attorney, to execute deeds or do any other thing on its behalf in any place (whether inside or outside the State).[5] The attorney can be granted general powers or powers only in respect of specific matters (acts incidental to the carrying out of his express authority are also binding on the company). A deed signed by an attorney on behalf of the company binds the company and has the same effect as if it were under its common seal. The attorney may never exceed the authority granted by the company.

Doctrine of *"Ultra Vires"*

A private limited company has no objects clauses. Its capacity is unlimited.[6] Thus, much of what follows in the first half of this chapter applies to the DAC, and not to the LTD. The DAC retains the old two document format — the memorandum of association and articles of association – and continues to be limited by the objects set out in its memorandum of association.[7] This means that the doctrine of *ultra vires*, which has been abolished for the LTD by virtue of s 38 of Companies Act 2014, still applies to the DAC. How many companies will elect to become DACs, thus retaining their objects clauses? It is anticipated that the majority of companies in Ireland will take the form of the LTD, and thus, much of what follows will be less important than it used to be for Irish businesses.

At common law, any transaction entered into by a company which was *ultra vires* was not enforceable: the third party, unable to enforce the contract, often lost out. This was a strict rule. The phrase *ultra vires* means "beyond the powers" and is the opposite of *"intra vires"*.[8] The Companies Act 1963 modified the doctrine of *ultra vires*.[9] That modification has been abandoned in favour of a new formula, found at s 973 of Companies Act 2014, which states that persons dealing with a DAC which acts *ultra vires*

---

[5] *ibid*, s 41.
[6] For the arguments behind this move, see *Reform of the Ultra Vires Rule, A Consultative Document*, (1986) by Dr Dan Prentice of Pembroke College, Oxford, which is noted by the CLRG in its First Report.
[7] Companies Act 2014, s 972.
[8] The phrase "ultra vires the company" is correct but the phrase "ultra vires the directors" should not be used.
[9] Companies Act 1963, s 8.

will not be prejudiced but the DAC's directors may be held to account for causing the DAC to perform an *ultra vires* act. The action would be against the directors *in personam* (i.e. not an *in rem* action which would set aside the transaction). Section 973(5) removes the doctrine of constructive notice, stating that: "A party to a transaction with a DAC is not bound to enquire as to whether it is permitted by the DAC's objects". Also new is the company's ability to ratify the *ultra vires* transaction by special resolution,[10] something which reverses the old common law position.[11]

The Main Objects Rule

In the late nineteenth century, the courts decided that if a *main* object could be ascertained among all the objects clauses in a company's memorandum, then all the other objects there would be treated as ancillary. This is "the main objects rule". The effect of this is that the ancillary objects can only be pursued while the main object is being pursued. The ancillary objects are treated as "limited and controlled" by the main object.[12] So if you have broadly stated objects which are followed by specific objects, the courts will say that the narrower objects are the main objects. In *Re German Date Coffee Co Ltd*[13] Lindley LJ said that when trying to find what the main object of a company was "the governing principle" is to look at "the real object" of the company, which he specified meant "the thing for which the people subscribe their money".[14]

Getting Around the Main Objects Rule

Companies found this rule a bit of a straightjacket. Draftsmen were told to get around it. The first way of getting around it was to list all the objects as usual, and then add a line at the very end that said "each of these objects is independent, and none of them are more or less important that the others". This clause at the very end of the objects was called the "Independent Objects Clause". This innovation was approved by the

---

[10] Companies Act 2014, s 973(3).

[11] The classic case on this common law rule was *Ashbury Railway Carriage and Iron Co Ltd v Riche* (1875) LR 7 HL 653. The object of the company in was to make and sell railway carriages. The directors bought a licence to build a railway line in Belgium. This was *ultra vires* and therefore void.

[12] *Per* Salmon J in *Anglo-Overseas Agencies Ltd v Green* [1961] 1 QB 1 at 8.

[13] (1882) 20 Ch D 169.

[14] *ibid* at 188.

House of Lords in *Cotman v Brougham*.[15] The main object of company in that case was "developing rubber plantations". The object in question was underwriting an allotment of shares.

The second way of getting around the main objects rule came in *Bell Houses Ltd v City Wall Properties Ltd*.[16] What the "Bell Houses Clause" says is that if the directors honestly believe that a certain activity which is not part of the company's objects would be of benefit to the main object of the company, then the company can extend its reach into that area: it doesn't matter that it is not specifically provided for. The main business of Bell Houses Ltd was buying vacant sites and building houses on them. The board delegated all business matters to Randal Bell, the chairman of Bell Houses and he gathered a good understanding of how property development is financed. City Wall Properties Ltd agreed to pay Bell Houses Ltd £20,000 as a "procuration fee" because Bell Houses introduced City Wall to a financier who provided them with a huge amount of bridging finance for one of their projects. City Wall declined to pay the fee, taking the view that the contract was *ultra vires* Bell Houses. Danckwerts LJ held that Randal Bell's knowledge of property development financing was of benefit to the main object of the company, and allowed the plaintiff to enforce the contract. A typical Bell Houses Clause looks like this:

> "To carry on any other business whatsoever which can, in the opinion of the company or the board of directors, be advantageously carried on in connection with or as ancillary to any of the above businesses or the general business of the company."[17]

You can see that it has to be carried on in connection with or as ancillary to any of the company's businesses.

Objects and Powers, Express and Implied

A DAC may have a list of objects in its memorandum of association. Some of these the courts will not consider to be *objects*, rather, they will consider that they are *powers*. Because they are there, written down in the

---

[15] [1918] AC 514.
[16] [1966] 2 QB 656.
[17] MacCann & Courtney, *Annotated Companies Acts 1963 – 2012*(Bloomsbury 2012) at p 53.

memorandum of association, they will be considered "express powers". But the company's powers do not end with what is expressly stated. It has "implied powers" too: these powers are incidental to the stated objects, or must be there as a consequence of them. Examples of implied powers are: the power to appoint agents; to hire employees, borrowing money; giving security for borrowing; paying pensions to former employees; paying gratuities to employees. It should be noted that a DAC is not stuck with the objects it starts out with. It can alter its objects by special resolution.[18]

PART II

Actual and Ostensible Authority

A company may enter into contracts, and directors may be empowered to sign on its behalf. But what if a director enters into a contract when he was not empowered to do so. Will the company be bound in that case? What if the signatures of two directors were needed, and one went ahead and signed on behalf of the company? Can the company tell the party to the contract: "sorry, he shouldn't have done that; it's not valid". Will the contracting party be able to say "tough, it *is* valid" and enforce the contract? These are the questions we deal with now, the question of actual and ostensible authority. This question can still arise in the context of the LTD, because the LTD has unlimited contractual capacity, but its officers will not always have an unlimited capacity to bind it. That is the difference between corporate authority and corporate capacity.

It is a "branch of the law [that] has developed pragmatically rather than logically".[19] The idea of actual authority is an uncomplicated one. Usually it will be written down. The terms will set out the scope of the actual authority. Diplock LJ defined actual authority as "a legal relationship between principal and agent created by a consensual agreement to which

---

[18] Companies Act 2014, s 974. If there are a minority of dissenters they can try to reverse the change. If they have 15% of the issued share capital they can apply to court within 21 days of the resolution. The key thing is — if you alter — it must be done by the members in good faith for the benefit of the company as a whole. See *Allen v Gold Reefs of West Africa Ltd* [1900] 1 Ch 656. Good faith is a subjective test: "It is not the business of the court to manage the affairs of the company" (Scrutton LJ in *Schuttleworth v Cox Bros & Co* [1927] 2 KB 9).

[19] [1964] 2 QB 480 at 502.

they alone are parties".[20] What kind of authority can a party expect from the board, an individual director, the company secretary? When it acts collectively the board has authority to enter contracts.[21] The board can appoint a managing director: usually, this person will have individually the same power as the board has collectively.[22] With regard to an individual director, the law says that he has very little authority when acting on his own to enter into contracts. The role of chairman of the board can vary from something akin to a managing director, to something little more than ceremonial: when uncertain, it is best practice to assume the chairman has no more authority than to sign the minutes. Company secretaries can usually enter contracts for the company which are of an administrative nature, things which concern day-to-day matters.[23]

If everything proceeds as it should, and the person in question has actual authority to sign a contract, then the contract will be binding on the company. A trickier point is the concept of "ostensible authority." Arguments over whether or not people have had ostensible authority are the arguments that have become case law. It is tricky because it usually appears to the outside person — the one entering the contract with the company — that the person they're dealing with has the full authority to do what he is purporting to do. It is only later that they are told by the company, or by its liquidator, that in fact that person didn't have the requisite authority, and unfortunately for them contract is therefore unenforceable. The concept of "ostensible authority", however, means that this consequence will not necessarily follow. Before we consider the leading case the following should be noted: if a person is to argue that he believed so-and-so had ostensible authority to do something, he is deemed to have constructive notice of the DAC's articles. If, for example, the DAC does not permit the appointment of a managing director, it will be fruitless for a plaintiff to argue that the defendant company had conferred ostensible authority upon the agent in question.

The leading case is *Freeman & Lockyer (a firm) v Buckhurst Park Properties (Mangal) Ltd.*[24] Diplock LJ, who gave the leading judgment, set a four point

---

[20] *ibid:* see also Costello J in *Williamson Ltd v Bailieborough Co-op*, Unreported, High Court, 31 July 1986.
[21] Companies Act 2014, s 158.
[22] *ibid*, s 159.
[23] See *Panorama Developments (Guildford) Ltd v Fidelis Furnishing Fabrics Ltd* [1971] 3 All ER 16.
[24] [1964] 2 QB 480.

test for establishing whether ostensible authority has been created. But first, the facts. The plaintiffs were a firm of architects. They did work for the defendant, a property company. The case arose out of the failure of Mr Shiv Kumar Kapoor's vision for a magnificent English country house in Sussex, the kind of place they could have used in *The Remains of the Day* or *Downton Abbey*. The estate was called Buckhurst Park — and Mr Kapoor wanted to develop it. Like many a man he was certain he would succeed as a property developer, if only he had the money to get started. But he didn't. So he approached another man, Mr Hoon, who advanced £40,000. They contracted to buy the estate in September 1958. The following month they formed a limited company to run the development operation. Mr Kapoor and Mr Hoon were the directors (together with a nominee of each man). The idea was to complete the purchase and sell it on. It was a magnificent way to make money. But then they weren't able to sell it on nice and quickly, as they had intended. What steps could they take? Mr Kapoor decided to hire architects to do some work on the estate and to get planning permission in respect of it. The firm he hired was Freeman and Lockyer. They did the work and it came to £291 and six shillings. When Buckhurst Park Properties (Mangal) Ltd refused to pay them they sued the company and Mr Kapoor. Practically, they wanted to succeed against the company, because Mr Kapoor had disappeared. Consequently they were unable to even serve him with proceedings.

The articles of the company provided for the appointment of a managing director, but this was never acted upon. No managing director was ever *formally* appointed by the four-man board of directors. The company said that Mr Kapoor didn't have the authority to enter into the contract with Freeman and Lockyer, so they couldn't come looking for their £291 from it, and they should instead try to recover it from Mr Kapoor.

Did Kapoor have ostensible authority? The case was first heard by a County Court. It found

> "that Kapoor, although never appointed as managing director, had throughout been acting as such in employing agents and taking other steps to find a purchaser; and that Kapoor was so acting was well known to the board."

The company appealed these two points.

Ostensible authority will come into being as a result of a representation by the company, and that "the representation...operates as an estoppel",[25] i.e. the company cannot turn around and say "we are not bound by what was agreed". Often, the concept people most struggle with is the "representation". It sounds like an active thing, and it sounds like it must take the form of words. But this is not the case. As Diplock LJ said, the most common form of representation is conduct. When we know this, we can readily understand that a *failure to act* is a form of conduct too. The courts have also decided that a representation can be tacit, i.e. it can take the form of a *failure to speak up*, or to set the record straight.

Diplock LJ's Four Point Test

With this in mind there are four conditions:

> "which must be fulfilled to entitle a contractor to enforce against a company a contract entered into on behalf of the company by an agent who had no actual authority to do so."

It is essential that these are applied step-by-step to any fact scenario where the possibility of ostensible authority is being considered. It must be shown:

1. "that a representation that the agent had authority to enter on behalf of the company into a contract of the kind sought to be enforced was made to the contractor (a representation may be tacit, i.e. a failure to set the record straight, as it was in *Ulster Factors v Entonglen Ltd*.[26] In *Armagas Ltd. v. Mundogas SA*[27] there was no representation);

2. that such representation was made by a person or persons who had "actual" authority to manage the business of the company either generally or in respect of those matters to which the contract relates (usually the board);

3. that he (the contractor) was induced by such representation to enter into the contract, that is, that he in fact relied upon it; and

---

[25] [1964] 2 QB 480 at 503; the making of the representation "is itself an act of management of the company's business", at 505.
[26] [1997] IEHC 34.
[27] [1985] 3 All ER 795.

4. that under its memorandum or articles of association the company was not deprived of the capacity either to enter into a contract of the kind sought to be enforced or to delegate authority to enter into a contract of that kind to the agent."[28]

Applying these points to the facts above Diplock LJ said:

1. "The judge found that the board knew that Kapoor had throughout been acting as managing director in employing agents and taking other steps to find a purchaser. They permitted him to do so, and by such conduct represented that he had authority to enter into contracts of a kind which a managing director or an executive director responsible for finding a purchaser would in the normal course be authorised to enter into on behalf of the company. Condition (1) was thus fulfilled.

2. the articles of association conferred full powers of management on the board. Condition (2) was thus fulfilled.

3. The plaintiffs, finding Kapoor acting in relation to the company's property as he was authorised by the board to act, were induced to believe that he was authorised by the company to enter into contracts on behalf of the company for their services in connection with the sale of the company's property, including the obtaining of development permission with respect to its use. Condition (3) was thus fulfilled.

4. The articles of association, which contained powers for the board to delegate any of the functions of management to a managing director or to a single director, did not deprive the company of capacity to delegate authority to Kapoor, a director, to enter into contracts of that kind on behalf of the company. Condition (4) was thus fulfilled."[29]

There Must be a Representation

Unfortunately for the plaintiff in *Kett v Shannon & English*[30] there was no representation. The case is a short, simple one, more like a tort than a company law case. Henchy J approved of *Freeman & Lockyer*, saying that

---

[28] [1964] 2 QB 480 at 505-506.
[29] *ibid* at 509.
[30] [1987] ILRM 364.

Diplock LJ had dealt with the law "illuminatingly", and quoted Robert Goff LJ's summary in *Armagas* of ostensible authority, as he understood it from *Freeman & Lockyer*. In *Kett v Shannon & English* a mechanic loaned a car to Mr Shannon on a short-term basis. While driving it, Mr Shannon ran into the plaintiff, who was out walking. The second defendant, Mr English, was the garage owner. The question for the Supreme Court was whether the mechanic had ostensible authority to loan the car (because if he did, Mr English could be held liable for Mr Shannon's negligent driving).[31] The plaintiff didn't succeed, because she could not show that the garage owner had made any representation to Mr Shannon that his mechanic had the authority to loan cars on his own initiative. Henchy J said "there should have been a representation *of some kind* by [Mr English] to [Mr Shannon] that the mechanic had authority to lend" the car in question.[32]

The Rule in *Turquand*

The rule in *Turquand* is so old and so embedded in the law that there is no need to know the facts of the case. In *ACC Bank plc v McCann & Griffin* Hogan J said that the rule in *Turquand*:

> "reflects the principle that, generally speaking, a third party is entitled to rely as against the company on the validity of acts done or resolutions passed or documents executed by or on behalf of the company without the necessity of inquiring whether the company complied with its own memorandum and articles of association or other associated procedural rules, such as the presence of a quorum or the appointment of officers."[33]

---

[31] The plaintiff's claim against Mr Shannon settled for £42,000, but he wasn't insured when driving the car. Her injuries were serious, and if she were awarded damages against Mr English she could actually recover them, because he was insured. Otherwise she would have to take a smaller sum from the Motor Insurance Bureau in lieu of what she should have been able to recover from Mr Shannon.

[32] [1987] ILRM 364 at 366; see also *Bondina Ltd v Rollaway Shower Blinds Ltd* [1986] BCLC 177; *Rafsanjan Pistachio Producers Co-op v Reiss* [1990] BCLC 352; *SMC Electronics Ltd v Akhter Computers Ltd* [2001] 1 BCLC 433; *Hopkins v TL Dallas Group Ltd* [2005] 1 BCLC 543; *Ford v Polymer Vision* [2009] 2 BCLC 160; *GHLM Trading Ltd v Maroo & Ors* [2012] 2 BCLC 369.

[33] [2012] IEHC 236 at para 21. See also Blayney J in *Re Motor Racing Circuits Ltd* (Unreported, Supreme Court, 31 January 1997) at 7, and also *Ulster Investment Bank Ltd v Euro Estates & Drumkill Ltd* [1982] ILRM 57 at 67 where Carroll J said the bank was entitled to rely on

An example of the principle at work is *AIB v Ardmore Studios International*,[34] where Finlay J said that a reading of the memorandum and articles of the company "would…not raise any suspicion of an invalidity in the meeting". The company was trying to avoid summary judgment in the sum of just over £40,000. The loan had been drawn down, but again, it was alleged that no resolution authorizing the borrowing had been passed by the directors. It was contended for the company that the lack of meeting and resolution was not merely an irregularity but "a total gap" which even a party dealing *bona fide* with the company could not ignore. Finlay J, however, gave summary judgment, because it seemed to him that "these frailties or defaults" were "classical example of an irregularity in the internal management of the company".

Limitations to the Rule in *Turquand*

The rule in *Turquand* will not save a transaction where an agent has acted outside his *ostensible* authority. Further to this, the outsider must *rely* on the articles of the company[35]: if, for example, the outsider is claiming that he assumed Mr X was the managing director of the company, he must have consulted the company's constitution and found that it had capacity to *appoint* a managing director.

The rule is subject to three limitations. The first is where unusual circumstances put the outsider (or "third party") on notice: an example of this was *Underwood v Bank of Liverpool & Martins*[36] where Mr Underwood was lodging the cheques paid to his company into his personal account. The Bank of Liverpool tried to argue that Underwood had, or must have had, authority to put the company cheques into his personal account. The Court of Appeal rejected the argument because a situation where an agent for a company was paying the company's cheques into his own account was so unusual as to put the bank on inquiry. They should have asked if the company had a separate bank account, and if it had, why the cheques were being directed into Mr Underwood's account. Failure to do this constituted negligence on the part of the bank. The second limitation is

---

the rule "and to assume that the mortgage prepared by it and which on its face is duly executed in accordance with the articles, is the deed of the company."

[34] Unreported, High Court, 30 May 1973,

[35] *Rama Corporation Ltd v Proved Tin & General Investments Ltd* [1952] 1 All ER 554.

[36] [1924] 1 KB 775.

that while a party may assume an ordinary resolution has passed, he cannot assume a special resolution has, because it is open for him to check it in the CRO to confirm whether it has or not. All special resolutions of all companies are recorded there. So the second limitation is that *Turquand* will not help a party where the irregularity is a matter of public record.[37] The third limitation is that, obviously enough, if the outsider is actually aware that an internal procedure hasn't been followed, then he can't call on *Turquand* to save his contract.[38]

---

[37] *Irvine v Union Bank of Australia* (1877) 2 Ap Cas 366 (Privy Council).
[38] *Cox v Dublin City Distillery Co (No 2)* [1915] 1 IR 345.

CHAPTER FOUR

DIRECTORS: CORPORATE GOVERNANCE ISSUES

Directors: Corporate Governance Issues

A private limited company need only have one director.[1] Much was made of this as a reform which the 2014 Act brought it, but it may be less significant in practical terms, since certain documents will need to be signed off on by a director and a secretary, and in certain cases the one person cannot occupy those two roles.[2] The common occurrence in Ireland is that some companies, which have essentially been run by one person, have a spouse or a sibling listed as the second director simply to make up the statutory requirement. This token presence will probably not be eliminated by the new Act, but the token person may migrate from being a director to merely being a secretary.[3] The Companies Act 2014 states that company secretaries have certain duties — it does not state *what they are* in the case of private limited companies — and it states that directors have a duty to ensure that the person appointed as secretary "has the skills or resources necessary to discharge his or her statutory and other duties".[4] Other forms of companies — the DAC, the PLC, the company limited by guarantee — have a two director minimum.

Appointment of Directors

It should be noted that every rule in relation to the appointment of directors applies only to the extent that an individual company's constitution does not provide otherwise. As a general rule, a person should not be a director of more than 25 private companies limited by shares.[5] A director's remuneration is determined by the board.[6] The rules governing the formal appointment of directors are set out in s 144 of Companies Act 2014. Directors must consent to their appointment: the first directors of a

---

[1] Companies Act 2014, s 128; default in this is a category 3 offence and the fine may be imposed on the company.

[2] Companies Act 2014, s 134. Also, see s 129: "Where a company has only one director, that person may not also hold the office of secretary of the company."

[3] This could, in an insolvency situation, lead to a court being more reluctant to restrict or disqualify them.

[4] Companies Act 2014, s 129(4); the obligations of a company secretary in a PLC are, by contrast, specified, in s 1112(2). The vague "duties of secretary" are set out in s 226: "The duties of the secretary of a company shall, without derogating from the secretary's statutory and other legal duties, be such duties as are delegated to the secretary, from time to time, by the board of directors of the company."

[5] Companies Act 2014, s 142; this does not include PLCs or companies which have a "real and continuous" link with economic activity in the State.

[6] Companies Act 2014, s 155; tax-free payments to directors are prohibited by s 156.

company will be determined in writing by the subscribers of the constitution (or a majority of them); new directors may be voted in at a general meeting.[7] Motions for the appointment of directors at general meetings should be voted on separately, unless the meeting agrees unanimously to deal with them all on the one vote.[8] In the case of a single-member company, the sole member may appoint a person to be a director of the company simply by serving a notice in writing on the company which states that the named person is appointed director.[9] If it emerges that some formal step in the appointment process was not taken, this nonetheless does not invalidate any action they took during their tenure up to that point.[10]

There are few restrictions on persons becoming company directors. Bodies corporate may not be company directors (any purported attempt to appoint one will be void).[11] No minor may be appointed as a company director (any minor who was a company director prior to the commencement of Companies Act 2014 — on 1 June 2015 — automatically ceased to be a director).[12] Undischarged bankrupts may only become company directors with the leave of the court.[13]

There is no statutory requirement for directors to hold shares in the company but if the constitution of the company says there is such an obligation, the directors must take up the shares within two months of that appointment (or a shorter time, if the constitution specifies so).[14] All companies must have one director who is resident in a European Economic Area ("EEA") State. There is, however, a way around this. If none of the company's directors are an EEA resident, the company can lodge a bond to the value of €25,000 with the CRO. The bond would provide that if the company failed to pay any fine arising from the Taxes Consolidation Act 1997, the fine could be paid out of the bond.[15]

---

[7] Companies Act 2014, s 144(4).

[8] *ibid*, s 145.

[9] *ibid*, s 144(5).

[10] *ibid*, s 135.

[11] *ibid*, s 130.

[12] *ibid*, s 131.

[13] *ibid*, s 132; pursuant to s 133, if the Director of Corporate Enforcement has reason to believe that a director or secretary of a company is an undischarged bankrupt then he or she has the power to require that person to produce a sworn statement of their financial position.

[14] Companies Act 2014, s 136.

[15] This is dealt with in ss 137 and 138. There is one way for a company to be exempted from the requirement to have one EEA resident director: if it can show that it has "a real and

Removal of Directors

Section 146(1) of Companies Act 2014 states that a company can remove a director by ordinary resolution "before the expiration of his or her period of office notwithstanding anything in its constitution or in any agreement between it and him or her".[16] The rules governing this process are set out in the subsections of s 146. Obviously, fair procedures should be observed and nothing in s 146 will prevent a person from seeking compensation or damages in respect of the termination of their appointment.[17] If a director becomes bankrupt or is deemed to be the subject of a disqualification order, that person must immediately vacate their office.[18] Directors are also obliged to vacate their office if "the health of the director is such that he or she can no longer be reasonably regarded as possessing an adequate decision making capacity,"[19] though, in practical terms, it may be difficult to determine when this line is crossed, and it may be hotly contested. A simpler scenario is the vacation of office if the director is absent from directors' meetings for more than six months without the permission of the other directors.[20]

The Register of Directors and Secretaries

Every company must keep a register of its directors and secretaries.[21] The register contains the following details in relation to each director: (a) present forename and surname and any former forename and surname; (b) date of birth; (c) his or her usual residential address[22]; (d) his or her nationality[23]; (e) his or her business occupation, if any; and (f) particulars of any other directorships of bodies corporate, whether incorporated in the

---

continuous link with one or more economic activities that are being carried on in the State" then it may be exempted from the requirement (see s 140). The decision is a matter for the Revenue and the CRO. The tests for determining whether a director is resident in the State are set out at s 141. One test is satisfied if a person has spent 183 days in Ireland in a given year (those days don't have to be consecutive).

[16] This rule does not authorise the removal of a director holding office for life.

[17] Companies Act 2014, s 147.

[18] *ibid*, s 148.

[19] *ibid*, s 148(2)(b).

[20] *ibid*, s 148(2)(e).

[21] *ibid*, s 149 (this also applies to assistant and deputy secretaries if there are any).

[22] If a person's safety or security is at risk, they may not need to provide this piece of information, pursuant to s 150(11).

[23] Pursuant to s 151(1) a company must state each director's name, former name (if any) and nationality (if not Irish, in all business letters on or in which the company's name appears and which are sent by the company to any person. Failure to do so is a category 4 offence.

State or elsewhere, held by him or her or which have been held by him or her (this only applies to directorships held within the last five years). The company's shareholders have the right to inspect this register and request copies of it,[24] just as they have the right to inspect the contracts of service of all directors (and, if a director's contract is oral, the written memorandum setting out the terms of that contract).[25] The information that must be recorded in relation to secretaries is more basic, and is set out in s 149(5).

Directors' General Power of Management

It is a basic principle of company law that the root authority in the company rests with the shareholders, but they immediately confer it upon the directors, who become the day-to-day managers of the company. It would be impractical if all the shareholders retained an ability to guide the affairs of the company in everyday matters. The root power of the shareholders is set out in s 25(2) of Companies Act 2014:

> "From the date of incorporation mentioned in the certificate of incorporation, the subscriber or subscribers to the constitution, together with such other persons as may from time to time become members of the company, *shall be a body corporate* with the name contained in the constitution, having perpetual succession and a common seal."

Some matters are so fundamental that the members of the company must ratify them by voting. For example, directors cannot approve of the company providing financial assistance in the purchase of its own shares: a special resolution is needed. Likewise, s 238 of Companies Act 2014 requires a similar process (though the resolution required is an ordinary one) if a director wishes to be involved with a substantial property transaction with the company, or vice versa (see Chapter 6).

Directors' general power of management is set out in s 158 of Companies Act 2014: this replaces the old provision — model regulation 80 of Companies Act 1963 — which was dubbed "the cornerstone of corporate governance". With regard to this, there is an oft-quoted *dictum* of Lord Wilberforce in *Howard Smith v Ampol* where he said that:

---

[24] Companies Act 2014, s 149(3) – the rights set out in ss 215-217 apply to this register.
[25] Companies Act 2014, s 154(1) and (2).

"directors, within their management powers, may take decisions against the wishes of the majority of shareholders, and indeed the majority of shareholders cannot control them in the exercise of these powers while they remain in office."[26]

Section 158(1) states:

"The business of a company shall be managed by its directors, who may pay all expenses incurred in promoting and registering the company and may exercise all such powers of the company as are not, by this Act or by the constitution, required to be exercised by the company in general meeting, but subject to—

(a) any regulations contained in the constitution;

(b) the provisions of this Act; and

(c) such directions, not being inconsistent with the forego-ing regulations or provisions, as the company in general meeting may (by special resolution) give."

In practice, the key element is that in the day-to-day management of the company the directors are supreme and cannot be interfered with. These day-to-day powers can be limited or particularized by the company's constitution and the directors' powers are, of course, subject to compliance with the Companies Act 2014.[27] Thus, s 158(a) and (b) are uncontroversial. What causes some difficulty is the practical meaning of s 158(c). How much power does it leave the members? What is meant by "directions"? Courtney says that this issue has been "the subject of some speculation".[28] It is difficult to see why this provision was retained, as: (1) it an almost unheard of issue in the LTD; and (2) in the rare cases where members try to force the directors to act in a certain way, the courts have clearly stated that the directors' general powers of management cannot be overridden by the shareholders.[29]

---

[26] [1974] AC 821 at 837.

[27] For example, the matters covered by the Summary Approval Procedure require the sanc-tion of a special resolution by the members.

[28] Courtney, *Law of Companies* (3rd ed, Bloomsbury, 2012) at p 791 (para 13.132); English case law uses the term "regulations" rather than "directions", and Irish law spoke of "regula-tions" before the Companies Act 1963.

[29] The paucity of case law is shown in the cases cited in *Ryanair v Aer Lingus* [2011] 3 IR 69; see also *Scott v Scott* [1940] 1 Ch. 794; *Automatic Self-Cleansing Filter Syndicate Co v Cuninghame* [1906] 2 Ch. 34; *Clark v Workman* [1920] 1 IR 107; *Breckland Group Holdings Ltd v London and*

It would seem, in conclusion, that a consideration of what powers s 158(c) might reserve to the members is a purely academic question.

In *Breckland Group Holdings Ltd v London and Suffolk Properties*[30] the directors were going to give the go-ahead to commencing legal proceedings. The members sought an injunction to stop them passing this resolution. Harman J refused them. He said that the English equivalent of s 158 "confides the management of the business to the directors and in such as case it is not for the general meeting to interfere".[31] That's the most up-to-date English case on this point. Fourteen years before that, the House of Lords said in *Alexander Ward and Co v Samyang Navigation*[32] that:

> "the directors, and no one else, are responsible for the management of the company, except in the matters specifically allotted to the company in general meeting. This is a term of the contract between the shareholders and the company."[33]

Similarly, in a ninety-five year old Irish case Ross J came to a similar conclusion: "once given the company cannot interfere in the subject-matter of the delegation unless by special resolution".[34]

The correct view would seem to be that if the powers of the directors have not been modified by the company's constitution — if they are as set out in Parts 2 to 14 of Companies Act 2014 — then the shareholders cannot interfere in their exercise of them; they may only issue directions with regard to areas where there is no specific power plotted out.

Can Shareholders Force a Dividend?

Where the directors have been given specific powers by the articles, the shareholders cannot act in disregard of these powers by issuing directions, be it by way of a members' directive or a purported special resolution. For example, (subject to the constitution of the company) if the directors don't

---

Suffolk Properties Ltd [1989] BCLC 100; *Alexander Ward and Co Ltd v Samyang Navigation Co Ltd* [1975] 2 All ER 424; *Gramophone and Typewriter Ltd v Stanley* [1980] 2 KB 89.

[30] [1989] BCLC 100.

[31] *ibid* at 106.

[32] [1975] 2 All ER 424.

[33] *ibid* at 432.

[34] *Clark v Workman* [1920] 1 IR 107 at 114, citing *Automatic Self-cleansing Filter Co. v Cunninghame* [1906] 2 Ch. 34.

want to register a transfer of shares the shareholders can't direct them to do so. If the directors don't want to declare a dividend the shareholders can't direct them to do so.

Some of these issues arose in *Ryanair Ltd v Aer Lingus plc*.[35] Ryanair held 29.82% of the shares in Aer Lingus. The directors of Aer Lingus had recommended that no dividend be paid for the year. Ryanair tabled a resolution that Aer Lingus should declare and pay a dividend of €30m. It was trying by a resolution to override the recommendation of the directors on a matter of management. Ryanair also wanted no more payments to be made into Aer Lingus's employee pension scheme without prior shareholder approval. Aer Lingus refused to table the resolutions. McGovern J upheld their refusal. On the pension scheme issue McGovern J stated:

> "the board has been given power to determine what (if any) pension benefits the Company will provide and to determine what payments are to be made to the Company's pension scheme. Since this power is given to the directors under the Articles of Association, the members, in general meeting, cannot, by ordinary resolution, seek to override or fetter that exclusive power. If the directors cannot or will not exercise a power vested in them, then the general meeting may do so. But that has not happened here."[36]

If powers are delegated to directors then directions to them in those areas will be nullities. If something could be argued to fall outside the management of the business, then members may be able to issue directions in that respect. If shareholders of an LTD want to specifically limit the power of directors they must ensure that the desired modification is set out on the company's constitution.

An older example of the principle is *Scott v Scott*,[37] where the members passed two resolutions, one instructing a firm of auditors to investigate the company's affairs and the other ordering the payment of a weekly sum pending the payment of a dividend for the current year. Both were invalid

---

[35] [2011] 3 IR 69.
[36] *ibid* at 77.
[37] [1943] 1 All ER 582.

because they were attempts to usurp the powers of directors, in particular in this case, the power to decide the financial direction of the company.[38]

When Shareholders' Power Comes to the Fore Again

There are three situations where members' powers come to the fore again. The first is when there are no directors capable of acting, by which we mean they all die or become incapacitated at the same time. A very old case — *Mahony v East Holyford Mining Co*[39]— saw such a situation: what happens then is that the members can decide who among them will act as director for the time being. In *Alexander Ward and Co v Samyang Navigation*[40]— which we came across above — the plaintiff company issued a claim against the defendant Korean company for £160,000, at a time when the plaintiff had no directors and held no general meetings. A ship belonging to the Korean company was lying in Scottish waters. A Scottish court issued a summons for the payment of the sum in the name of two men, Ward and Irons, and a warrant for the "arrestment" of the ship. The defendant raised a preliminary point: it said that the plaintiff had no directors and so it couldn't have been authorised to bring the proceedings. Before the case came on for hearing, the plaintiff went into liquidation. The liquidator ratified the acts which Ward and Irons had done on the company's behalf. The Court said the action could go ahead. That a company was without directors didn't mean it was unable to exercise its powers of management. Any act could be done on its behalf, and ratified later by the shareholders. An attempt to recover a debt was an act capable of being ratified (the principle is the important part; in this case it so happened that it was the liquidator ratifying the act, rather than the shareholders in general meeting).

The second situation is where the directors go beyond their delegated authority. This happened in *Re Burke Clancy & Co Ltd*,[41] when the directors borrowed more money than the company's articles allowed them to. The members didn't mind, and approved the accounts at the general meeting. They were perfectly entitled to do this because the power to borrow that

---

[38] As to whether the refusal to declare a dividend could amount to conduct that would come within s 205 of the Companies Act 1963, see *Re Sam Weller & Co* [1990] BCLC 80 in Chapter 14.

[39] (1875) LR 7 HL 869.

[40] [1975] 2 All ER 424.

[41] Unreported, High Court, Kenny J, 23 May 1974.

amount was beyond the scope that had been given to the directors but borrowing itself was *intra vires* the company.[42] The Companies Act 2014 now permits the ratification of *ultra vires* transactions by DACs.[43]

The final situation is where directors act in breach of their duties (this is different from above, where they acted beyond their delegated authority). The best known case is *Bamford v Bamford*,[44] where the Court of Appeal stated that it was "tolerably plain" law that if directors carry out acts which for whatever reason are not technically valid[45] they can call a general meeting, make "a full and frank disclosure" and

> "obtain absolution and forgiveness of their sins; and provided the acts are not ultra vires the company…everything will go on as if it had been done all right from the beginning."[46]

There is no need for a special resolution to do this: an ordinary one will do.

Delegation by Directors

The directors are permitted to delegate their powers to "such person or persons as they think fit, including committees". Committees to which directors' powers are delegated must conform to any regulations that may be imposed on them by the directors. Directors may appoint "one or more of themselves to the office of managing director (by whatever name called)".[47] Two things arise here. First, the Act recognises the importance of the substance of the role: the given title is not the crucial factor when determining whether someone is or was a managing director. Second, it presents the possibility that more than one person could be the company's managing director, something that, in practice, is likely to be an unattractive possibility. The directors may confer upon a managing director any of the powers exercisable by them collectively. The powers of the MD might exist concurrently with the board or might act to the exclusion of the board's powers.

---

[42] See also *Grant v United Kingdom Switchback Railways Company* (1888) 40 Ch D 135.

[43] Companies Act 2014, s 973(3).

[44] [1970] 1 Ch 212.

[45] For example, if there is no quorum, if the directors aren't properly appointed, if they were actuated by improper motives.

[46] *Bamford v Bamford* [1970] 1 Ch 212, *per* Harman LJ at 237 and 238 (the allegation was that the directors hadn't made an allotment of shares *bona fide*.

[47] Companies Act 2014, s 159.

Directors' Meetings

The rules governing directors' meetings have always been loose to allow for flexibility. Historically, there is one example of a directors' meeting being held on a corridor. The Companies Act 2014 states that directors may "meet together for the dispatch of business, adjourn and otherwise regulate their meetings *as they think fit*".[48] Any questions should be decided by majority. If the question is tied the chairperson —who will have been appointed by the directors[49] — has a casting vote. Any director may call a directors' meeting at any time. The key issue in that regard is that all directors are entitled to "reasonable notice". If one director is out of the country, the others may decide that it is not necessary to give him or her notice.[50] The Act does not say if the agreement to do this must be unanimous: the company's constitution might. The only persons who have the right to object to lack of reasonable notice are directors.[51] It is up to the directors to fix a quorum: if they don't fix one, the default quorum is two (unless it is a sole member company, in which case the quorum is, obviously, one). In order to pass a resolution, however, the directors do not even need to meet: they may decide to use the written resolution procedure which provides that as long as all of the directors who are entitled to receive notice of directors' meetings sign a resolution in writing it is as valid as if it had been passed at a directors' meeting.[52] There is one formal obligation, however: the keeping of minutes of the directors' meetings. The Act requires a minute book to be kept which records: (a) all appointments of officers made by its directors; (b) the names of the directors present at each meeting of its directors and of any committee of the directors; (c) all resolutions and proceedings at all meetings of its directors and of committees of directors. Failure to comply with this is a category 4 offence. The minutes have to be entered "as soon as may be". Once the minutes are signed by the chairperson of the meeting at which the proceedings were had they become "evidence of the proceedings".[53] There comes into being a rebuttable presumption that the meeting was duly held and convened.

---

[48] Companies Act 2014, s 160.
[49] See s 160(8).
[50] Companies Act 2014, s 160(4).
[51] *ibid*, s 160(5).
[52] *ibid*, s 161.
[53] *ibid*, s 166(3).

CHAPTER FIVE

DIRECTORS' DUTIES

Director by Whatever Name Called: *De Jure, De Facto* and Shadow Directors

The Companies Act 2014 defines a director as "any person occupying the position of director by whatever name called".[1] The definition lays emphasis on the substance of what a person's activities in the company are: a person may not be *called* a "director", or formally appointed as one, but may well be carrying out the functions of a director. For twenty-five years the concept of the "shadow director" has been given a statutory definition. That definition is carried over into Companies Act 2014. A shadow director is "a person in accordance with whose directions or instructions the directors of a company are accustomed to act."[2] There is one saver: a person shall not be treated as a shadow director if the true (*"de jure"*) directors are accustomed to act on his or her advice "by reason…that they do so on advice given by him or her in a professional capacity." This is the same definition as is found in the English Companies Acts.[3] A body corporate is not to be regarded as a shadow director of any of its subsidiaries.[4] In *Re Hocroft Developments*[5] McKechnie J undertook a large review of the case law in this area, and added some guidance to the statutory phrasing (the implementation of the instructions must be "causatively connected to the communication;" the making of such communication and the reliance on it must be *habitual*; the instructions "must be repetitive, customary and recurring"; the instructions should not be "infrequent, rare or occasional"; the communication "must have an obligatory or imposing force…behind it"; and so on).

> "The scope of the affected business must be such as to demonstrate a real influence over a wide ranging area of the company's affairs; although not its total affairs."[6]

No one point is decisive in deciding whether a party was a shadow director. All the circumstances will be considered. In *Re Devona Ltd*[7] — a

---

[1] Companies Act 2014, s 2; for a discussion of the meaning of "director" see *Re Mumtaz Properties Ltd; Wetton v Ahmed* [2011] EWCA Civ 610, [2011] All ER (D) 237 (May).
[2] s 221(1); the giving of advice is not enough, it must be acted on: *Ultraframe (UK) Ltd v Fielding* [2005] EWHC 1638 (Ch).
[3] See Companies Act 2006, s 251(1).
[4] Companies Act 2014, s 221(2). A body corporate may not be appointed a director but may be found to have been a shadow director.
[5] [2009] IEHC 580.
[6] *ibid* at 40, *per* McKechnie J.
[7] *Pyne v Van Deventer* [2012] IEHC 263.

misguided application by a liquidator to have a person in a managerial role deemed a shadow director for the purposes of securing his restriction — Dunne J drew on the series of points enunciated by McKechnie J and found *Hocroft* "a useful exposition of the principles to be considered" in these applications.[8]

The law in relation to *de facto* directors in England developed in the context of decisions relating to applications to disqualify persons from acting as directors. In Ireland, the question arose first in relation to restriction (*Re Lynrowan Enterprises Ltd*[9]). The concept of a "de facto director" is given statutory definition in Companies Act 2014. A *de facto* director is "a person who occupies the position of director of a company but who has not been formally appointed as such".[10] Again, a person will not be regarded as a *de facto* director merely because they give professional advice to the directors. Part 5 of Companies Act 2014 deals with the duties of directors: wherever "director" is written in Part 5, it includes shadow directors and *de facto* directors. ie, they are obliged to observe the duties imposed on *de jure* directors.

McKechnie J considered the law relating to de facto directors in *Hocroft*. He stated: "I think that no one test is decisive but that all the relevant factors must be considered"[11] (in saying this, McKechnie J was agreeing with Jacob J in *Secretary of State for Industry v Tjolle*,[12] which was endorsed by Walker LJ in *Re Kaytech International*[13]). The critical issue, McKechnie J said, was "whether the person has assumed the status and function of a director" (and in this he was specifically agreeing with Finlay Geoghegan J in *Re First Class Toy Traders Ltd; Gray v McLoughlin*[14]). There is a passage in *Re Lynrowan Enterprises Ltd*[15] which states that if the person's role can be explained in another way, by pointing to a role which they occupied that wasn't that of director, for example, then "the person in question should not be made amenable to…restriction."

---

[8] [2012] IEHC 263 at 17 ([2012] 2 ILRM 430); see also *Secretary of State for Trade and Industry v Deverell* [2001] Ch 340, Morritt LJ.
[9] [2002] IEHC 90.
[10] Companies Act 2014, s 222.
[11] [2009] IEHC 580 at para 58.
[12] [1998] BCC 282.
[13] [1999] BCC 390.
[14] [2004] IEHC 289.
[15] [2002] IEHC 90.

De Facto and Shadow: A Difference?

Is there a difference between a *de facto* and a shadow director? The answer is not as clear-cut as one would expect, with Irish judges breathing a sigh of relief when the facts of a case do not require them "to tease out any of the difficult questions which may arise as to the distinction between *de facto* directors and shadow directors".[16] In *Re Hydrodam (Corby) Ltd* Millett J said that *de facto* and shadow directorship "do not overlap. They are alternatives and in most and perhaps all cases are mutually exclusive".[17] Millett J stated that an application by a liquidator which did not distinguish between the two was "embarrassing".[18] In *Re Kaytech International plc* Robert Walker LJ added "a tentative comment" to this:

> "...the two concepts do have at least this much in common, that an individual who was not a de jure director is alleged to have exercised real influence (otherwise than as a professional adviser) in the corporate governance of a company. Sometimes that influence may be concealed and sometimes it may be open. Sometimes it may be something of a mixture, as the facts of the present case show."[19]

Lewison J in *Ultraframe (UK) Ltd v Fielding* has stated that

> "in most cases...it seems to me that it is unlikely...that a person will be simultaneously a shadow director and a de facto director; although he may be both in succession."[20]

The law in England on this point is not rigid and is circumstance-specific; the same can be said about the corresponding law in Ireland. Laffoy J in *Fyffes v DCC*[21] doubted that both were mutually exclusive, and McKechnie J agreed with her, saying

> "when discussing both types of director, conceptually or theoretically, the firmness of [Millett J's] view may be justified,

---

[16] *Stapleton v Doran* [2011] IEHC 528 at para 69, *per* Hogan J.
[17] [1994] 2 BCLC 180 at 183.
[18] *ibid at 182.*
[19] [1999] 2 BCLC 351 at 423.
[20] [2005] EWHC 1638 (Ch) at 337 (27 July 2005).
[21] [2009] 2 IR 417.

but in the context of a given case, it may have to soften, as a finding under both heads may potentially be justified."[22]

The law as it stands in Ireland is as stated by McKechnie J, with the proviso that a liquidator "should always particularize his claim", not least because the respondent must know what case he is to meet.

General Duty to Comply with the Companies Act

Every director has a duty to ensure the Companies Act is complied with by his company.[23] When a person consents to become a company director he should sign his name to the following statement, which must be delivered to the CRO: "I acknowledge that, as a director, I have legal duties and obligations imposed by the Companies Act, other statutes and at common law". There is no duty to employees, other that a duty to "have regard" to them while there are performing their functions. What this means in practical terms, no one really knows. It is a hollow duty that cannot be enforced by the employees themselves (the duty to the employees is owed to the company).[24]

The technical meaning of "in default" of an obligation under the Act is set out in s 270 of Companies Act 2014, which states that

> "an officer who is in default is any officer who *authorises* or who, in breach of his or her duty as such officer, *permits* the default mentioned in the provision."

"Default" includes a refusal to do a thing or a contravention of a provision.[25] If proceedings are taken against an officer for a default, it must be proved that the respondent was aware of the "basic facts concerning the default" in question. If this is proved, there is a presumption that the respondent permitted the default unless the respondent shows that he took all reasonable steps to prevent it or that, by reason of circumstances beyond the respondent's control, was unable to do so.[26]

---

[22] [2009] IEHC 580 at para 61.
[23] Companies Act 2014, s 223.
[24] *ibid*, s 224(2).
[25] *ibid*, s 270(2).
[26] *ibid*, s 271(2).

Any provision contained in the constitution of a company or a contract with a company which would purport, in respect of any officer of a company, to exempt from or indemnify against any liability will be void[27] (this does not preclude the company from purchasing and maintaining insurance in respect of any liability for any of its officers[28]). The good news for company officers is that if proceedings are issued against them for negligence, default, breach of duty or breach of trust but the court is of the view that the officer acted "honestly and reasonably" the court may excuse them and relieve them from all or part of their liability in respect of the wrong.[29] Interestingly, if a company officer anticipates that such a claim — in respect of any negligence, default, breach of duty or breach of trust — might be made against him he may apply to court in advance to be relieved of liability in respect of the wrong concerned.[30] The same "honestly and reasonably" arguments would have to be put forward by the applicant, and believed by the court.

Directors and secretaries have a transparency duty: they must notify the company in writing of their interests in shares or debentures of the company.[31] The rules in relation to "disclosable interests" are set out in ss 256–269 of Companies Act 2014.

Directors' Report for Financial Year

Depending on the size of the company, directors may be obliged to prepare a directors' report for every financial year.[32] The obligation applies when the company's balance sheet total for the year exceeds €12.5m and the amount of its turnover for the year exceeds €25m.[33] If the company falls into this category, then the directors' report must be prepared. In it the directors have to state, among many other things, the following: the principal activities of the company during the course of the year; a statement of the measures taken by them to secure compliance with the

---

[27] *ibid*, s 235.
[28] *ibid*, s 253(4).
[29] *ibid*, s 233.
[30] *ibid*, s 234.
[31] *ibid*, s 261. The mode of notification is set out in s 265 and is new, as of 1 June 2015. While elements of the enforcement of these obligations are taken from s 58 of Companies Act 1990, the obligation as set out is new. Failure to comply with the these rules is a category 3 offence.
[32] Companies Act 2014, s 325.
[33] *ibid*, s 225(7), subject to s 943(i).

books and records requirements[34]; the amount of any interim dividends paid by the directors during the year and the amount, if any, that the directors recommend should be paid by way of final dividend[35]; particulars of any important events affecting the company which have occurred since the end of that year; a fair review of the business of the company[36]; a description of the principal risks and uncertainties facing the company; information on the acquisition or disposal of own shares[37]; information on interests in shares or debentures[38]; a statement that the director has taken all steps to make himself or herself aware of any relevant audit information and to establish that the company's statutory auditors are aware of that information.[39] Together with this directors' report the directors must include a statement acknowledging that they are responsible for securing the company's compliance with its relevant obligations. They must confirm that an appropriate compliance policy statement has been drawn up: that "structures" are in place to secure compliance and that the structures have been reviewed during the year.[40]

Do Directors Owe Duties to Shareholders?

It is a key tenet of company law that directors owe their duties to the company[41] and each of these duties is owed by the director to the company alone.[42] If a director breaches any of the above duties the breach will not of itself affect the validity or the enforceability of any contract or other transaction (other than by the director who breached his duty). A party who suffered loss or damage can pursue a third party where the third party was an accessory to a director's breach of duty or knowingly received a benefit from the breach.[43]

---

[34] Set out in ss 281 to 285.

[35] Companies Act 2014, s 326(1).

[36] ibid, s 327(1).

[37] ibid, s 328.

[38] ibid, s 329.

[39] ibid, s 330(b).

[40] ibid, s 225(3).

[41] Percival v Wright [1902] 2 Ch 421; Peskin v Anderson [2001] 1 BCLC 372, Court of Appeal; if the company in turn owes fiduciary duties to a client, it is possible for a director of the company also to owe fiduciary duties to that client: see Satnam Investments Ltd v Dunlop Heywood & Co Ltd [1999] 3 All ER 652, [1999] 1 BCLC 385, Court of Appeal (fiduciary duty owed by way of contractual and equitable obligations; duty breached when information offered to a third party); and JD Wetherspoon plc v Van de Berg & Co Ltd [2007] EWHC 1044 (Ch), [2007] All ER (D) 82 (May).

[42] Companies Act 2014, s 227.

[43] ibid, s 227(2).

Directors do not owe fiduciary duties to shareholders, collectively or individually, solely by virtue of the fact that the hold the office of director. For over a hundred years, for example, since *Percival v Wright*, it has been held that

> "[t]he directors of a company are not trustees for individual shareholders, and may purchase their shares without disclosing pending negotiations for the sale of the company's undertaking."[44]

The logic is that directors should not be over-exposed to the risk of a multiplicity of legal actions by dissenting minority shareholders. The rule is a broad one, and as a general rule it still holds good, though it has been given some qualifications. In *Stein v Blake and others (No 2)*[45] the Court recognised the possibility of special circumstances in which a director may owe a fiduciary duty to a shareholder personally (the shareholder was induced by the director to sell his shares at an undervalue, and this gave him a personal remedy against the director; this is different from a shareholder suffering a loss by simple diminution in value of his shareholding, something which gives rise to no cause of action).

The hallmarks of a fiduciary relationship are trust, confidence and loyalty. One of the most important things to bear in mind in this area is just how fact-specific a finding of fiduciary duties can be. To give two examples: In *Wetherspoon plc v Van de Berg & Co Ltd*[46] the Court considered whether three directors of the defendant owed fiduciary duties to the claimant. It held that while one director did, two directors did not, a finding which illustrates the fact-sensitive nature of the question. The second example is this: Usually, fiduciary duties between commercial co-venturers will not arise in the absence of agency or partnership, but in *Murad v Al-Saraj*[47] the claimants successfully argued that the defendant owed them fiduciary duties in relation to a joint venture to acquire a hotel, where there was a relationship between the joint venturers of trust and confidence, where the defendant had acted in some respects as the claimant's agent, and where the claimants had no relevant experience and trusted the defendant

---

[44] [1902] 2 Ch 421, headnote.
[45] [1998] 1 BCLC 573 at 576, 579.
[46] [2009] EWHC 639 (Ch).
[47] [2004] EWHC 1235 (Ch).

with extensive discretion.[48] Again, a set of special circumstances had caused the fiduciary duties to arise.

The reason a director owes duties to the company is because he directs and controls it: that legal relationship gives rise to the duties, and no such legal relationship exists between the director and the shareholder, and so a shareholder would have to establish a "special factual relationship"[49] between himself and the directors in order to successfully bring home a case of breach of fiduciary duty. In *Peskin v Anderson*, Mummery LJ identified two examples of events which may bring the directors into "direct and close contact with the shareholders" in a manner capable of generating fiduciary obligations,

> "such as a duty of disclosure of material facts to the shareholders, or an obligation to use confidential information and valuable commercial and financial opportunities, which have been acquired by the directors in that office, for the benefit of the shareholders, and not to prefer and promote their own interests at the expense of the shareholders."[50]

In *Coleman v Myers*[51] — a New Zealand case — the Court rejected the established rule that directors owe no fiduciary duties to shareholders because the company was a family-run company, and because the shareholders often looked to the directors for guidance the directors were found to have had a duty to them (which they breached by withholding share value information). Woodhouse J gave general guidance on the factors which would influence a court to find a fiduciary relationship and, in Ireland, in *Crindle Investments v Wymes*[52] Keane J approved them. These were:

---

[48] For a discussion of this, see *Ross River Ltd v Waveley Commercial Ltd* [2014] 1 BCLC 545.

[49] *Per* Mummery LJ, *Peskin v Anderson* [2001] 1 BCLC 372 at 379.

[50] [2001] 1 BCLC 372 at 379.

[51] [1977] 2 NZLR 225. The headnote states that the court found that the two directors, a father and son, owed fiduciary duties to the shareholders, many of whom were relatives, because of "(1) the family character of the company; (2) the position of father and son in the family and in the company; (3) their high degree of inside knowledge; (4) the way in which they went about the take-over and the persuasion of shareholders. Because of these reasons they were obliged not to make to shareholders statements on matters material to the proposed dealing which were either deliberately or carelessly misleading, and to disclose material matters as to which they knew or had reason to believe that the shareholder whom they were trying to persuade to sell was inadequately informed."

[52] [1998] 2 ILRM 275.

"dependence on information and advice, the existence of a relationship of confidence, the significance of some particular transaction for the parties, and the extent of any positive action taken by or on behalf of the director to promote it".[53]

Keane J stated: "in particular circumstances a company director may indeed be in a position where he owes a fiduciary duty to individual shareholders".[54]

One situation which is not in doubt is where directors to some extent step outside their normal role and make certain representations to shareholders: this will create the fiduciary relationship. This is what happened in *Allen v Hyatt*,[55] where the directors made a profit from the sale of shares which they had bought, having induced shareholders to sell them their shares and having concealed their intention to sell them on. The directors were probably thinking that they could act like this by virtue of the rule in *Percival v Wright*, but the fact that they had not dealt with the shareholders at arm's length and had "held themselves out to individual shareholders as acting for them" meant that the situation was "widely different" and the directors had, by their actions, turned themselves into agents of the shareholders.[56]

In *Brunninghausen v Glavanics*[57]— an Australian case — the Court found that Brunninghausen had a fiduciary duty to Glavanics when buying back shares that he had issued to Glavanics. The two men were related by marriage. Each had their own company. Brunninghausen had made Glavanics a director of his company, and had given him a shareholding in exchange for services, and Glavanics had ever remained a director in name only. Over time the two men fell out. When Glavanics decided leave Australia and sell his shareholding to Brunninghausen, he simply asked for "a fair price" for the shares, and said he would not check the company's books and records, its

---

[53] *Crindle Investments et al v Wymes et al* [1998] 2 ILRM 275 at 288.
[54] *ibid.*
[55] (1914) 30 TLR 444 (Privy Council).
[56] *Allen v Hyatt* (1914) 30 TLR 444. Just because a relationship exists between a shareholder and director doesn't automatically mean that the latter owes a fiduciary duty: whether that duty arises depends on the facts of each case. The leading authority on who a fiduciary is: "someone who has undertaken to act for or on behalf of another in a particular manner in circumstances which give rise to a relationship of trust and confidence" — and what a fiduciary owes — "the obligation of loyalty" — are the comments of Millett LJ in *Bristol and West Building Society v Motthew* [1996] 4 All ER 698 (at 711–712).
[57] (1999) 32 ACSR 294.

turnover and so on, but would trust his former friend. Brunninghausen bought Glavanics' shares at a massive undervalue: when this was discovered and Glavanics litigated the matter, the Supreme Court of New South Wales found that Brunninghausen had, essentially, cheated Glavanics. The Court felt that that the merits of the general rule in *Percival v Wright* were "greatly diminished"[58] where there are very few members and directors in the company, and where their relationships are not impersonal but close, and directors deal directly for the purchase or sale of shares. Among the relevant factors for the Court — again showing the fact-sensitive nature of each finding — were: (1) the position of Brunninghausen as sole effective director; (2) the existence of only one other shareholder; (3) their close family association (they had married two sisters); (4) the intervention of their mother-in-law; (5) the exclusive advantage which Brunninghausen's position conferred on him to receive any offers to purchase the company's business from third parties.[59] Taking this into consideration, and stating that the principle in *Percival v Wright* was correct in general, the Court found that the principle couldn't be applied in this case, because to state that Brunninghausen owed a duty only to the company would be "meaningless" and

> "lack all practical content. The company could not suffer any loss from the breach of such a duty, and had no interest in its loyal and disinterested performance."[60]

In this situation, a recognition of a duty to the other shareholder was reasonable because that duty would not compete with the duty owed by Brunninghausen to the company.[61] The Court found that a duty owed by directors to shareholders was not at all a novel concept: the duty could be seen at play whenever directors made a call on unpaid share capital (the duty to treat all shareholders equally[62]), or whenever they allotted new shares (a duty not to issue shares for the purpose of altering the balance of voting power in the company[63]).

---

[58] *ibid* at 302.

[59] *ibid* at 303–304.

[60] *ibid* at 304.

[61] It was this fear of parallel duties that Lord Cullen had in mind in *Dawson International plc v Coats Paton plc* [1989] BCLC 233.

[62] The Court cited *Nocton v Lord Ashburton* [1914] AC 932 at 955–6 and *Galloway v Hallé Concerts Society* [1915] 2 Ch 233.

[63] The Court cited Lord Wilberforce in *Howard Smith Ltd v Ampol Petroleum Ltd* [1974] AC 821 at 835 and 837–8; see also *Re a company (Case No 005136 of 1986)* [1987] BCLC 82 at 84–85; and *Re Chez Nico (Restaurants) Ltd* [1992] BCLC 192 at 208; and *Platt v Platt* [1999] 2 BCLC

In conclusion, the general rule is clear. It was stated in *Percival v Wright*. In *Dawson International* Lord Cullen repeated that directors had "but one master, the company", and that were the law to be otherwise, the existence of parallel duties could lead to conflict.[64] The other fear, as expressed by Neuberger J, in *Peskin v Anderson*, was that parallel duties would represent the placing of "an unfair, unrealistic and uncertain burden on a director."[65] The law developed over the course of the twentieth century to admit of specific circumstances where a fiduciary duty might exist — *Allen v Hyatt*, *Brunninghausen v Glavanics*, *Coleman v Myers*, *Stein v Blake* — so that certain events may bring directors into the "direct and close contact with the shareholders" discussed above, which acts to generate fiduciary obligations.

Duty to Creditors

Directors do owe a duty to creditors when the company is insolvent and when it is in that "grey area", approaching insolvency. The safest advice is to say that when a company is experiencing financial difficulties which may put the creditors' money or interests at risk, the directors have a duty to consider or act in the interests of the company's creditors.[66] This was enunciated in an Australian case of the mid-1980s — *Kinsela v Russell Kinsela Property Ltd*[67]— and adopted in three important Irish decisions after that, *Parkes v Hong Kong & Shanghai Bank Corp*,[68] *Re Frederick Inns Ltd*[69] and *Jones v Gunn*.[70] When the company is solvent, it is often the interests of the shareholders which the directors consider, but when a company is insolvent, in the words of the Court in *Kinsella*, "the interests of the creditors intrude". This is logical and fair because when a company is headed for liquidation the shareholders have no more claim on the assets

---

745 where a director bought shares from his two shareholding brothers on the basis of misrepresentation and in breach his fiduciary relationship to them (this decision was affirmed by the Court of Appeal on the basis of misrepresentation only at [2001] 1 BCLC 698).

[64] *Dawson International plc v Coats Paton plc* [1989] BCLC 233 at 243.

[65] *Peskin v Anderson* [2000] 2 BCLC 1 at 14.

[66] See *Roberts v Frohlich* [2011] 2 BCLC 625.

[67] [1986] 4 NSWLR 722. Street CJ stated at 730: "where a company is insolvent the interests of the creditors intrude. They become prospectively entitled, through the mechanism of liquidation, to displace the power of the shareholders and directors to deal with the company's assets."

[68] [1990] ILRM 341.

[69] [1994] 1 ILRM 387.

[70] [1997] 2 ILRM 245 and [1997] 3 IR 1.

until the creditors' claims are satisfied.[71] As Templeman LJ explained in *Winkworth v Edward Baron Development Co*:

> "...a company owes a duty to its creditors, present and future. The company is not bound to pay off every debt as soon as it is incurred and the company is not obliged to avoid all ventures which involve an element of risk, but the company owes a duty to its creditors to keep its property inviolate and available for the repayment of its debts ... A duty is owed by the directors to the company and to the creditors of the company to ensure that the affairs of the company are properly administered and that its property is not dissipated or exploited for the benefit of the directors themselves to the prejudice of the creditors."[72]

Fiduciary Duties

Directors are employees of the company, and as such owe a duty of loyalty and fidelity to their employer.[73] They are quasi-trustees of the company's profits and they have a fiduciary relationship to the company because they act as its agent. The fiduciary duties of directors were previously found in common law pronouncements but the Companies Act 2014 codifies them in s 228, in a list that is nonetheless not intended to be an exhaustive one. All of the law which interpreted the common law duties is still to be used as a guide in interpreting the codified duties in the Act.[74] A company director must:

(a) Act in good faith in what the director considers to be the interests of the company (company directors may, however, have regard to the interests of a particular shareholder if they were appointed or nominated by that shareholder[75]);

(b) Act honestly and responsibly in relation to the conduct of the affairs of the company;

---

[71] See also *West Mercia Safetywear v Dodd* [1988] BCLC 250.

[72] [1986] 1 WLR 1512 at 1516; see also *Re MDA Investment Management Ltd, Whalley v Doney* [2004] 1 BCLC 217 at [70] per Park J; for an example of a failure to have regard to the interests of creditors leading to disqualification, see *Re Genosyis Technology Management Ltd, Wallach v Secretary of State for Trade and Industry* [2007] 1 BCLC 208.

[73] Non-executive directors, however, may not be "employees"; they may draw directors' fees but not have a contract of employment. Each case will depend on its own facts.

[74] Companies Act 2014, s 227(5).

[75] *ibid*, s 228(4).

(c) Act in accordance with the company's constitution and exercise his or her powers only for the purposes allowed by law;

(d) Not use the company's property, information or opportunities for his or anyone else's benefit unless—(i) this is expressly permitted by the company's constitution; or (ii) the use has been approved by a resolution of the company in general meeting;

(e) Not agree to restrict his power to exercise an independent judgment unless: (i) this is expressly permitted by the company's constitution; (ii) the director considers in good faith that it is in the interests of the company for a transaction or engagement to be entered into and carried into effect, a director may restrict his power to exercise an independent judgment in the future by agreeing to act in a particular way to achieve this[76]; (iii) the director's agreeing to such has been approved by a resolution of the company in general meeting;

(f) Avoid any conflict between the director's duties to the company and the director's other (including personal) interests unless he is released from his duty to the company in relation to the matter concerned, whether in accordance with provisions of the company's constitution in that regard or by a resolution of it in general meeting;

(g) Exercise the care, skill and diligence which would be exercised in the same circumstances by a reasonable person having both: (i) the knowledge and experience that may reasonably be expected of a person in the same position as the director; and (ii) the knowledge and experience which the director has;
and

(h) In addition to the duty to have regard to the interests of its employees in general,[77] have regard to the interests of its members.

A number of these points are well represented in the case law. For guidance as to s 228(1)(b) — what constitutes honest and responsible behaviour — readers should turn primarily to the case law on restriction and disqualification (Chapter 7).

---

[76] *ibid*, s 228(2).
[77] Set out in s 224.

No Profits, No Conflicts of Interest

Section 228(1)(d) states that a director may not use the company's property, information or opportunities for his or her own or anyone else's benefit unless: (i) this is expressly permitted by the company's constitution; or (ii) the use has been approved by a resolution of the company in general meeting. There is a good deal of case law on this area.

Any person with a fiduciary duty is not entitled to make a profit from their position, unless that is expressly provided for. Since directors are in a fiduciary position this inflexible rule applies to them, for, as Lord Herschell put it in *Bray v Ford*[78] "human nature being what it is, there is a danger a person holding a fiduciary duty can be swayed by his interest rather than his duty".[79] Much the same thing was said in *Aberdeen Railway Co v Blaikie Brothers*.[80] The most famous case in this area is *Regal (Hastings) Ltd v Gulliver*,[81] where directors made a profit from their position and did not reveal this to the company shareholders. Had they revealed it, there was the chance that the shareholders would have absolved them, and let them keep it. But they did not give the shareholders that opportunity, and so the Court held that they had to "disgorge" — or give back — the profits.

As Viscount Sankey stated:

> "At all material times they were directors and in a fiduciary position, and they used and acted upon their exclusive knowledge acquired as such directors. They framed resolutions by which they made a profit for themselves. They sought no authority from the company to do so, and, by reason of their position and actions, they made large profits for which, in my view, they are liable to account to the company."[82]

---

[78] [1896] AC 44.

[79] *ibid* at 51–52.

[80] [1854] 1 Macq 461. Lord Cranworth stated that no fiduciary "...shall be allowed to enter into engagements in which he has, or can have, a personal interest conflicting, or which may possibly conflict, with the interests of those whom he is bound to protect." The headnote states: "The director of a railway company is a trustee, and, as such, is precluded from dealing, on behalf of the company, with himself, or with a firm of which he is a partner."

[81] [1967] 2 AC 134.

[82] *ibid* at 139.

The directors' state of mind doesn't matter in these cases. They will be asked to account for the money they made whether they made it *bona* or *mala fide*. *Regal (Hastings)* was approved most recently in *AIB plc v Diamond*[83] where Clarke J cited Lord Russell, when he stated that

> "[t]he liability arises from the mere fact of a profit having…been made. The profiteer, however honest and well-intentioned, cannot escape the risk of being called upon to account."

In *Parolen Ltd v Doherty and Lindat Ltd*[84] Clarke J recognised that the strict rule in *Regal (Hastings)* can lead to injustice but it wasn't something he could decide in that case, rather, he said that the law would have to remain as it was until the matter came before the High Court in a full plenary hearing. In *Bhullar v Bhullar*[85] Jonathan Parker LJ said that where directors purchased a property without informing the company of the existence of the opportunity to acquire it, there was no need to ask anything but the following simple question: "was the fiduciary's exploitation of the opportunity such as to attract the application of the rule?" The Court of Appeal held that the rule expounded in *Regal (Hastings)* was "universal and inflexible".

Statutory Duty to Declare Interest in Contracts

Section 228(1)(f) states that a director must avoid any conflict between his duties to the company and his other interests (including personal) unless he is released from his duty to the company in relation to the matter concerned (whether in accordance with provisions of the company's constitution in that behalf or by a resolution of it in general meeting). Contracts between directors and the company are voidable unless the shareholders have approved them. Section 231 of Companies Act 2014 provides that if a director is directly or indirectly interested in a contract which the company proposes to enter he has a duty to declare his interest. He must make that declaration at the meeting of directors at which the question of entering into the contract is first taken into consideration. There is no latitude. If the director had no interest at that time, but

---

[83] [2011] IEHC 505.
[84] [2010] IEHC 71.
[85] [2003] 2 BCLC 241.

subsequently gains one, then he must make the declaration at the very next directors' meeting.

Directors Competing with Their Companies

In *Spring Grove Services (Ireland) Ltd v O'Callaghan*[86] Herbert J stated that:

> "[a] director of a company owes strict obligations of good faith, fair dealing and honesty to the company of which he is a director. Aspects of these obligations commonly referred to as fiduciary duties include a duty not to compete with the company, a duty to act in the best interests of the company and a duty not to use confidential information obtained as a director otherwise than for the benefit of the company."

Where a director is an employee of the company, then whether his contract is oral or in writing, he owes an implied duty of loyalty which lasts as long as his contract is in being (directors and managing directors usually will be employees: non-executive directors are usually not; they may be paid directors' fees, but will have no day-to-day management role. When things go wrong and the company is wound-up, the courts have recently begun to take the view that the non-executive director will have had less of a role in the company's downfall, because his role is not "co-extensive" with the executive directors, being as he is a boardroom presence rather than an active manager[87]).

Severity of the Rule

The severity of the no conflict rule was shown in *Industrial Development Consultants Ltd v Cooley*.[88] The defendant was managing director of the plaintiff, a construction specialist. The defendant had been offered the role of MD partly because of his contacts in the gas industry. There were no restrictive covenants in the defendant's contract of employment and no provisions regarding notice periods. A public body — a Gas Board — was

---

[86] Unreported, High Court, 31 July 2000. Most textbooks begin with *Moore v M'Glynn* [1894] 1 IR 74. This is a case that touches the point only by analogy, because it deals with a trust. It is better to begin with *Spring Grove Services*.

[87] See the comments of Hardiman J in *Re Tralee Beef & Lamb Ltd* [2008] 3 IR 347 at 359–360. This should be borne in mind when considering whether a non-executive director should be restricted.

[88] [1972] 2 All ER 162; [1972] 1 WLR 443 (it is an *ex tempore* judgment of Roskill J).

contemplating building four gas depots (at a cost of over £2m). The plaintiffs wished to obtain the contract. In the course of negotiations it became clear to the defendant, Mr Cooley, that the Gas Board did not like the plaintiff's organisation. Some months later the Gas Board had settled on a location for the depots and a new chairman was in charge. He was told that the defendant was either in, or was thinking of getting into, private practice. The new chairman telephoned the defendant and set up a meeting at the Gas Board's offices:

> "It became plain to the defendant at the meeting that if he was to obtain the work from the board it was necessary to secure his release from the plaintiffs as quickly as possible."[89]

Over the weekend the defendant worked on a number of documents which related to the proposed work with the Gas Board (these were detailed proposals concerning the work). On the Monday, he met the founder of the plaintiff company, Mr Hicks, and made certain untrue representations to him about his health which led Hicks to believe that Mr Cooley was on the verge of a breakdown. This took place in mid-June, and the result was that on 1 August the defendant was released from his contract with the plaintiff. Five days later he was offered a contract with the Gas Board to do work which was more or less the same work which the plaintiffs had unsuccessfully pitched for the previous year. The plaintiffs took an action against the defendant seeking an account of profits to the defendant which resulted from the breach of fiduciary duty. The plaintiffs argued that from the middle of June he set about obtaining the contract for himself. The defendant contended that the only remedy was in damages, but no damage had occurred since the plaintiffs would never had obtained the work for themselves. The Court stated:

> "There is no doubt that the defendant obtained that very valuable contract with the Eastern Gas Board at the beginning of August 1969. The plaintiffs seek to say that he is accountable to them for the whole of the benefit of the contract so obtained, for all fees and all remuneration which he has received or will hereafter receive thereunder. The basis of the plaintiffs' claim for such an account of the defendant's benefit under that contract can be put in this way. They say his terms of service

---

[89] [1972] 2 All ER 162 at 165–6.

with the plaintiffs between the beginning of 1968, when he joined the plaintiffs, and the end of July or the beginning of August 1969, when he left, required him to devote the whole of his services to the plaintiffs. They say that from about the beginning or middle of June 1969 onwards, instead of devoting the whole of his time and endeavour to giving the plaintiffs his advice and all his services as he should, he was in fact, in breach of his duty, seeking to obtain business for himself, particularly this Eastern Gas Board business. They say that his duty required him to obtain that business for and only for the plaintiffs. Put in another, way, the plaintiffs say he allowed his duty and his interests to conflict."[90]

Roskill J went on:

"There can be no doubt that the defendant got this Eastern Gas Board contract for himself and got it as a result of work which he did whilst still the plaintiffs' managing director. It is, of course, right to say that the contract for that work was not concluded until after he had left the plaintiffs... He was still their managing director not only at the time when he met [the chairman of the Gas Board] on 13 June but when he prepared the documents over the ensuing weekend, sending them off on 17 June so as to get this work for himself... It is plain that at the meeting of 13 June the defendant became possessed of knowledge and information which was not possessed by his employer, the plaintiffs, knowledge which the plaintiffs would have wished to possess...the defendant...was prepared to obtain his freedom by fair means or if necessary by foul... When one looks at the letters of 17 June and the associated documents, there is disclosed the plainest conflict of interest between the defendant as potential architect or project manager of the Eastern Gas Board and as managing director of the plaintiffs. Finally I ought to say that I am sure Mr Hicks would not have agreed to give the defendant the carte blanche release claimed by the defendant if he had known the full facts about the Eastern Gas Board project."[91]

---

[90] *ibid* at 167–8.
[91] [1972] 2 All ER 162 at 168–9.

The Court found that the defendant was liable to account.[92] He had not used the plaintiff's property or confidential information in obtaining the job for himself. But he had misused his position as director.[93] It was no argument to say that the defendant received notice of the business opportunity in his private capacity, because he was MD of the plaintiff company at the time he received it. He had a duty to pass on to the plaintiffs any information which was relevant for them to know. In the Court's view: "it is the basic principle which matters."[94]

In Canada, it was held that a director who declared a business opportunity to the board was, if the board rejected it, allowed to personally take advantage of that opportunity: the crucial thing was that the opportunity had been brought to the board's attention, been considered, and been decided against (*Peso Silver Mines Ltd v Cropper*[95]). This is not the law in Ireland, which takes its cue from the UK, where the rule is as inflexible as ever. In *JJ Harrison (Properties) Ltd v Harrison*,[96] for example, Chadwick LJ stated

> "[a] director assumes the duties of a trustee in relation to the company's property. If he takes possession of that property his possession is coloured from the start by the trust and confidence by which he obtained it. His obligations as a trustee to that property do not arise out of the transaction by which the property became his, but out of his preexisting duties as a director."[97]

---

[92] Roskill J did not state the extent of the liability to account; he did say that if he had awarded damages instead, he thought that the plaintiffs had only a 10% chance of obtaining the contract, and so "If I am wrong in making an order for account I should have given the plaintiffs as damages whatever would represent a 10% chance."

[93] Roskill J considered *dicta* in *Bell v Lever Bros Ltd* and *Boardman v Phipps* ([1966] 3 All ER 721 at 756 (*per* Lord Upjohn), which in turn cited *Bray* v. *Ford* ([1896] AC 44 at 51 and *Aberdeen Ry. Co. v Blaikie Brothers* (1854) 2 Eq Rep 1281 at 1286, and *Regal (Hastings), Keech v Sanford* [1588–1774] All ER Rep at 230.

[94] *Per* Roskill J, [1972] 2 All ER 162 at 176: "It is an overriding principle of equity that a man must not be allowed to put himself in a position in which his fiduciary duty and his interests conflict. The variety of cases where that can happen is infinite. The fact there has not previously been a case precisely of this nature with precisely similar facts before the courts is of no import. The facts of this case are, I think, exceptional and I hope unusual. They seem to me plainly to come within this principle."

[95] (1966) 58 DLR 1.

[96] [2002] 1 BCLC 162.

[97] *ibid* at 175.

The strictness of the English approach was again evident *O'Donnell v Shanahan*,[98] where the Court again stated that a director's duty "is one of undivided loyalty".[99]

The usual remedy is that the director must account to the company: he must give back the money he has wrongly made. The logic is this: the courts treat the money made by the director as actually belonging to the company, with the director merely a constructive trustee for the company.[100] The company will take proceedings for breach of fiduciary duty, breach of the duty of fidelity owed by an employee to his employer, for an account of profits and/or for damages. It is possible that a court will award damages only. The Court favoured an award of damages in *Aerospares Ltd v Thompson & Ors*[101] because the plaintiff was seeking to recover unascertained loss of earnings over an indefinite period stretching into the future as a result of the directors having poached the company's clients.

Use of Confidential Information

There might be a clause in the contract that prohibits competition, or which prohibits the use of confidential information. The director will, however, be able to make the most of such information once his contract comes to an end, unless that information can be classed as a "trade secret" or "confidential information".[102] That principle was decided in *Faccenda Chicken Ltd v Fowler*,[103] which Clarke J accepted and applied in *The Pulse Group v O'Reilly*,[104] stating "the only enduring obligation on the part of an employee after his employment has ceased is one which precludes the employee from disclosing a trade secret."[105]

---

[98] [2009] BCC 822.

[99] [2009] 2 BCLC 666 at 685; see also *Gencor ACP Ltd v Dalby* [2000] 2 BCLC 734; both judgments were given by Rimer LJ.

[100] See *CMS Dolphin Ltd v Simonet* [2001] 2 BCLC 704.

[101] Unreported, High Court, Kearns J, 13 January 1999.

[102] Whether the information was a trade secret will depend on whether the employee regularly handled confidential information and recognised it as such, the nature of the information, whether the employer had stressed the confidentiality of the information, whether the relevant information could easily be isolated from other non-confidential information which was part of the same package of information.

[103] [1986] 1 All ER 617.

[104] [2006] IEHC 50.

[105] *ibid* at para 3.5.

Directors Competing and Poaching Workforce

In *British Midland Tool Ltd v Midland International Tooling*[106] a number of the plaintiff's directors had grown dissatisfied and decided to leave and set up a rival company, taking some of the plaintiff's employees with them. These four directors (who set up the rival company) kept their plan secret from the other directors. The Court stated:

> "The situation was one, quite simply, where to the knowledge of three of the six members of the board of BMT, a determined attempt was being made by a potential competitor to poach the former company's workforce. The remaining three at best did nothing to discourage, and at worst actively promoted, the success of this process. In my judgment this was a plain breach of their duties as directors. Those duties required them to take active steps to thwart the process. Plainly their plan required the opposite. Active steps should have included alerting their fellow directors to what was going on."[107]

It should be noted that the Court was of the view that there as an active duty on the part of the non-breaching directors to report those committing the breach of duty. It was argued that such a duty did not exist, that a duty to report could only extend to a subordinate employee and not exist among equals. This argument was rejected. Passive standing by while the workforce was poached was itself a breach of the directors' fiduciary duties.

Where a Director's Spouse/Partner is a Company Rival

Fairbrother v Stiefel Laboratories (Ireland) Ltd[108] provides an example of a director whose loyalty was called into question when it came to light that his wife was running a rival company. It is an employment rather than a company law case. It came before the Employment Appeals Tribunal and the sole question for the Tribunal was whether the company had acted reasonably in dismissing the plaintiff. The case report is short. There isn't a great deal of legal analysis. Whether there was actually a conflict of interest was not examined. The sole question was whether the company

---

[106] [2003] 2 BCLC 523.
[107] *ibid* at 561.
[108] (1985) UD665/1985.

had acted reasonably in dismissing Dr Fairbrother and the EAT found that it had. Dr Fairbrother's position of responsibility, authority and control in the company was an important factor in the Tribunal's conclusion.

Another conflict of interest/reasonable dismissal case is *Conachey v Little Chic Knitwear*.[109] Martin Conachey worked for Little Chic Knitwear for sixteen years before he was dismissed: he was a sales director, and spent four days each week on the road, selling the company's products. It was a company based in Cork, which manufactured children's and young women's knitwear products made of acrylic. After returning from sick leave Mr Conachey was told by the company accountant that the company wasn't in good financial health and he should think about leaving. He approached a State body — the IDA — about a company which was "on the market" which manufactured pure wool school knitwear for the Cork area. Two months later he was suspended on suspicion of carrying products from a company other than Little Chic. He said he wasn't. His boss put him "under intense pressure" to resign after Conachey refused to answer questions as to whether or not he had approached the IDA. The Employment Appeals Tribunal held that his dismissal was not unfair because an employer was "entitled to insist that an employee does not interest himself in a company which will compete with the business of the employer" and that his failure to answer the questions — it seems — led the Tribunal to conclude that he had not acted reasonably.

---

[109] (1985) UD342/85.

CHAPTER SIX

DIRECTORS AND CONFLICT OF INTEREST TRANSACTIONS

Substantial Property Transactions

If a director had a free hand to sell to the company an asset that belonged to him, he might be tempted to cause the company to purchase it at an overvalue: if the transaction involved the director buying property of the company, he might be tempted to cause the company to sell the property at an undervalue. As MacCann and Courtney politely put it, where there are conflicts of interest or loyalty, directors' judgment "may be distorted".[1] For this reason, directors do not have a free hand in such transactions: they are subject to statutory control, set out in s 238 of Companies Act 2014. The Act states that a company must not enter into an "arrangement" under which:

(a) a director of the relevant company or of its holding company, or a person connected with such a director, acquires or is to acquire, one or more non-cash assets of the requisite value from the relevant company[2], or

(b) the relevant company acquires or is to acquire, one or more non-cash assets of the requisite value from such a director or a person so connected unless the arrangement is first approved: (i) by a resolution of the relevant company in general meeting; and (ii) if the director or connected person is a director of its holding company or a person connected with such a director, by a resolution of the holding company in general meeting.[3]

Carnwarth J, in *British Racing Drivers' Club Ltd v Hextall Erskine & Co*,[4] spoke of the English equivalent to our section, and said that:

> "[t]he thinking behind that section is that if directors enter into a substantial commercial transaction with one of their number, there is a danger that their judgment may be distorted by conflicts of interest and loyalties, even in cases where there is no actual dishonesty. The section is designed to protect

---

[1] MacCann & Courtney, *Annotated Companies Acts 1963–2012* (Bloomsbury Professional, 2012) at p 1222.

[2] According to s 238(5) this part of the rule does not apply in relation to any arrangement under which a person acquires (or is to acquire) an asset from a company of which he is a member if the arrangement is made with that person *in his character as such member.*

[3] Companies Act 2014, s 238(1).

[4] [1997] 1 BCLC 182; applied in *Dadourian Group International v Simms* [2007] EWHC 454 (Ch) and *Redbus LMDS Ltd v Jeffrey Green And Russell (a firm)* [2006] EWHC 2938 (Ch).

a company against such distortions. It enables members to provide a check. Of course, this does not necessarily mean that the members will exercise a better commercial judgment; but it does make it likely that the matter will be more widely ventilated, and a more objective decision reached."[5]

Important Definitions and Qualifications

There are a number of technical factors which must be considered under this part of company law. For ease of reading, they are outlined below in bullet-point format, from (a) to (m).

(a) An "arrangement" is an extremely broad term which catches all imaginable kinds of transactions, even ones which are not contractually binding (for example, an understanding or an agreement between parties)[6];

(b) Because of the inclusion of "connected persons" in s 238(1)(a) the scope of persons who can be caught by the section is very wide. The Act defines connected persons in s 220. A person is connected with a director of a company if the person is: (a) that director's spouse, civil partner,[7] parent, brother, sister or child,[8] or business partner[9]; (b) the trustee of any trust, the principal beneficiaries of which are that director, the spouse (or civil partner) or any children of that director or any body corporate which that director controls. A body corporate is also deemed to be a connected person if it is controlled by that director or by another body corporate that is controlled by that director. Control, in this regard, means that the director is "alone or together with any other director": (a) interested in one-half or more of the equity share capital of that body; or (b) entitled to exercise or control the exercise of one-half or more of the voting power at any general meeting of that body.

---

[5] [1997] 1 BCLC 182 at 197.
[6] For that example, I am indebted to MacCann and Courtney, *Companies Acts 1963–2012* (annotated), (Bloomsbury Professional, 2012), at p 1222
[7] As defined in the Civil Partnership and Certain Rights and Obligations of Cohabitants Act 2010.
[8] "Child", in relation to a director, is deemed to include a child of the director's civil partner who is ordinarily resident with the director and the civil partner.
[9] "Partner" as defined by s 1(1) of the Partnership Act 1890.

(c) The resolution required by s 238(1) is an ordinary resolution. Finlay Geoghegan J has said, "[t]he mischief sought to be avoided appears confined to the protection of shareholders with a right to vote. It does not have any wider ambit".[10] There doesn't need to be formal approval by the shareholders; as long as they all agree on the course of action, according to the principle known as the *Duomatic Principle*, this agreement will be "tantamount to a resolution"[11];

(d) "Non-cash asset" means any property or interest in property other than cash and "cash" includes foreign currency;

(e) For the purposes of s 238 a non-cash asset is of the "requisite value" if at the time the arrangement in question is entered into its value is not less than €5,000 but, subject to that, exceeds €65,000 or 10% of the amount of the relevant company's "relevant assets";

(f) The amount of a company's relevant assets is either the value of its net assets, which is determined by reference to the company's entity financial statements[12]; or if no entity financial statements have been prepared, the amount of a company's relevant assets will be the amount of the company's called-up share capital;

(g) To illustrate the cash amounts: no arrangement worth less than €5,000 is caught by s 238. All arrangements over €65,000 are caught by s 238;

(h) What happens if the value of the asset falls between those two stools? That is where the "10% of the amount of the company's relevant assets" comes into it. If the relevant assets of the company are €100,000, and the proposed arrangement between director and company has a value of €15,000, then the arrangement will be caught by the section, because it concerns something worth more than 10% of the company's relevant assets. Take a second example. If the company's relevant assets are €630,000 and the transaction is for an asset worth €50,000, will the transaction be caught? While €50,000 is "substantial" in layman's terms, it is not substantial for

---

[10] *Kerr et al v Conduit Enterprises Ltd* [2011] 3 IR 1 at 17.

[11] The principle is known in Ireland by its English name "Duomatic" and by the Irish case where the principle was established, *Buchanan Ltd v McVey* [1954] IR 89. For a recent application, see *Kerr v Conduit Enterprises Ltd* [2011] 3 IR 1 at 13 – 20.

[12] These are prepared under s 290 of Companies Act 2014 and laid before the members in accordance with s 341.

the purposes of the section and this company. It is less than €65,000 and less than 10% of the company's relevant assets;

(i) The rule set out in s 238(1) does not apply in the following three circumstances. It does not apply if the non-cash asset in question is or is to be acquired: (i) by a holding company from any of its wholly owned subsidiaries; or (ii) from a holding company by any of its wholly owned subsidiaries; or (iii) by one wholly owned subsidiary of a holding company from another wholly owned subsidiary of that holding company;

(j) A non-cash asset includes a reference to the creation or extinction of an estate or interest in (or a right over) any property and also a reference to the discharge of any person's liability other than a liability for a liquidated sum;

(k) The rule set out in s 238(1) does not apply if the arrangement is entered into by a company which is being wound-up unless the winding up is a members' voluntary winding-up;

(l) The rule set out in s 238(1) does not apply if the arrangement involves the disposal of a company's assets by a receiver[13];

(m) If a prohibited arrangement has gone through, the burden of proving that the non-cash asset is of the requisite value rests on the person who is asserting that a breach occurred.

Consequences of Section 238 Breach and Breach of General Duties

From a practical point of view, it seems that the greatest problem presented by s 238 is that people don't realise it applies, and fail to obtain shareholder approval because of this, leaving the transaction vulnerable at a later stage.[14] Breach of s 238 means that any arrangement — and/or any transaction entered into in pursuance of the arrangement (whether by the company or any other person) — will be voidable at the instance of the company.[15] This rule is subject to three exceptions. The arrangement will not be voidable if:

---

[13] This is new, brought in by Companies Act 2014.

[14] Such was the case in *Joint Receivers and Managers of Niltan Carson v Hawthorne* [1998] BCLC 298 (see Hodgson J at 320, where "there would not have been the slightest difficulty in obtaining approval").

[15] *Duckwari plc v Offerventure Ltd & Anor (No2)* [1999] BCC 11.

(a) Restitution of any money or any other asset which is the subject-matter of the arrangement or transaction is no longer possible, or if the company has been indemnified by any other person for the loss or damage suffered by it[16]; or

(b) Any rights acquired *bona fide* for value and without actual notice of the contravention by any person who is not a party to the arrangement or transaction would be affected by its avoidance; or

(c) The arrangement is affirmed by a resolution of the company in general meeting passed within a reasonable period of time after the date on which the arrangement is entered into[17]; and, if it is an arrangement for the transfer of an asset to or by a director of its holding company or a person who is connected with such a director, is affirmed by a resolution of the holding company in general meeting passed within a reasonable period of time after that date.

Where a director breaches any of the directors' duties set out in s 228 of the Companies Act 2014, liability under either of the following headings can be imposed:

(a) He can be made to account to the company for any gain which he makes directly or indirectly from the breach of duty;

(b) He can be made to indemnify the company for any loss or damage resulting from that breach.[18]

The same can be imposed on connected persons who breach s 238 or s 239 of the Companies Act 2014 (unless the directors can show that he "took all reasonable steps to secure the company's compliance" with the sections and unless he can show that at the time of the transaction he "did not know the relevant circumstances constituting the contravention").[19]

Prohibition of Loans to Directors and Connected Persons

The second potential conflict of interest area which is subject to statutory regulation is where a director causes a company to make a loan to him.

---

[16] On the indemnity point, see s 232 of Companies Act 2014.
[17] For discussion of a reasonable period see *Re Duckwari plc* [1997] 2 WLR 48.
[18] Companies Act 2014, s 232 (1).
[19] Companies Act 2014, s 232(2) and (6).

This is prohibited, along with certain other kinds of transactions, but the general rule is subject to qualification. Section 239 states that a company must not, as a general rule:

(a) Make a loan or a quasi-loan to a director of the company or of its holding company or to a person connected with such a director[20];

(b) Enter into a credit transaction as creditor for such a director or a person so connected,

(c) Enter into a guarantee or provide any security in connection with a loan, quasi-loan or credit transaction made by any other person for such a director or a person so connected.

Arrangements which seek to circumvent the general rule, by causing another person to enter into the kind of transaction which would contravene s 239(1) in place of the company, are also prohibited.[21]

The logic of the rule was explained in *Re Ciro Citterio Menswear plc*:

"Directors have an important responsibility in relation to the funds under their control. That responsibility is hedged around with legal obligations and criminal offences…If the directors agree that the one in credit will provide his credit for the benefit of the other so as to create a loan, then that is permissible and easily achieved, but it does require some sort of agreement that that is what should happen, and it requires real transactions to take place and to be documented. The company has a right to expect that such matters are properly documented and that the transaction is properly carried out. The directors are not entitled to deal with matters informally and sort it out later."[22]

Knowledge, on the part of one director, that a practice has built up where another director takes loans from the company, and failure to act by the director who is not engaging in the practice, may be enough to make that director liable to repay some or all of the loaned money to the company.[23]

---

[20] See *Re T O'Reilly (Electrical Suppliers) Ltd* [2014] IEHC 463 for consideration of large loans to a director in the context of restriction applications.

[21] Companies Act 2014, s 239(3).

[22] *Per* Anthony Mann QC (sitting as a Deputy Judge of the High Court) [2002] 1 BCLC 672 at 683; the important finding in the case was that because a prohibited loan stands until it is avoided by the company, it cannot be said that the director automatically becomes a constructive trustee of the money.

[23] *Neville v Krikorian* [2007] 1 BCLC 1; see also *Queensway Systems Ltd v Walker* [2007] 2 BCLC 577.

Qualifications of the Rule in Section 239

Section 239 of the Companies Act 2014 sets out the general rule that loans by the company to directors or connected persons are prohibited, but there are a number of qualifications to this:

(a) If the company uses the Summary Approval Procedure the prohibitions in s 239 against the making of loans or quasi-loans, the entering into of credit transactions or guarantees or the provision of security, do not apply[24];

(b) The rule in s 239 does not apply if the value of the arrangement is less than 10% of the company's relevant assets.[25] The arrangement mentioned here includes the granting by a person of a loan, quasi-loan, the entering into a credit transaction as creditor, the provision of security in connected with a loan or credit transaction, the entering into a guarantee. If the arrangement was made for the benefit of a person, and the court is of the view, when the company is being wound up, that that arrangement contributed materially to the company's inability to pay its debts, that person may be fixed with personal liability for some or all of the debts of the company[26];

(c) As stated above, the amount of a company's relevant assets is either the value of its net assets, which is determined by reference to the company's entity financial statements,[27] or if no entity financial statements have been prepared, the amount of a company's relevant assets will be the amount of the company's called-up share capital.

(d) Intra-group transactions are not prohibited (i.e. the carrying out of those transactions by a company with a holding company, a subsidiary or a subsidiary of its holding company)[28];

(e) Nothing in the s 239 rule is to be read as preventing the company from providing any of its directors with funds to meet vouched expenditure: (i) for the purposes of the company; or (ii) for the

---

[24] Companies Act 2014, s 242.

[25] *ibid*, s 240.

[26] *ibid*, s 247.

[27] These are prepared under s 290 of Companies Act 2014 and laid before the members in accordance with s 341.

[28] Companies Act 2014, s 243.

purpose of enabling him or her properly to perform his or her duties as an officer of the company[29];

(f) Nothing in the s 239 rule is to be read as preventing the company from making the kind of loans, guarantees, provision of security, etc, which the company would enter into "in the ordinary course of its business" and he value of the transaction is not greater, and the terms on which it is entered into are no more favourable, in respect of the person for whom the transaction is made, than that or those which the company ordinarily offers.[30]

Consequence of Section 239 Breach

If a company breaches s 239 the arrangement is voidable at the instance of the company unless:

(a) Restitution of any money or any other asset which is the subject matter of the arrangement or transaction is no longer possible (or the company has been indemnified for the loss or damage suffered by it); or

(b) Any rights acquired *bona fide* for value and without actual notice of the contravention by any person other than the person for whom the transaction or arrangement was made would be affected by its avoidance.[31]

Any officers who have been responsible for the s 239 breach are subject to category 2 penalties.[32]

Directors with Interests in Contracts

The law does allow directors to have an interest in contracts which their companies might be about to sign but s 231 of Companies Act 2014 imposes a duty on them to declare their interest, either in a contract or a proposed contract with the company, "whether directly or indirectly" (the rule does not apply in relation to an interest that cannot reasonably be regarded as likely to give rise to a conflict of interest).

---

[29] *ibid*, s 244(1). Note that s 244(2) states: "Where a company enters into any transaction that is permitted by s 244(1) any liability falling on any person arising from any such transaction shall be discharged by him or her within 6 months after the date on which it was incurred" and contravention of this is a category 4 offence.

[30] Companies Act 2014, s 245(1) and (2).

[31] *ibid*, s 246.

[32] *ibid*, s 248.

The section says that they must declare "the nature" of their interest and it doesn't matter how small it might be. The rest of the section is taken up with the practical steps to complying with this requirement. If they have an interest in a proposed contract, they should make their declaration "at the meeting of the directors at which the question of entering into the contract is first taken into consideration". If the director didn't have an interest in the contract at the time of the meeting when it was being considered, or if he acquires an interest in the contract after it has been entered into, the step he has to take is the same: once he acquires an interest he has to declare it at the very next meeting.

What will be deemed a sufficient declaration of interest in relation to a possible conflict of interest? The director must give the other directors "a general notice" to the effect that:

(a) He or she is a member of a specified company or firm and is to be regarded as interested in any contract which may, after the date of the notice, be made with that company or firm, or

(b) He or she is to be regarded as interested in any contract which may, after the date of the notice, be made with a specified person who is connected with him or her.

If the director does this, then he or she will have made a sufficient declaration of interest.[33] The notice must be given at the meeting of directors otherwise it will not be effective. If he doesn't give the notice at the meeting of directors — if, for example, he was not in attendance — he can satisfy the requirement by taking "reasonable steps" to ensure that the matter is brought up and read at the next meeting of the directors.[34] Once the declaration of interest is made it must be entered into "a book kept by the company for this purpose".[35] This book can be consulted free of charge by all members of the company, as well as any director, secretary, or statutory auditor. It has to be kept at the registered office of the company. It must be produced at every general meeting of the company and any meeting of the company directors if any directors requests in sufficient time to enable the book to be available at the meeting.[36] All s 239

---

[33] *ibid*, s 231(4); these rules were previously found in s 194 of Companies Act 1963.
[34] Companies Act 2014, s 231(5).
[35] *ibid*, s 231(6).
[36] *ibid*, s 231(7).

transactions and arrangements with a director are deemed to be things in respect of which a director has a declarable interest under s 231.[37]

What happens if the director doesn't declare his interest? If the company goes ahead and enters the contract, it may avoid it if it chooses.[38] If he has made profits from the contract, he will be liable to account for them.

Rebuttable Presumptions

The Companies Act 2014 introduces two rebuttable presumptions. The first is that if a director has made a loan to a company and the terms of the loan are not it writing, the loan is repayable on demand and that the amount has borne interest.[39] This rule applies is civil proceedings where it is claimed that a company has made a loan or quasi-loan to: (a) a director of the company; or (b) a director of its holding company; or (c) a person connected with a director of any such company.[40] If the terms of the loan are in writing (or partially in writing) but the terms are ambiguous with respect to the time at which the loan is to be repaid then it is presumed that the loan is repayable on demand, until the contrary is proved.[41]

In the reverse situation, where it is claimed that a transaction or arrangement entered into by a director of a company with the company constitutes a loan by the director to that company — and it is not in writing, or only partly in writing, or there is ambiguity — then it is presumed that the transaction or arrangement *does not* constitute a loan to the company.[42] This presumption is rebuttable. It applies where the transaction or arrangement took place between the director and the company's holding company. It applies to connected persons.[43] It applies to quasi-loans. There is also a presumption that the loan bears no interest and is not secured and that the loan is subordinate to all other indebtedness of the company.[44]

---

[37] *ibid*, s 231(10).
[38] See *Aberdeen Railway Co v Blaikie Bros* (1854) 1 Macq 461, *Bristol & West Building Society v Mothew* [1996] 4 All ER 698; and *Newgate Stud Co v Penfold* [2008] 1 BCLC 46.
[39] Companies Act 2014, s 236(2).
[40] *ibid*, s 236(1).
[41] *ibid*, s 236(3)(a).
[42] *ibid*, s 237.
[43] *ibid*, s 237(1)(b).
[44] *ibid*, s 237(3)(a) and (b) and (c).

RESTRICTION AND DISQUALIFICATION

PART I

The Aim is Not to Punish

Tucked into the Compliance and Enforcement part of the Companies Act 2014 are two significant remedies against delinquent directors and company officers: restriction and disqualification. It is a little difficult to talk about these measures without using words like "sanction" and "punishment" but those words have been banished by judges from this area of the law. Whatever restriction is, is it not a punishment. Time and time again, judges have emphasised that these measures are there "to protect the public" and not to punish the delinquent director. Why the courts have taken such pains to make this distinction is hard to justify: but it is there.

Why the punishment of directors is not an *equally* high priority if the conduct has gone beyond mere commercial error or misjudgement, is not evident. Two passages in particular are recited like a mantra. The first is the part of Browne-Wilkinson VC's judgment in *Re Lo-Line Motors Ltd*[1] which begins:

> "The primary purpose of the section is not to punish the individual but to protect the public against the future conduct of companies by persons whose past record as directors of insolvent companies have shown them to be a danger to creditors and others."

The second comes from *Business Communications v Baxter and Parsons*[2] where Murphy J said "[o]f course one must be careful not to be wise after the event. There must be no 'witch hunt' because the business failed as businesses will". The resulting regime is one which leans towards what might be called a very humane and understanding approach to corporate behaviour which is less than impeccable.

Locus Standi

So, first, a few definitions. An insolvent company is one which is unable to pay its debts as they fall due. A director of an insolvent company is any person who was a director in the twelve-month period prior to the

---

[1] [1988] Ch 477.
[2] Unreported, High Court, Murphy J, 21 July 1995, at 17.

company's liquidation: this includes shadow directors.[3] A number of parties have standing to make a restriction application—the Director of Corporate Enforcement, a receiver of the company's property, for example—but the most common applicant is the company's liquidator.[4] The director, the respondent to the application, may be fixed with the costs of not only of the application but also of the costs incurred by the applicant in investigating the matters which were the subject of the application[5]: this element will depend on how deserving of restriction the director is.[6]

The liquidator is obliged to apply for the restriction of directors of an insolvent company to which he is appointed unless he is relieved of this duty by the Director of Corporate Enforcement.[7] It is a category 3 offence for a liquidator to fail to comply with this rule.[8] Unless the DCE allows for a greater time, the restriction application must be made not later than the expiry of two months after the date on which the DCE has notified the liquidator that he is not relieved of the obligation to make the application in respect of the director.[9]

The Capital Requirement

Restriction seems to talk a tough game, but depending on a person's resources or connections, it can be made toothless. The period for which a person may be restricted is five years. There is no judicial discretion on this point. It is a five-year period, no more, no less, and it begins on the day when the declaration of restriction is made.[10] It seems to be a broad interdiction: the statute says that if restricted, a person

---

[3] For an application brought outside the time limit see *Coyle v Hughes* [2003] 2 IR 627; for a refusal to allow a late application see *Re Higgins Civil Engineering and Construction Ltd* [2013] IEHC 31 (Herbert J, 30 January 2013).

[4] Companies Act 2014, s 820(1).

[5] *ibid*, s 820(2).

[6] Since *USIT (Ireland)* [2005] IEHC 481 the courts have on occasion awarded costs against unsuccessful liquidators personally.

[7] Companies Act 2014, s 683(1), (2), (3).

[8] *ibid*, s 683(3).

[9] *ibid*, s 683(4).

[10] When it begins—whether on the date of the order or whether it dates from the commencement of the winding-up—was argued in *Duignan v Carway* [2001] 4 IR 550

"shall not... be appointed or act in any way, directly or indirectly, as a director or secretary of a company, or be concerned in or take part in the formation or promotion of a company".[11]

But there is an "unless provision". This refers to what is known as the "capital requirement". If a company has a minimum paid up share capital of €100,000 then a "restricted director"—such would be their official title— would not be prohibited from acting "in any way, directly or indirectly, as a director or secretary of a company", and so on.[12] This minimum capital requirement holds good for all companies except PLCs, where the requirement is five times as large.[13] The company which accepted a restricted director onto its board would be officially referred to as a "restricted company". Certain procedures involving the Summary Approval Procedure, which call for a certain amount of trustworthiness, are not open to it,[14] but in all other respects the company would be the same. Another matter to be noted is that the court has a very broad discretion to give relief to a restricted director "on such terms and conditions as it sees fit"; if a director were to apply for relief he is obliged to give 14 days' notice to the liquidator who took the application to restrict him.[15]

Defences to Restriction

The court "shall" restrict a person "unless" it is satisfied that:

(a) The person concerned has acted honestly and responsibly in relation to the conduct of the affairs of the company in question, whether before or after it became an insolvent company;

(b) He or she has, when requested to do so by the liquidator of the insolvent company, cooperated as far as could reasonably be expected in relation to the conduct of the winding-up of the insolvent company; and

(c) There is no other reason why it would be just and equitable that he or she should be subject to a restriction order.

---

[11] Companies Act 2014, s 819.
[12] The restricted director is obliged to inform the company which proposes to hire him of his status, per s 825.
[13] Companies Act 2014, s 819(3)(a)(i).
[14] See ss 827–834.
[15] Companies Act 2014, s 822.

Of these three points (a) is the key one, (b) is a new addition, brought in by Companies Act 2014 and (c) is almost never addressed in the case law. There is no Irish case where a director has satisfied the conditions under (a) and yet been restricted under subsection (c). It is so difficult to see this happening that subsection (c) seems a pointless retention. Prior to the enactment of Companies Act 2014 directors' duties already extended to assisting the liquidator and the "just and equitable" ground allowed the court to taken into account the director's behaviour after the winding-up began. A disgruntled director, for example, might file an inadequate or inaccurate statement of affairs, simply to make the liquidator's life difficult. That behaviour, however, was always capable of being dealt with under the rubric of irresponsibility.[16]

The burden of proof is on the director, something the Supreme Court has said is "draconian".[17] It is rare for a finding of dishonesty to be made: directors are usually restricted for irresponsibility.

The Test for Judging Behaviour

The most cited case in Irish restriction applications is *La Moselle Clothing Ltd v Souhali*.[18] The facts are never rehearsed, only the five point test of Shanley J, which according to Hardiman J has taken on an "almost canonical status".[19] This was not something which Shanley J could have predicted when he enunciated his five points, noting at the time that the points "necessarily overlap".[20] They were approved by the Supreme Court in *Re Squash (Ireland) Limited*[21] and are as follows. The court should have regard to

1. The extent to which the director has or has not complied with any obligation imposed on him by the Companies Acts[22];

---

[16] See the case of Barry Muncaster in *Re Tansoft Ltd* [1991] BCLC 339; For assessment of post-liquidation behaviour see also *Re CMC (Ireland) Ltd*, 4 March 2005, Clarke J.

[17] Per Hardiman J, *Re Tralee Beef & Lamb Ltd; Kavanagh v Delaney* [2008] 3 IR 347 at 354.

[18] [1998] 2 ILRM 345.

[19] *Re Tralee Beef & Lamb Ltd* [2008] 3 IR 347 at 358.

[20] [1998] 2 ILRM 345 at 352.

[21] [2001] 3 IR 35 at 40, where McGuinness J said the considerations were "very well set out" by Shanley J

[22] It should be remembered that the duty to keep proper books is joint and several; see *Re Vehicle Imports Ltd*, Unreported, High Court, Murphy J, 23 November 2000, and *Re Capital Auto Group* [2005] IEHC 434 (Peart J). For regular attendance at board meetings

2. The extent to which his conduct could be regarded as so incompetent as to amount to irresponsibility;

3. The extent of the directors' responsibility for the insolvency of the company;

4. The extent of the directors responsibility for the net deficiency in the assets of the company disclosed at the date of the winding-up or thereafter;

5. The extent to which the director in his conduct of the affairs of the company has displayed a lack of commercial probity or want of proper standards.

Point 1 refers to the proper keeping of company records and financial information, the proper holding of board meetings and passing of resolutions. Good corporate governance, in short. Financial records which are not particularly detailed are acceptable: the important thing is that they are detailed enough to allow auditors to understand the financial life of the company, detailed enough to allow directors to make well-informed commercial decisions. Keeping proper records has long been seen as an indication of responsibility which will go a good way to discharging the onus on directors in restriction applications.[23] While some delegation is acceptable, it is always ultimately a joint and several responsibility of each director: no individual director has been allowed to claim that he was not responsible for looking after that aspect of the business.[24] Technical breaches of the Companies Act, while less likely to result in restriction without more, may still justify the making of an order.[25] The making of an unfair preference in favour of one particular creditor or group of creditors is prohibited by the Companies Act and may lead to restriction.[26] Failure to file a statement of affairs and failing to explain why can merit restriction.[27]

---

see *Re Cavan Crystal Group Ltd*, Unreported, High Court, Murphy J, 26 April 1996. On the failure to make returns see *Re Newcastle Timber Ltd* [2001] 4 IR 586. For failure to comply with s 194 of the Companies Act 1963 see *Re XNet Information Systems Ltd* [2004] IEHC 82.

[23] *Re Costello Doors Ltd*, Unreported, High Court, Murphy J, 27 July 1995.

[24] *Re Vehicle Imports Ltd*, Unreported, High Court, 23 November 2000; *Re Capital Auto Group Ltd* [2005] IEHC 434; on delegation, see the comments of Finlay Geoghegan J in *Re 360 Networks (Ireland) Ltd* (21 December 2004); on directors who say they were merely making up the numbers see the comments of Carroll J in *Re Hunting Lodge* [1985] ILRM 75.

[25] *Re Xnet Information Systems* [2004] IEHC 82 (Finlay Geoghegan J); *Re Newcastle Timber Ltd* [2001] 4 IR 586; *Re Tansoft Ltd* [1991] BCLC 339.

[26] *Re Swanpool* [2006] 2 ILRM 217.

[27] *Re Dunleckney Ltd* [2001] 1 IR 103.

Point 2 is a difficult one because it is not easy to say where ineptitude changes its colouring and becomes irresponsibility. Being incompetent is not the same as being irresponsible, though the consequences of the behaviour may be the same. The case law rarely addresses this point in much detail, in part because of the strength of the pronouncements which allow and forgive "mere misjudgment" and commercial error. Whenever incompetence is mentioned the courts usually say it must be "gross" before it could attract restriction. Engaging in a plan which is overly optimistic will not be found to be incompetent if professional advice was sought and taken. Shanley J, citing *Continental Assurance Co of London plc v Burrows*,[28] said that

> "a director's ability to see the 'writing on the wall' (e.g. an inability to see from a perusal of the company's management accounts that the company was trading while insolvent) may result from sheer incompetence and justify a restriction."[29]

In *Coyle v Callanan*[30] a liquidator sought to have two directors restricted on the basis that they had breached the financial assistance provisions of company law but the Court declined to do so because the directors had received and acted on express legal advice which told them that the course of action was safe. In *Re MDN Rochford Construction Ltd*[31] the directors were restricted for "flying blind", i.e. failing to keep proper books of account and failure to take decisions based on a true and accurate picture of the company's state of health. In *Re First Class Toy Traders*[32] experienced businessmen who began trading through an undercapitalised company were not restricted, in part because they personally guaranteed the company's debts.

For Point 3 the courts will look for a causal link between wrongdoing by the director and the insolvency of the company: this must be done, however, without the use of hindsight. For Point 4 the courts will look for dishonest behaviour, such as issuing false invoices to avoid VAT,

---

[28] [1997] 1 BCLC 48.
[29] [1998] 2 ILRM 345 at 352.
[30] [2006] 1 IR 447; *see also Stafford v O'Connor* [2007] IEHC 246; *Re Gerdando Ltd* [2014] IEHC 187 (Barrett J, 1 April 2014); and *Re McNulty's Interchange Ltd* [1988] 4 BCC 533 (which was a disqualification application but turned on the taking of professional advice).
[31] Unreported, High Court, MacMenamin J, 18 August 2009.
[32] [2004] IEHC 289.

continuing to draw excessive or any remuneration when the company is insolvent,[33] diverting business opportunities or seeking to trade using phoenix companies, and deliberately putting off the company's liquidation to the detriment of creditors. There is little unique to point 5, which overlaps considerably with the previous points.

Recent Irish case law has not shed any further light on the above, but one difference is perceptible: the regime seems more forgiving of errors of judgment.[34] Even reproachable faults such as non-payment of monies owing to the Revenue have been forgiven in recent times, where there is evidence of a belated but genuine attempt to address this.[35]

NEDs and Restriction

The position of non-executive directors is an uncertain one. They must act honestly and responsibly, of course, but to what extent will they be liable to be restricted in the event of insolvency? There is a terrible lack of judicial comment on this in Irish case law and little guidance from the UK.[36] The Supreme Court has acknowledged that there is "usually a real difference" between executive and non-executive directors. According to Fennelly J:

> "There will usually be a real difference between the duties of executive and non-executive directors. The latter will usually be dependent on the former for information about the affairs and of the finances of the company, a fact which will impose correspondingly larger duties on the former."[37]

Unfortunately the Supreme Court was reluctant to say any more on this point, passing over an opportunity to provide any guidelines whatsoever.[38]

---

[33] *Re Stanford Services Ltd* [1987] BCLC 607.

[34] See *Re M.K. Fuels Ltd* [2014] IEHC 305 (Barrett J, 30 May 2014) and, as regards the first respondent, and *Re Zuccini Café and Restaurant Ltd* [2014] IEHC 369 (Barrett J, 25 July 2014).

[35] *Re Access Cleaning Services Ltd* [2014] IEHC 317 (Barrett J, 30 May 2014); this should be contrasted, however, with *Re Noxtad* [2014] IEHC 278.

[36] A NED may be restricted for using the company credit card inappropriately, as in *Re Zuccini Café and Restaurant Ltd* [2014] IEHC 369.

[37] *Re Mitek Holdings* [2010] 3 IR 374 at 397.

[38] It may be that the Court was too focused on smoothing over the debacle of *Re Tralee Beef and Lamb* [2008] 3 IR 347, where Hardiman J overturned a High Court restriction on the basis that the common law duties of directors could not be taken into account by a judge in a restriction application, because to do so would be an "amplification" of the *La Moselle* test.

PART II

Disqualification

If a director is "disqualified" it means he cannot be appointed or act as a director or other officer, or be in any way, whether directly or indirectly, concerned in the promotion, formation or management of most types of company.[39] A disqualified person is also barred from being appointed or acting as a statutory auditor, receiver, liquidator or examiner. In the main, disqualification applications are taken by liquidators or the Director of Corporate Enforcement against directors.[40]

Disqualification is reserved for the more serious cases of corporate delinquency. While the application will usually be brought by a liquidator or the DCE, the court has the power to disqualify a person of its own motion. The court has a wide discretion in deciding the disqualification period (the statute says "for such period as it sees fit"). The court can decide to restrict the subject of the application, rather than disqualify him.[41] The law as it was previously set out in s 160 of Companies Act 1990 is re-enacted in s 842 of Companies Act 2014; there are almost no changes.

Section 842 of Companies Act 2014

The key concept is "unfitness". This is retained, along with all the other categories at s 842(a) to (i). The most important categories are (a) to (d) and the greatest amount of people have standing to bring applications under these grounds. These are members, contributories, officers, employees, creditors and the various kinds of insolvency practitioners who may be acting in relation to the company.[42] The only new element is that any applicant may be ordered to provide security for costs for the application. Section 842(a) to (d) states:

---

[39] Companies Act 2014, s 838. A private company limited by shares; a DAC; a PLC; CLG, an unlimited company; an unregistered company—set out in s 819(6).

[40] In *Cahill v Grimes* [2002] 1 IR 372 the respondent was a liquidator.

[41] Companies Act 2014, s 845; this happened in *Re Newcastle Timber Ltd* [2001] 4 IR 586, a rather lenient judgment; the court may order that the disqualified person bear the costs of the application (s 846), and related costs (where the application is made by the DCE or the DPP).

[42] Companies Act 2014, s 844.

(a) that the person has been guilty...of any fraud in relation to the company, its members or creditors;

(b) that the person has been guilty...of any breach of duty as an officer, etc;

(c) that a declaration that the person was guilty of trading recklessly or fraudulently has been made[43];

(d) that the conduct of the person...makes him unfit to be concerned in the management of a company.

Deterrent Element

The courts sometimes say, just as they do with restriction, that disqualification is not designed to punish the individual, but to protect the trading public. They also say, without seeming to recognise any logical conflict, that disqualification must sometimes have a deterrent element to it. Therefore, even if a director has turned over a new leaf, can show the court that "that was then, this is now", the court should still, in certain grave cases, impose a disqualification order. In *Re Westmid Packing Services Limited*[44] the UK Court of Appeal stated:

> "...there are occasions when disqualification must be ordered even though, by reason of the director's recognition of his previous failing and the way he has conducted himself since the conduct complained of, he is in fact no longer a danger to the public at all. In such cases it is no longer necessary for the director to be held 'off the road' for the protection of the public, but other factors come into play in the wider interest of protecting the public, i.e. a deterrent element in relation to the director himself and a deterrent element as far as other directors are concerned. Despite the fact that the Courts have said disqualification is not a 'punishment', in truth the exercise that is being engaged in is little different from any sentencing exercise. A period of disqualification must reflect the gravity of the offence. It must contain deterrent elements."

---

[43] This happened in *Re PSK Construction Ltd* [2009] IEHC 538 (seven years for the executive director, and five years for the NED for her complicity in making under-declarations to the Revenue Commissioners for a five month period).

[44] [1998] 2 All ER 124, *per* Lord Woolf MR.

In *Re CB Readymix Ltd; Cahill v Grimes*[45] a liquidator who was improperly appointed had deliberately destroyed the books and records of the company. This was a very serious matter which merited disqualification, particularly in the context of comments made by the respondent in the High Court. The respondent stated that he was "determined to screw the Revenue, no matter what it took", that he was "prepared to blow up anyone who got in my way" and that he was "going to make an example of" the properly appointed liquidator. The respondent was disqualified for a period of seven years. He appealed to the Supreme Court, defending his conduct with a grace that was "attractive but alarming".[46] It seems from the judgment that even given the foregoing, the court might have been ready to consider reducing the period of disqualification, if it were not for the fact that the respondent utterly failed to appreciate the gravity of what he had done.

In *DCE v Collery*[47] a senior official in a merchant bank who had knowingly assisted a company to conduct its affairs in Ireland so as to defraud the Revenue was disqualified for nine years. The Court said that although the respondent was an officer of a solvent bank and not an insolvent company, he should be judged by the principles of unfitness which had been developed to judge the conduct of directors of insolvent companies. *DCE v Stakelum*[48] arose from the same facts as *Collery*. The respondent, a chartered accountant and experienced business advisor, was disqualified for five years, on the basis of unfitness, for helping to assist a company called Ansbacher to defraud the Revenue. While the Court found that he did not give "knowing assistance" he nonetheless "operated a system that was inexplicable on any normal basis and can only have been designed to hide funds from the Revenue authorities".[49]

Mitigating Factors

A director faced with a disqualification application will not be able to successfully advance the argument that as he was not paid for his role, he should be held to a lesser standard, or that this should be considered a

---

[45] [2002] 1 IR 372.
[46] *ibid* at 382.
[47] [2007] 1 IR 580, Finlay Geoghegan J. The application was not contested.
[48] [2007] IEHC 486, McGovern J.
[49] At para 13

mitigating factor. Nor will a director who has passed the age of retirement be permitted to advance that as a mitigating factor.[50] It is no argument to say that the failure to file annual returns is a mere technical breach of the Companies Act.[51] In *Re FAI Finance Corporation Ltd*[52] the respondent was the former Managing Director of the company and was disqualified for a four year period after he failed to prevent multiple matters which led to an insolvency with a €50m deficit. The disqualification period would have been six years but for the fact that he acknowledged his role and made certain repayments to the company, both of which were considered mitigating factors.

In *Re Bovale Developments*[53] two brothers, developers, were guilty of "systematic falsification" of books of account and of understating their gross remuneration by €6m.[54] A managing partner in PwC stated in evidence that over the course of a thirty-five year career in public accounting he had never seen such a failure to maintain proper books and records. Finlay Geoghegan J stated that the breaches merited a fourteen year disqualification—which would have been the longest ever given in Ireland[55]—if it were not for mitigating factors. The brothers made a voluntary disclosure of their wrongdoing to the Revenue in 2000: they had been tax compliant since 2001; they said they had "learned from their mistakes". A seven year period was imposed. In *DCE v McGowan*[56] the Supreme Court refused to disqualify the respondents despite their failure, for a period of thirteen years, to comply with their legal obligations to file prescribed returns with the Registrar of Companies. Fennelly J said that a disqualification order was not warranted as it would "not, at this stage,

---

[50] *DCE v Liwosz* [2014] IEHC 611 (Cregan J)—first respondent for seven years, second respondent for six because he came late to the directorship, after some key, faulty, decisions were made. The directors had permitted the breach of High Court orders, filed certain financial statements late and failed to file others entirely.

[51] *Re Clawhammer* [2005] 1 IR 503; for a surprising contrast to this, see the more recent *Re Walfab Engineering Ltd; DCE v Walsh* [2014] IEHC 365 (High Court, Barrett J, 23 July 2014); see also *Re Chercrest; DCE v Slattery* [2014] IEHC 363 (Barrett J, 23 July 2014).

[52] [2010] IEHC 225.

[53] [2013] IEHC 561.

[54] For a UK case where a director continued to pay himself excessive remuneration after the company was obviously insolvent, see *Re Firedart Ltd; Official Receiver v Fairall* [1994] 2 BCLC 340 (six-year period).

[55] For UK cases of 12 to 15 years, see *Official Receiver v Stern and another (No 2)* [2002] 1 BCLC 119; *Official Receiver v Doshi* [2001] 2 BCLC 235; *Official Receiver v Vass* [1999] BCC 516.

[56] [2008] 4 IR 598.

serve any useful purpose and would probably disrupt the ongoing business of the company".[57]

Leniency of the Irish Courts in Disqualification Matters

The Irish courts are reluctant to disqualify directors. The Supreme Court has said that restriction is bad enough.[58] Each case will turn on its own facts and there may be times when disqualification is not appropriate because a person has actually learned their lesson,[59] or when a very short period of two years only is appropriate, where the nature of the business—start-ups, venture capitalism—involves as many, if not more, failures as successes.[60] A disqualified director can always apply to court for relief.[61] Taking this into account, however, there does seem to be an aversion to disqualification on the part of the Irish courts. In interpreting simple concepts like "commercial probity" the courts have set the bar high. Furthermore, negligence must be "gross" or incompetence must be "total" for a person to be disqualified. In *Re Kentford Securities Limited*[62] O'Donnell J stated:

> "given the penal consequences of a disqualification order for any director or other officer, a court must feel a high degree of confidence before making any such disqualification order."

There are no reported cases of two-year periods of disqualification; rather than a two-year disqualification, it seems the Irish courts would rather reduce the disqualification to a restriction. This lenient attitude can be seen in *DCE v Byrne*,[63] *DCE v Seymour*,[64] *DCE v Boner*[65] and *DCE v McCann*[66] (as well as *DCE v McGowan*[67] above). Anyone wishing to dispute this view

---

[57] [2008] 4 IR 598 at 612.

[58] [2008] 3 IR 347, *per* Hardiman J: it is "gravely damaging to the reputation of a person" who is "afflicted" by a restriction, and is something of a "stigma".

[59] *Re Dawson Print Group Ltd* [1987] BCLC 601.

[60] *Re Pamstock Ltd* [1994] 1 BCLC 716.

[61] *Re Clenaware Systems Ltd* [2013] EWHC 2514 (Ch) (Barker J, 9 August 2013).

[62] *Director of Corporate Enforcement v McCann* [2011] 1 IR 585 at 601.

[63] [2009] 2 ILRM 328.

[64] [2013] 1 IR 82.

[65] [2008] IEHC 151. *DCE v Brennan* [2008] IEHC 132 was another case arising out of NIB. The Court found the respondent failed "to supervise and control" these matters while a senior General Manager of the Bank but judgment did not specify a disqualification period.

[66] [2007] IEHC 1 (Peart J).

[67] [2008] 4 IR 598.

would surely point to *DCE v D'Arcy*,[68] where the respondent was disqualified for ten years, but it is submitted that this case was anomalous in this regard.

The first three of the cases just cited arose from revelations in the late 1990s that National Irish Bank[69] had facilitated tax dodging through undeclared off-shore bank accounts.[70] Bogus non-resident accounts with fictitious names were opened and maintained in the bank's branches. In *DCE v Byrne*[71] a disqualification of four years was entirely set aside. One of the respondent's duties was to produce a circular and a laminated sheet for all branches to explain what should be done to comply with the relevant procedures, to outline what documents were required for the off-shore accounts, and so on. Denham J agreed that the circulars and the laminated sheet "might have been drafted more clearly" but said that "at its height this criticism is a drafting criticism" and that, essentially, people should not be disqualified for poor drafting.[72] The only other matter was whether the respondent ought to have realised a potential retrospective tax liability, after nearly a year in the job. Denham J could be said to have side-stepped the issue by saying that the respondent should not be judged with the benefit of hindsight. In setting aside the order, the learned judge disregarded the deterrent element and took into account "the fact that the effect of a disqualification order may be greater on a professional person"[73]: it is difficult to make sense of this, given the fact that disqualification only concerns persons acting in a professional capacity.

In *DCE v Seymour*[74] the respondent, a former chief executive of National Irish Bank, saw his nine year disqualification period reduced to a five year restriction by the Supreme Court. He had been asked to step in as chief executive when the chief executive resigned suddenly. He was

---

[68] [2006] 2 IR 163. The unfitness was exacerbated, the Court said, by the fact that the wrongdoing took place in a bank rather than an ordinary corporate entity. This was very much the exception to the general run of the NIB proceedings.

[69] Now Danske Bank.

[70] The Revenue dealt with more than 15,000 individual cases, recouped €800m in voluntary disclosure from 14,000 account holders, and recouped €1bn from its decade long investigation into the matter (*Irish Independent*, 17 April 2014).

[71] [2009] 2 ILRM 328.

[72] *ibid* at 343.

[73] *ibid* at 344.

[74] [2013] 1 IR 82.

only supposed to be chief executive for a few weeks and he came to realise he had inherited an organisation "that had been managed in an autocratic fashion". He successfully argued that it was unrealistic to criticize him on a complex point of tax law. Macken J said that no one else at the bank in a position of authority "deduced that there was a calculated effort taking place to evade taxes that would inevitably, or even likely, lead to a retrospective tax liability on the part of" the bank and that he appellant "took steps to try and counteract the problems he did recognise".[75] The Supreme Court did not think it fell to him to stamp out entirely the bad practices in his organisation. The point was that he made some efforts, and where he failed, his failures were not such as they would amount "to the level of incompetence necessary to meet the test for a disqualification order". In *DCE v Boner*[76] a Regional Manager in NIB was aware, as he acknowledged, of certain practices, such as the improper charging of interest, but he avoided disqualification, because he did make attempts to address the problems.

In *DCE v McCann*[77] the High Court was prepared to impose no disqualification order on the basis that the improper conduct had happened "all those years ago" at the behest of the respondent's employer and that since then the respondent had enjoyed "good standing". The Supreme Court disagreed, remitting the matter to the High Court, but with instructions that only a short period be imposed, and that conditions may be attached to the order to make it less burdensome to the respondent, for whom the experience of defending the application had been a costly and "a chastening one."[78] Given such precedent it may well seem to members of the public that a director must work hard to be disqualified.

---

[75] *ibid* at 139.
[76] [2008] IEHC 151. *DCE v Brennan* [2008] IEHC 132 was another case arising out of NIB. The Court found the respondent failed "to supervise and control" these matters while a senior General Manager of the Bank but judgment did not specify a disqualification period.
[77] [2007] IEHC 1 (Peart J).
[78] [2011] 1 IR 585, *per* O'Donnell J at 609. The respondent audited the accounts of a company called Kentford Securities Ltd between 1989 and 1993, and this company was another Des Traynor outfit used to help clients such as Charles Haughey evade taxes.

CHAPTER EIGHT

DIRECTORS' PERSONAL LIABILITY ON INSOLVENCY

Reckless and Fraudulent Trading: The Statute

Given the fact that so few directors find themselves disqualified, it is little wonder that even fewer find themselves made personally liable for company debts because they have traded either recklessly or fraudulently. In a country where the courts view restriction as something to which grave stigma attaches, and where a disqualification order will not be made where the irresponsibility displayed is something less than of "a high degree", it stands to reason that the imposition of personal liability for reckless or fraudulent trading will be rare in the jurisprudence. The concept of civil liability for reckless trading did not even exist in Irish law until 1990, and in the quarter century since it was introduced only three written judgments deal with the issue: in two of them, no liability was imposed. In 1993 the High Court stated that this part of our law

> "involves a radical departure from previous company law and is exceptional and draconian in nature. A court should therefore require strong clear evidence before applying the section."[1]

Given the foregoing, it could be said that this area is the closest we have to a purely academic topic in Irish company law.

The law is to be found in the Companies Act 2014, s 610. The court has the power to declare "if it thinks it proper to do so" that certain persons be made personally responsible, "without any limitation of liability, for all or any part of the debts or other liabilities of the company as the court may direct".[2] The application can be made only in the course of the winding-up of the company or if the company is in examinership. The company must be unable to pay its debts for the application to be made.[3] The application may be brought by the liquidator or examiner of the company, a receiver of the property of the company, or any creditor or contributory of the company. If the applicant is a creditor or contributory, that person must be able to show the court that he has suffered loss or damage as a consequence of the conduct complained of.[4] With regard to reckless trading, a potential respondent to the application must have been an

---

[1] [1993] IR 191 at 217.
[2] Companies Act 2014, s 610(2).
[3] Companies Act 2014 s 610(4)(a) which refers to s 570.
[4] Companies Act 2014, s 610(4)(b).

officer of the company, and while an officer must have been "knowingly a party to the carrying on of any business of the company in a reckless manner".[5] Recklessness is not merely an exhibition of carelessness: for a court to find that directors have acted recklessly in the conduct of the company's affairs, there must be evidence of "a wilful disregard of a clear risk to creditors".[6] One judge, in giving guidance to the vexed question of what constitutes recklessness, has suggested the phrase "culpable want of care on the part of a director".[7] A respondent must have had a clear understanding of the risk involved for creditors and gone ahead taking that risk not really caring about the creditors."[8] Put another way, because the statute includes the word "knowingly", it must be shown that a director was:

> "party to carrying on the business in a manner which the director knows very well involves an obvious and serious risk of loss or damage to others, and yet ignores that risk, because he does not really care whether such others suffer loss or damage or because his selfish desire to keep his own company alive overrides any concern which he ought to have for others."[9]

With regard to fraudulent trading, an application can be brought against

> "*any person* [who] was knowingly a party to the carrying on of any business of the company with intent to defraud creditors of the company, or creditors of any other person or for any fraudulent purpose."[10]

The inclusion of "knowingly a party" in both definitions means that the test must be a subjective one, and so the bar is set incredibly high, and it is extremely difficult for an applicant to prove the respondent's state of mind. Because of this, the Act offers guidance on when a person shall be deemed to have been knowingly a party to reckless conduct of the business. For some reason, there is no equivalent guidance with regard to fraudulent conduct: there is no "deemed fraudulent conduct".

---

[5] *ibid*, s 610(1)(a).
[6] [1993] 3 IR 191 at 218.
[7] Peart J in *Re USIT World Plc* [2005] IEHC 285.
[8] *ibid*.
[9] [1993] 3 IR 191 at 222.
[10] Companies Act 2014, s 610(1)(b).

Deemed Recklessness

A person will be deemed to have been knowingly a party to the carrying on of any business of the company in a reckless manner in two circumstances. First, if the person ought to have known that his or her actions or those of the company would cause loss to the creditors of the company, having regard to that person's general knowledge, skill and experience. Second, if the person was a party to the contracting of a debt by the company and did not honestly believe on reasonable grounds that the company would be able to pay the debt when it fell due for payment as well as all its other debts (this takes into account the contingent and prospective liabilities). When considering this second aspect, the court must have regard to whether the creditor in question was aware of the company's financial ill health at the time and whether, notwithstanding this awareness, still assented to the incurring of the debt.[11] Thus, the conduct of an officer may not warrant the making of an order under s 610(1), but may warrant the making of an order for "deemed recklessness" under s 610(3). In considering behaviour with regard to s 610(1) the court considers whether or not a person has been knowingly a party to the carrying on of any business of the company in a reckless manner: in considering behaviour with regard to s 610(3) the court considers whether there are any "additional circumstances" in which an officer may be deemed to have been knowingly a party to the carrying on of any business of the company in a reckless manner.[12]

Continued Trading when Solvency Doubtful

When considering whether the directors acted honestly and responsibly the court does not require that decisions taken must turn out later to have been the right ones. The issue is "whether it was irresponsible to have taken the decision at the time".[13] When should directors cease trading when solvency is becoming doubtful? Peart J answered the question thus:

> "I think that it is important to note that it is not incumbent on a board of directors, at the first moment at which it is becoming

---

[11] Companies Act 2014, s 610(5).
[12] *Per* Finlay Geoghegan J [2009] IEHC 538 at para 28.
[13] Peart J in *Re USIT World Plc* [2005] IEHC 285.

apparent that debts may not be capable of being paid as they fall due, to immediately call in the liquidator and cease trading. Many companies will experience for many reasons unrelated to the general health of the company a downturn in profitability over a quarter, two quarters or even three quarters. That in my view does not mean that even where a risk of insolvency downstream is warned or anticipated, some reasonable effort at rescuing the situation may not be permitted to be undertaken. To attempt to trade out of a difficulty is not an irresponsible act. Care of course must be taken to ensure that effective and realistic steps are taken and that creditors' interests are kept to the fore, rather than that a careless or reckless gamble is taken without proper advice and planning to an achievable end. Some sort of short term emergency fire-fighting must be permitted to take place without those efforts, provided they are reasonable and responsible, from being made. Many companies have survived and prospered after temporary setbacks."[14]

In Whose Favour is Liability Imposed?

If the court were to impose personal liability on a respondent then it has a wide discretion to stipulate where the money will go, for example, some of it might be directed to a particular creditor or class of creditors.[15] Whether the court has the power to displace the order of priorities of secured creditors is not clear, but the wording of the statute seems to suggest it does.

The Defence to a Recklessness Application

As usual in these matters, if a respondent can show that he acted honestly and responsibly then, in the case of reckless conduct, it acts as the principle defence, and it is difficult to see a court imposing liability on anyone who can show that he acted honestly or responsibly. In the case of persons responding to allegations of fraudulent trading the statute does not offer them an "honestly and responsibly" defence, but that is still a line of defence which may be pursued, in tandem with the argument that they were not knowingly a party to any recklessness.

---

[14] *Re USIT World Plc* [2005] IEHC 285.
[15] Companies Act 2014, s 610(6).

Case Law on Reckless Trading

There are three Irish cases on reckless trading. The first is *Re Hefferon Kearns Ltd (No. 2)*,[16] where no liability was imposed. For fifteen years *Hefferon Kearns* was the *only* authority in the area. This may be because the action, which was taken by a creditor of an insolvent company, was, in the words of Lynch J, "a financial disaster for everybody". It may also be due to the fact that, unlike restriction and disqualification, the liquidator has discretion whether or not to bring the application, and there is little appetite for doing so. The taking of the action in *Hefferon* scuppered an examinership proposal and was ultimately a pyrrhic victory for the plaintiff. The defendants were found to have traded recklessly, but only for a period of thirteen days, during which no loss or damage had occurred to the plaintiffs: the Court considered the directors' conduct to have been honest and responsible overall and so, using its discretion, absolved them of liability. The outstanding lesson of the case is not the guidance it offers on recklessness in a commercial context, but the warning it gives against being blinded by emotion, for the plaintiffs were "furious" with the defendants and were "convinced that a fraud had been perpetrated"[17] on them, but their view was unwarranted, and had they taken a cooler view of the matter and allowed the examinership to have begun they would have at least retrieved *some* of what they were owed.

It is worth extracting from the judgment the examples of conduct which led Lynch J to absolve the directors. There were four directors. The plaintiffs were really only after the first and second named defendants, Hefferon and Kearns, and in Lynch J's view if Hefferon was not guilty of recklessness then none of the respondents was. Four mitigating factors emerged: (1) the borrowing of a significant sum of money with a view to improving the company's cash-flow, and the giving of a personal guarantee for that debt; (2) constant concern for the creditors, evidenced by a weighing up of the effects of a forced liquidation on creditors, with the view emerging that the better outcome for them would be to trade on rather than liquidate immediately (this decision was supported by the examiner, later on: the examiner stated that on a winding-up creditors

---

[16] [1993] 3 IR 191; referred to by Finlay Geoghegan J as "the principal authority" in *PSK Construction Ltd* [2009] IEHC 538 at para 25.
[17] [1993] IR 191 at 206.

would probably be £88,000 worse off than under a scheme of arrangement); (3) attempts to secure reliable funding for one of the company's projects; (4) a willingness, under a proposed scheme of arrangement, to surrender a personal shareholding in two related and still-profitable companies.

The second case is *Re PSK Construction Ltd*,[18] where Finlay Geoghegan J considered whether a decision to keep the business going by under-declaring and under-paying to the Revenue involved,

> "to the knowledge of each respondent, an obvious and serious risk of loss or damage to creditors, and yet this risk was ignored by reason of a desire to keep the Company alive."[19]

The Court took the view that the first respondent did know—at the time of taking the decision—that it involved an "obvious and serious risk of loss or damage" to creditors of the company.[20] The Court made this conclusion based on what the first respondent acknowledged he knew at the time. In relation to the second respondent, who characterised herself as a non-executive director, the Court concluded that she did not have such knowledge, partly because she took at face value the word of the first respondent that the under-declarations would be a temporary measure, and partly because the last set of accounts which she signed prior to the making of the decision showed the company to be in a positive financial situation. Further to this, the Court did not deem the second respondent to have been reckless because she did not have the general knowledge, skill and experience that would mean she ought to have known that the under-declaration would cause loss to the company's creditors: the responsibilities of the second respondent centred on the pricing of materials and stock and the administration of the office and related paperwork. She had no accounting expertise or qualifications.

Application by Creditor for Imposition of Liability

The third case, *Re Appleyard Motors Ltd (in voluntary liquidation)*,[21] is an example of a successful application made by a creditor. Interestingly, the

---

[18] [2009] IEHC 538.
[19] *ibid* at para 29.
[20] *ibid* at para 30.
[21] [2015] IEHC 28 (Binchy J, 21 January 2015).

respondents argued that notwithstanding the "strident criticisms" made of them by the applicant, personal liability should not be imposed because the liquidator of the company had not made the application. Essentially it was argued that if the respondents really did require sanction, it was a matter for the liquidator, and even then the appropriate application would be merely for restriction or disqualification. It was further argued that to impose liability upon the application of an aggrieved creditor would "encourage an entirely new type of claim", throwing overboard the "sensible, sober, realistic approach" of *Hefferon Kearns*.[22] That such arguments could have been made is worrying: the statute gives *locus standi* to creditors. It is unstateable to argue that because the liquidator did not decide to make the application, then the matter should fall away. It is also very telling that counsel submitted to the Court that conduct meriting "strident criticisms" should attract the lesser sanction of a restriction or disqualification order. The Court rightly rejected these arguments.

The failure to take sufficient professional advice and the failure to wind-up the company within a certain period was crucial to the Court's finding that the directors' conduct was not responsible: the Court imposed personally liability on the respondents, in favour of the applicant company, in the sum of €48,250, which was the loss sustained by the applicant in arising out of its dealings with Appleyard Motors in the weeks leading up to its liquidation. The Court held that while the respondents were not knowingly parties to the carrying on of any business of the company in a reckless manner, they could be deemed so by virtue of s 610(3).

Fraudulent Trading in General

The following have been found to amount to fraudulent trading: tax evasion, attempts to conceal the company's assets from creditors, incurring debts knowing there is little chance they will be repaid, the siphoning off of assets, the transfer of stock to an associated company when creditors are bearing down, the keeping of two separate books of account (one false, for the Revenue, and one true, for the use of the company's auditors or directors), false invoicing, the diversion of company money into bank accounts which are not recorded in the company's records, under-declaration of taxes and the use of those tax monies to fund continued trading.

---

[22] *ibid* at para 51.

Fraudulent Trading: Case Law

No one will feel overwhelmed by the amount of fraudulent trading cases successfully taken in Ireland. It may be that the task of proving fraudulent trading is just too challenging, putting off liquidators and other potential applicants, or it may be that the taking of such an application is simply seen as a waste of money. There are three strong authorities in the Irish jurisprudence.[23]

In *Re PSK Construction Ltd*[24] liability for fraudulent trading was imposed on the first respondent, as well as liability on the grounds of reckless trading. The purpose of under-declaring the company's tax liabilities to the Revenue was to make the Revenue believe the company's liability was less than it actually was, and that the company was fully discharging the monies it owed: this was found to be a fraudulent purpose. This action took place each month for six months. It was not relevant that the first respondent obtained no personal benefit from the wrongdoing.[25] As a result of the continued trading, which was funded fraudulently, the company suffered pure trading losses of approximately €159,149 per month. In total, the respondent was fixed with liability in the sum of €1,604,526: this was imposed for both the reckless and the fraudulent trading.[26]

Re Hunting Lodges Ltd[27] featured an attempt to defraud the Revenue, which was investigating the company's affairs. When the Revenue was bearing down on the directors, and had issued a summons claiming £200,000 in tax arrears, the company's directors, Mr and Mrs Porrit, arranged for the sale of a pub which was the company's main asset. The Revenue had warned the company's auditor that there should be no attempt to dispose of assets without paying the Revenue what it was owed: this was precisely

---

[23] In UK case law, see *Re William C Leitch Brothers Ltd* [1932] 2 Ch 7, *Morris v State Bank of India* [2004] 2 BCLC 236 and *Re Overnight Ltd; Goldfarb v Higgins & Ors* [2010] 2 BCLC 186. There is an unreported Irish case which Courtney mentions, at para 15.122 of his *Law of Companies* (3rd ed, Bloomsbury, 2012) called *Re Contract Packaging Ltd.* (Flood J) reported in *The Irish Times* (16–18 January 1992). In that case the liquidator discovered VAT fraud and a fraudulent system of book-keeping; certain deposit accounts were not included in the company's audited accounts. This was with a view, on the part of the directors, to siphoning off money and defrauding the Revenue.

[24] [2009] IEHC 538.

[25] *ibid* at para 40.

[26] *ibid* at para 43.

[27] [1985] ILRM 75.

what the directors tried to do. The sale price of the pub was recorded as £480,000 but there was a secret arrangement for the payment of an additional £200,000 directly to Mr Porrit: the company was hopelessly insolvent at this time. This secret part of the purchase price was lodged by Mr Porrit in a building society account under a false name, the mandate documents for which were signed by him and his wife—also using false names. The sale was completed just after the Revenue sent a letter which stated that if matters weren't regularized, winding-up proceedings would be brought. The Revenue did appoint a liquidator. He took proceedings on the basis of the transaction, and Carroll J said that this single fraudulent transaction was enough, where the intent was to defraud the Revenue, to amount to fraudulent trading for the purposes of the Companies Acts. Thus, *Hunting Lodges* is authority for the proposition that a single fraudulent transaction is sufficient to ground an application under the fraudulent trading rules (it was argued for the Porrits that "trading" implied more than one transaction). There were four respondents in *Hunting Lodges* and each of them took positive steps in the subterfuge. There is no requirement that a common design be shown: the courts look at each individual's behaviour and the entire circumstances when deciding whether to impose personal liability or not.

Re Aluminium Fabricators Ltd[28] is a three page report which is mainly about the admissibility of evidence under the court's power to summon persons for examination,[29] but we do learn that the two directors in control of the company—Phelan and Barrett—were "cynically" indifferent towards their creditors and were concerned "only with safeguarding and furthering their own personal interests at whatever cost to those with whom they were doing business". The liquidator had brought proceedings against them for fraudulent trading. Attempts had been made to put part of the company's assets out of the reach of creditors and for at least a period of several months, the company continued to trade, despite Phelan and Barrett knowing that the company could not meet its liabilities as they fell due. O'Hanlon J stated that

> "[t]he privilege of limitation of liability…cannot be afforded to those who use a limited company as a cloak or shield beneath

---

[28] [1984] ILRM 399.
[29] Companies Act 1963, s 245.

which they seek to operate a fraudulent system of carrying on business for their own personal enrichment and advantage"[30]

O'Hanlon J made a declaration that they were knowingly parties to the carrying on of the business with the intent to defraud the creditors. Phelan and Barrett were made personally liable without any limitation for all the debts and other liabilities of the company.

Imposition of Liability for Failure to Keep Proper Accounts

A company is obliged to keep ("or cause to be kept") adequate accounting records.[31] There are four characteristics which define what adequate records are. They must correctly record and explain the transactions of the company. They must "enable, at any time, the assets, liabilities, financial position and profit or loss of the company to be determined with reasonable accuracy". They must enable the directors to ensure that any financial statements of the company (which are required to be prepared under the financial reporting framework) and any directors' report (which must be prepared for each financial year, see s 325) comply with the requirements of the Companies Act 2014. Finally, they must be sufficiently detailed to allow the company to be audited.[32] The company's accounting records must be kept on a continuous and consistent basis.[33] These general rules are further fleshed out in s 282(3), which states that the accounting records must contain entries from day to day of all sums of money received and spent by the company, as well as an indication of what the money was received for and what it was spent on, and if the company deals in goods there should be a record of all transactions involving the purchase and sale of goods. These records must be kept for a minimum of six years.[34]

If an insolvent company is being wound-up and the officers have failed to ensure that the company complied with the above duties, the court has the power to declare, "if it thinks it proper to do so", that such officer or officers shall be personally liable for all or part of the company's debts.

[30] [1984] ILRM 399 at 401.
[31] Companies Act 2014, s 281.
[32] ibid, s 282(1)(a)–(d).
[33] ibid, s 282(2).
[34] ibid, s 285.

The crucial consideration, however, is not merely the insolvency of the company or the default of the officers with regard to the accounting records, it is whether the court considers that their failure to keep proper accounting records did any one of the following three things:

(i) Contributed to the company's inability to pay all of its debts; or
(ii) Resulted in substantial uncertainty as to the assets and liabilities of the company; or
(iii) Substantially impeded the orderly winding-up of the company.

The court will not make an order imposing liability if it considers that the respondent took "all reasonable steps to secure compliance by the company" with the accounting provisions of the Act, or if the respondent can show the court that he had

> "reasonable grounds for believing and did believe that a competent and reliable person, acting under the supervision or control of a director of the company who ha[d] been formally allocated such responsibility, was (i) charged with the duty of ensuring that those sections were complied with, and (ii) in a position to discharge that duty."[35]

It is no excuse for one director to say that another director was the one in charge of looking after the books.[36]

The touchstone case when considering the above is *Re Mantruck Services Ltd*.[37] Shanley J said the Court should consider how much the director's involvement in the s 609 breach contributed to the financial loss, and ask whether that loss was reasonably foreseeable by the director. If s 609 had been breached but the loss had not been reasonably foreseeable, then Shanley J said that liability should only be imposed in exceptional cases. Shanley J held in *Re Mantruck* that the respondent's breach had caused the liquidator to spend a lot of time trying to piece together the books and records, work he wouldn't have had to do if the breach hadn't occurred. Thus, the respondent was made personally liable for the fees of the liquidator which could be traced to this part of his work. Further authority on this

---

[35] Companies Act 2014, s 609(8)(b).
[36] *Re Vehicle Imports Ltd*, Unreported, High Court, Murphy J, 23 November 2000.
[37] *Mehigan v Duignan* [1997] 1 ILRM 171.

point is *Re Dev Oil and Gas Ltd*,[38] a decision of Finlay Geoghegan J, where the Court found that the company did not keep accounts that allowed its transactions to be determined with any reasonable accuracy. The liquidator submitted that, had the books been in order, he would have expected to recover 70% of the company's debts: because the books were kept so badly, he only recovered 1.85% of them. Finlay Geoghegan J therefore made the respondent personally liable for 68% of the company's debts.[39]

In *Re Rayhill Property Company Ltd*[40] the liquidator had to deal with "bits and scraps" of information. Smyth J made the second respondent personally liable because even on his own evidence the book-keeping "was spasmodic and so infrequent and muddled with the affairs of other companies or enterprises".[41] This "led to a failure to meet the objectives intended to be achieved by the observance of the statutory requirements". Smyth J found "a causative connection" between this failure and the company's inability to pay its debts, i.e. if proper books had been kept, the directors would have known the true state of the company's affairs and the liquidation of the company might have been avoided. In *PSK Construction*[42] the liquidator calculated that as a result of the bad records, he and his team had spent additional hours on the liquidation that ran to €21,447. Finlay Geoghegan J made an order that both respondents be jointly and severally liable for that sum.

Thus, whenever an order has been made under the section it has been to cover the extra costs incurred by the liquidator, and not an order than an officer pay some or all of the liabilities of the company, which were incurred before the liquidation began.

Misfeasance

The court may impose personal liability on those who have been guilty of misfeasance "or other breach of duty or trust in relation to the company".[43] Such an application may be made by four categories of person: the DCE, the liquidator, any creditor or contributory of the company. Such an

---

[38] *Jackson v Devlin* [2008] IEHC 538.
[39] See also *Re Ashclad Ltd; Forrest v Harington and Culleton* [2000] IEHC 174.
[40] *Conroy v Corneill and Corneill* [2003] 3 IR 588.
[41] [2003] 3 IR 588 at 596.
[42] [2009] IEHC 538.
[43] Companies Act 2014, s 612(1).

application may only be made in the course of a winding-up. The section covers a multitude of persons. It covers officers past or present and stretches back to anyone who took part in the formation or promotion of the company (needless to say, there is no case law on this latter point). It encompasses liquidators, provisional liquidators, examiners or receivers of the company. The court is empowered first of all to examine the conduct of such persons, and then the power to order that such a person "repay or restore the money or property or any part of it respectively with interest at such rate as the court thinks just" or the power to order that such a person contribute whatever sum the court "thinks just" by way of "compensation in respect of the misapplication, retainer, misfeasance or other breach of duty or trust".[44] The misfeasance rule was extended by Companies Act 2014 to include directors of a holding company.[45]

The liquidator in *PSK Construction* included a misfeasance application, in relation to an allegation of stolen tarmacadam, but the issue was disputed by the first respondent on affidavit and the court made no ruling on it. It may be assumed that, in light of the success of the liquidator's applications in general, and the amount he was able to move to recover against the first respondent, that the Court found it unnecessary to consider liability under this heading.

In *Re Mont Clare Hotels Ltd*,[46] no liability was imposed for misfeasance. The alleged wrongdoing was twofold: the granting of a loan in "a very informal way" to a company of which the respondent was also a director, and the failure to seek repayment of this loan. Costello J made a number of observations. Firstly he said that he was

> "satisfied that [the respondent] may well have been guilty of errors of judgment in relation to this whole transaction but that he was not guilty of any fraud in relation to it, and it has not been shown that he did not believe that what he said would come to pass."

On a second occasion, an over-optimistic statement which might also be based on an error of judgment was not enough, in the eyes of Costello J,

---

[44] *ibid*, s 612(2)(a) and (b).
[45] *ibid*, s 613.
[46] *Jackson v Mortell*, Unreported, High Court, 2 December 1986.

to constitute misfeasance. In the most significant passage Costello J stated:

> "It is not every error of judgment that amounts to misfeasance in law and it is not every act of negligence that amounts to misfeasance in law. It seems to me that something more than mere carelessness is required, some act that, perhaps, may amount to gross negligence in failing to carry out a duty owed by a director to his company."[47]

A successful example of misfeasance proceedings is *Re Greendale Developments Ltd*.[48] There were two directors, Mr Burgess, a builder, and Mr Fagan, who claimed to have initiative and business acumen. Fagan was described by his co-director as "a very difficult and forceful man" and the High Court found that Burgess was "dominated" by him and "did his bidding until shortly before the company's collapse".[49] Part of that bidding was co-signing cheques despite expressing reluctance to do so. The company was wound-up on just and equitable grounds on the application of Burgess. A liquidator was appointed and he took misfeasance proceedings against Fagan on the basis that Fagan engineered a situation where he personally benefitted by payments and assets amounting to £456,062. Fagan tried to argue that the transactions in his favour had been ratified by the other shareholders. Keane J, in the Supreme Court, held that all of his acts were performed in his capacity as a director, and "at no stage did the three members of the company pass any resolution purporting to authorise the transactions in question" so there was "no doubt" that as a result of the impugned transactions "the company plainly suffered damage".[50] There was no provision in the memorandum or articles of the company that allowed it to make gratuitous dispositions. The payments had been *ultra vires* the company. The order of the High Court—that Fagan repay £456,062 to the liquidator—was upheld.

---

[47] 2 December 1986, Unreported, High Court, at 5 of the transcript

[48] [1998] 1 IR 8.

[49] *ibid* at 20; The liquidator brought proceedings against Mr Fagan and his wife, but Costello P (in the High Court) made no order against her because she was not an officer of the company and no reliefs had been sought against her as a promoter. For this reason, and for the sake of convenience, I have referred only to Mr Fagan.

[50] [1998] 1 IR 8 at 26.

CORPORATE GOVERNANCE: MEETINGS

Introduction

Corporate Governance is dealt with in Part 4 of the Companies Act 2014. This covers a broad range of matters, such as definitions of directors and secretaries,[1] rules relating to the appointment and removal of directors,[2] the remedies in case of oppression, rules governing the Summary Approval Procedure, rules governing directors' meetings, definitions of membership and rules relating to members' meetings.

General Meetings

The Annual General Meeting ("AGM") is the best known kind of meeting in company law. As a general rule, a company must hold an AGM once a year and no AGM should take place more than fifteen months after the last one. The Companies Act 2014 introduced one major exception to the AGM rule. The new model private company limited by shares—the LTD—can dispense with holding an AGM as long as all the members entitled to attend and vote at it and sign a written resolution[3] which contains three key pieces of information:

(a) The members acknowledge receipt of the financial statements that would have been laid before that meeting;

(b) The members resolve all matters as would have been resolved at that meeting; and

(c) The members confirm that there is no change in the company's statutory auditor.[4]

Anything required by the Companies Act 2014 to be done by the members of a LTD in a general meeting may be done via written resolution – dispensing with the need for a meeting—if the above procedure is followed.[5] The other kind of company which does not need to hold an AGM is the single-member company. All powers exercisable by a company in a general meeting are, in the case of a single-member company, exercisable by the sole member without the need to hold a general meeting for that purpose.[6]

---

[1] Companies Act 2014, s 128 and s 129.
[2] See Companies Act 2014, s 144 and s 146.
[3] See Companies Act 2014, s 193.
[4] Companies Act 2014, s 175(3).
[5] *ibid*, s 175(4).
[6] See Companies Act 2014, s 196.

All other general meetings of a company are known as "extraordinary general meetings".[7] They may be convened by the directors at any time of their choosing. EGMs can also be convened by members, either alone or acting together, as long as the convener(s) hold not less than 50% of the paid up share capital of the company which carries voting rights.[8] This statutory rule may be displaced by the company's constitution. The following rule, however, may not be displaced by the company's constitution: one or more members who hold a minimum of 10% of the company's paid up share capital can demand of the directors that the directors hold an EGM and the directors must comply.[9] This demand, called a "requisition", must state the objects of the meeting, and must be signed by all the requisitionists, and deposited at the company's registered office.[10] The directors have 21 days from the deposit of the requisition to decide a date for the EGM: this date must be no more than two months after the requisition date.[11] If the 21 day period elapses without the directors having set a date, the requisitionists can set a date: that date must be no more than three months after the requisition date. If the requisitionists incur any expenses in organising an EGM in these circumstances, the company must repay them their expenses, and the company shall cover the cost of this expense by retaining fees or other remuneration due to the directors.[12] Further to these rules, the Companies Act 2014 also grants the court powers to convene general meetings of the company, on foot of an application by a director, a member, a personal representative of a deceased member, or the assignee in bankruptcy of a bankrupt member.[13]

Location

A company may hold an AGM or EGM outside the State if it wishes.[14] If all of the members (who are entitled to attend and vote) do not consent to the holding of a meeting outside the State, the company has a duty—which is new—to

---

[7] Companies Act 2014, 177.

[8] *ibid*, s 178(2).

[9] *ibid*, s 178(3). The 10% requirement must be met as at the date that the requisition is deposited.

[10] Companies Act 2014, s 176(4): the requisition doesn't have to be a single document. It can be a number of documents, each requisitionist signing only one.

[11] Companies Act 2014, s 176(5).

[12] *ibid*, s 176(6).

[13] *ibid*, s 179.

[14] *ibid*, s 176(1).

"make, at the company's expense, all necessary arrangements to ensure that members can by technological means participate in any such meeting without leaving the State."[15]

Another innovation of Companies Act 2014 is that a general meeting does not need to be held in the one venue. It can be held in two or more venues—one or more of which could be outside the State. The key is that the meeting is conducted in all places at the same time, "using any technology that provides members, as a whole, with a reasonable opportunity to participate". The key concept here is that each member is able to fully hear what is being said and make contributions if they wish. This opens up the way for all kinds of new media to be utilised, as long as the participation is meaningful.

In *Byng v London Life Assurance Ltd*, a case that predates the internet, Mustill LJ considered the conditions for what might be called "a reasonable participation test". The Court was considering whether it was possible to have a meeting if the members were not present in the same room. What had happened in the case was that the room rented for the meeting was not big enough to house all the shareholders, and the directors had rented two additional "overflow rooms", which were fitted with audio-visual links. While not considering the question directly—Mustill LJ said that he was not considering "whether it was possible to convene a meeting which does not take place in any single location, and which consists only of the exchange of electronic impulses"—he said that if the shareholders in question "had been able to see, hear and communicate with the other participants I would have seen no intellectual and practical objection to regarding this as a 'meeting'".[16] Thus, if there is to be a test, it is submitted that it will be along these lines, and could be called a meaningful participation test.[17]

---

[15] *ibid*, s 176(3).

[16] *Byng v London Life Assurance Ltd* [1989] BCLC 400 at 414–415.

[17] For the Company Law Review Group's view, see its first report, at para 6.5.6, where it recommended that s 134 of 1963 Act be amended to reflect modern technology. The report is pre-Skype *et al*—it was published in 2001—and refers to videoconferencing, but the recommendation is that "any technology which gives members as a whole a reasonable opportunity to participate" should be allowed. See also *Re Mr. Binman & Ors* [2011] IEHC 401 at para 20, for an unsuccessful technical objection relating to the attendance, via telephone, of a non-executive director.

Notice

Notice of every general meeting of a company must be given to the following four categories of person:

(a) Every member;

(b) The personal representative of a deceased member of the company, which member would, but for his or her death, be entitled to vote at the meeting[18];

(c) The assignee in bankruptcy of a bankrupt member of the company (being a bankrupt member who is entitled to vote at the meeting); and

(d) The directors and secretary of the company.[19]

If a share is jointly held, notice will be properly given if it is given to the person whose name appears first in the register.[20] As a general rule, no other persons, other than those above, are entitled to notice of general meetings; this rule can be displaced by the company's constitution. Unless the company has availed of the audit exemption,[21] the company' statutory auditors are entitled to receive all notices of general meetings, attend and be heard at them (but they are only entitled to be heard "on any part of the business of the meeting which concerns them as statutory auditors").[22]

As a general rule at least 21 days' notice should be given of an AGM or an EGM which has a special resolution tabled, but this rule can be displaced by the company's constitution. If a special resolution is not tabled for an EGM then notice period is considerably shorter: seven days.[23] There are ways around these general rules, apart from the company's constitution. If a general meeting is called by a shorter notice than that just outlined, it will still be deemed to have been "duly called" if all the members entitled to attend and vote at the meeting (and if relevant, the company's statutory auditors) agree to this.[24]

---

[18] This should be posted, using a prepaid letter address to the representative(s) of the deceased. See also Companies Act 2014, s 180(4).

[19] Companies Act 2014, s 180.

[20] *ibid*, s 180(2).

[21] ss 360–365, or, where relevant, s 399.

[22] Companies Act 2014, s 180(6)(a)–(c).

[23] *ibid*, s 181.

[24] *ibid*, s 181(2).

If there is a dispute about the notice period, the following test applies. If notice is given by ordinary prepaid post to the registered address of a member then the giving of the notice is deemed to have been effected on the expiration of 24 hours following posting.[25] Accidental omission of notice will not invalidate the business transacted at a general meeting, unless the company's constitution states otherwise.[26]

It is essential that the notice of a meeting specifies the following:

(a) The place, the date and the time of the meeting;

(b) The general nature of the business to be transacted at the meeting;

(c) In the case of a proposed special resolution, the text or substance of that proposed special resolution; and

(d) With reasonable prominence a statement that (i) a member entitled to attend and vote is entitled to appoint a proxy[27] (or, where it is allowed, one or more proxies), to attend, speak and vote instead of him; (ii) a proxy need not be a member; and (iii) the time by which the proxy must be received at the company's registered office or some other place within the State as is specified in the statement for that purpose.

Quorum

As a general rule, two members of the company will make a quorum. The members may be present by proxy and the quorum will still be good.[28] This is a general rule which can be altered by a company's constitution. No business can be transacted at any general meeting unless a quorum of members is present at the time when the meeting proceeds to business.[29] If the company is a single-member company then, of course, one member present in person or by proxy at a general meeting of it is a quorum.

---

[25] *ibid*, s 181(3); see also s 181(4), which states: "In determining whether the correct period of notice has been given by a notice of a meeting, neither the day on which the notice is served nor the day of the meeting for which it is given shall be counted."

[26] Companies Act 2014, s 181(6).

[27] The form set out at s 184 of Companies Act 2014 must be used. The rules on proxies are set out in ss 183 and 184. The rules in relation to the representation of bodies corporate at general meetings are set out at s 185.

[28] Companies Act 2014, s 182(2).

[29] *ibid*, s 182(1).

If the meeting has been requisitioned by members and there is not quorum present within 15 minutes after the appointed time then the meeting is automatically dissolved.[30] In all other cases where a quorum is not present within 15 minutes, the meeting either adjourns to the same day in the next week, at the same time and place or it adjourns to a different day, time and place, determined by the directors. If at the adjourned meeting a quorum is not present within half an hour after the time appointed for the meeting, the members present become the quorum.[31]

The Business of the AGM

There are six topics which must be covered at the company's AGM[32]:

(a) The consideration of the company's statutory financial statements and the report of the directors and, unless the company is entitled to and has availed itself of the audit exemption,[33] the report of the statutory auditors on those statements and that report;

(b) The review by the members of the company's affairs;

(c) Save where the company's constitution provides otherwise (i) the declaration of a dividend (if any) of an amount not exceeding the amount recommended by the directors; and (ii) the authorisation of the directors to approve the remuneration of the statutory auditors (if any);

(d) Where the company's constitution provides, the election and re-election of directors;

(e) The appointment or re-appointment of statutory auditors (save where the company is entitled to and has availed itself of the audit exemption); and

(f) The remuneration of the directors (where the company's constitution so provides).

Section 187 of Companies Act 2014 provides a set of rules—which can be displaced by the company's constitution—for the conduct of proceedings at meetings. These include default rules on the appointment of a chairperson, what business may be transacted at an adjourned meeting

---

[30] *ibid*, s 182(5).
[31] *ibid*, s 182(5)(b)(ii).
[32] *ibid*, s 186.
[33] *ibid*, s 360 or s 365.

and the notice requirement for meetings which are adjournment for more than thirty days.

The first port of call in decision-making is a show of hands. A resolution is put to the meeting. A show of hands is called for. The chairperson makes a declaration that the resolution has been carried, carried unanimously, lost, and so on, and makes an entry in the minute book to that effect.[34] Where there is equality of votes the chairperson has a casting vote. On a show of hands, every member present in person and every proxy has one vote.[35] A member is entitled to demand a poll, but only if his voting rights represent 10% of the company's total voting rights, or if his shares confer the right to vote and are shares "on which an aggregate sum has been paid up equal to not less than 10% of the total sum paid up on all the shares conferring that right".[36] If an individual member does not meet this threshold, he can still demand a poll if he can convince two other members, or their proxies, to support his demand.[37] The default rule on a poll is that:

> "every member shall, whether present in person or by proxy, have one vote for each share of which he or she is the holder or for each €15 of stock held by him or her, as the case may be."[38]

For a member to be entitled to vote at a general meeting, he must have paid any calls made by the directors on his shares; a member could be denied the right to vote if he hasn't paid up any sums owning on a call.[39] This is a matter that a member or director could raise at the general meeting in question: the objection cannot be made after the meeting has taken place and the vote been cast. Any such objection would have no force.[40] If an objection is made, it should be made to the chairperson, whose decision on the matter shall be final and conclusive (like all these rules, this is subject to displacement by the company constitution).[41]

---

[34] Companies Act 2014, s 187(7).

[35] *ibid*, s 188(2)(a).

[36] *ibid*, s 189(2)(c) and (d).

[37] *ibid*, s 189(2)(b).

[38] *ibid*, s 188(2)(b); in the case of joint holders, the person whose name appears first in the register of members will be known as the "senior", and the vote of the senior who tenders a vote, whether in person or by proxy, must be accepted to the exclusion of the votes of the other joint holders. See also s 190.

[39] Companies Act 2014, s 188(6).

[40] *ibid*, s 188(7).

[41] *ibid*, s 188(8)

Minutes

Companies have an obligation to enter the minutes of all general meetings and the terms of any resolutions passed at them into books which are kept for that specific purpose.[42] Failure on this front is a category 4 offence. Wherever the word "book" is used, it may be understood that the company is permitted to record the matters on computers: the rule is that the matters must be kept in such a form as "is capable of being reproduced in a legible form".[43] If there is more than one such book, they should all be kept "at the same place". Members' rights of inspection, rights to request copies, and so on, apply to the minute books.[44] Minutes which are signed by the chairperson of the relevant meeting are "evidence of the proceedings" which took place.[45] Anyone alleging that matters recorded in minutes which are signed by the chairperson are not true and accurate must prove their case because there is a statutory assumption that such matters duly recorded and signed are true and accurate.[46]

Ordinary and Special Resolutions

An ordinary resolution means a resolution:

> "passed by a simple majority of the votes cast by members of a company as, being entitled to do so, vote in person or by proxy at a general meeting of the company."[47]

A special resolution[48] means a resolution that is

> "passed by not less than 75% of the votes cast by such members of the company concerned as, being entitled to do so, vote in person or by proxy at a general meeting of it"[49]

---

[42] *ibid*, s 199.

[43] *ibid*, s 214(1).

[44] *ibid*, s 199(2), referring to the rights in ss 215–217.

[45] Companies Act 2014, s 199(3).

[46] *ibid*, s 199(4).

[47] *ibid*, s 191(1).

[48] In a rare case, a practitioner might come across the term "extraordinary resolution". This will only be found in documents which were created before 1 April 1964, and any such reference is deemed to be a reference to a special resolution.

[49] Companies Act 2014, s 191(3) and (2).

A special resolution requires a notice period of 21 days to be given to the members before the vote is to take place.[50] Another thing to consider is whether the terms of a special resolution can be amended at the meeting where it is to be voted on. The answer is yes: the terms of *any* resolution can be amended by an ordinary resolution at a general meeting. The key thing is that the court could deem adequate notice of the intention to pass the amended resolution has been given.[51] Finally, if a resolution is passed at an adjourned meeting, does it get backdated? No. It will be deemed to have been passed on the date *on which it was in fact passed* and will not be deemed to have been passed on any earlier date.[52]

Unanimous Written Resolution Procedure

Resolutions do not necessarily have to be passed at a general meeting. There is a way around this, known as the written resolution. A resolution in writing signed by *all* the members of a company who are entitled to attend and vote on such a resolution at a general meeting shall be as valid and effective for all purposes *as if* the resolution had been passed at a general meeting of the company duly convened and held.[53] If the resolution is described as a special resolution, then that is fine: the written resolution procedure covers special resolutions. The key thing is the written resolution must have unanimous support. Wherever it says in Companies Act 2014 that a resolution must have been passed at a general meeting, the written resolution procedure can be used.[54] The only time this procedure cannot be used is when the resolution is to remove a director or a statutory auditor.[55]

At a practical level, a single sheet with the resolution doesn't have to be passed around all the members for them to sign, and they don't all have to sign it on the same day. The unanimous written resolution can be any

---

[50] There is almost always a way around these things: a majority of the members can agree to vote on a special resolution in cases where the 21 day minimum notice has not been given. By majority, the Act states that the members must hold together not less than 90% in nominal value of the shares which give the right to attend and vote, or represent not less than 90% of the total voting rights at that meeting of all the members. (Companies Act 2014, s 191(4)).

[51] Companies Act 2014, s 191(6).

[52] *ibid*, s 192.

[53] *ibid*, s 193(1)(a).

[54] *ibid*, s 193(2).

[55] *ibid*, s 193(11).

number of sheets, as long as they are gathered together and contain all the members' signatures, and the resolution will be said to have been passed on the date on which it was signed by the last member to sign.[56] When the resolution is not signed contemporaneously, two steps must be followed. First, signatories of the resolution should deliver to the company—e-mail or fax are fine—the documents which constitute the written resolution. That should be done within 14 days of its passing and signatories are obliged to take "reasonable steps" to make sure it does happen.[57] Second, the company must notify its members that the resolution has been passed: it should do this with 21 days of receiving the documents that constitute the resolution, and failure to do so is a category 4 offence.[58] The company must retain the documents as if they were minutes of a general meeting, and must keep them with the company's minute books.[59] Failure to do any of these housekeeping tasks will not invalidate the resolution: it will merely leave parties open to the possibility of a fine.[60]

Majority Written Resolutions

LTDs and DACs can now pass ordinary resolutions in writing by a majority. This rule is new and only applies to those two forms of company (and it does not apply to resolutions to remove a director or statutory auditor). The majority in question means

> "a member or members who alone or together, at the time of the signing of the resolution concerned, represent more than 50% of the total voting rights of all the members who, at that time, would have the right to attend and vote at a general meeting of the company".[61]

The signatories of a majority written resolution must ensure that the documents constituting the resolution are delivered to the company (e-mail or fax is fine). The resolution has no effect until this is done.[62] The company must retain these documents as if they were minutes of a meeting

---

[56] *ibid*, s 193(4).
[57] *ibid*, s 193(10); failure to do so is a category 4 offence.
[58] *ibid*, s 193(9).
[59] *ibid*, s 193(7).
[60] *ibid*, s 193(8).
[61] *ibid*, s 194(3).
[62] *ibid*, s 195(5).

and keep them with the minute books. There is an in-built delay to the majority written resolution procedure. Ordinary written resolutions passed by majority are deemed to have been passed "at a meeting held 7 days after the date on which it was signed by the last member to sign".[63] Special written resolutions passed by majority are deemed to have been passed "at a meeting held 21 days after the date on which it was signed by the last member to sign".[64] This in-built delay is subject to the rule that the resolution will have no effect unless the signatories ensure that the documents constituting the resolution are delivered to the company.

Forwarding Resolutions to the CRO

Companies must forward to the CRO a copy of every resolution passed within 15 days after the date of passing or making of it.[65] Every new resolution must be "embodied in, or annexed to" every copy of the company's constitution.[66] All members are entitled to receive copies of a resolution, upon the payment of a fee which may not exceed €10.[67]

Passing Resolutions Informally: Buchanan and Duomatic

The shareholders may validly pass a resolution without holding a meeting and without formally passing a resolution. The principle is either known as the "Buchanan principle" or the "Duomatic principle". The different names are simply due to the fact that the principle was first enunciated in Ireland in a case called *Buchanan Ltd v McVey*[68] and in England in a case called *Re Duomatic*.[69] While it is expressed in slightly different language in the two jurisdictions, the principle is "in substance, the same".[70] Speaking in the High Court in *Buchanan Ltd v McVey*, Kingsmill Moore J stated that:

> "[i]t is now settled law that neither meeting nor resolution is necessary. If all the corporators agree to a certain course then,

---

[63] *ibid*, s 194(9)(a).
[64] *ibid*, s 194(9)(b).
[65] *ibid*, s 198(1). For the avoidance of doubt, a full list of resolutions which require to be registered with the CRO is provided at s 198(4).
[66] Companies Act 2014, s 198(2).
[67] *ibid*, s 198(3).
[68] [1954] IR 89.
[69] [1969] 2 Ch 365.
[70] *Per* Finlay Geoghegan J [2011] 3 IR 1 at 16.

however informal the manner of their agreement, it is an act of the company and binds the company subject only to two pre-requisites. The two necessary pre-requisites are (1) that the transaction to which the corporators agree should be *intra vires* the Company; (2) that the transaction should be honest."[71]

This was approved in the Supreme Court. Finlay Geoghegan J approved it in *Kerr v Conduit*,[72] adding that the phrase "all the corporators" must be taken as "a reference to all shareholders with a right to both attend and vote at a general meeting of the company".[73] In *Re Duomatic* Buckley J stated that although the formal steps were not taken it was "[t]he fact that … they nevertheless did apply their minds" to the relevant question which was important.[74] In *Re New Cedos Engineering Co Ltd*[75] Oliver J said

> "the ratio of Buckley J's decision is that where that which has been done informally could, but for an oversight, have been done formally and was assented to by 100% of those who could have participated in the formal act, if one had been carried out, then it would be idle to insist upon formality as a pre-condition to the validity of the act which all those competent to effect it had agreed should be effected".

Summary Approval Procedure

There are seven kinds of activity which have restrictions placed on them. The new Summary Approval Procedure ("SAP") can be used to correctly embark on these courses of action. The seven restricted activities are as follows:

1.   Financial assistance for acquisition of shares[76];
2.   Reduction in company capital[77];

---

[71] [1954] IR 89 at 96.
[72] [2011] 3 IR 1 at 13.
[73] *ibid*, at 16.
[74] [1969] 2 Ch 365 at 373.
[75] [1994] 1 BCLC 797 at 814. For further judicial approval see also Mummery LJ in *Euro Brokers Holdings Ltd v Monecor (London) Ltd* [2003] 1 BCLC 506 at para 57; *Wright v Atlas Wright (Europe) Ltd* [1999] 2 BCLC 301; *Peña v Dale* [2004] 2 BCLC 508. For approval of Buchanan see Keane J in *Re Greendale Developments Ltd* [1998] 1 IR 8 at 21–22.
[76] Companies Act 2014, s 82.
[77] *ibid*, s 84.

3. Variation of company capital on reorganisation[78];
4. Prohibition on pre-acquisition profits or losses being treated in holding company's financial statements as profits available for distribution[79];
5. Prohibition of loans, etc., to directors and connected persons[80];
6. Mergers[81];
7. Procedure for and commencement of members' voluntary winding-up.[82]

Mergers require a slightly different set of rules and they are outside the scope of this work. In six other cases, the members can either: (i) permit the carrying on of a restricted activity that is otherwise prohibited; or (ii) fulfil the requirement specified in the provision concerned for the restricted activity to be authorised, by its members passing a special resolution and its directors making a certain declaration.[83]

The SAP is carried out as follows. The members confer authority for the carrying on of the restricted activity by passing a special resolution. The special resolution must be passed not more than 12 months prior to the commencement of the carrying on of the activity by the company. The written means for passing the resolution can be used.

The directors must make a declaration at a directors' meeting. The content of the declaration depends on the activity which is being pursued. The guidelines set out in ss 203 to 207 should be followed. For example, if the SAP is being used to begin a members' voluntary winding up the directors should state the total amount of the company's assets and liabilities as at the latest practicable date before the date of making of the declaration and that they, the directors, have made a full inquiry into the affairs of the company and that, having done so, have formed the opinion that the company will be able to pay or discharge its debts and other liabilities in full within such period not exceeding 12 months after the commencement

---

[78] *ibid*, s 91.
[79] *ibid*, s 118.
[80] *ibid*, s 239.
[81] *ibid*, s 464.
[82] *ibid*, s 579.
[83] *ibid*, s 201.

of the winding-up.[84] The directors' meeting must be held not earlier than 30 days before the date of the signing of the resolution by the last member to sign, if the written means for passing the resolution is used.[85]

Whatever the declaration, it must be delivered to the CRO within 21 days of the commencement of the restricted activity.

In three cases the directors' declaration will have no effect unless it is accompanied by a report drawn up by a person who is qualified at the time of the report to act as statutory auditor to the company. The report must state that person's opinion that the directors' declaration is "not unreasonable".[86] Those three cases are when the SAP is used for:

1. Variation of company capital on reorganisation;
2. Prohibition on pre-acquisition profits or losses being treated in holding company's financial statements as profits available for distribution;
3. Procedure for and commencement of members' voluntary winding-up.

Declarations made by directors which are made "without reasonable grounds" leave the declarants open to the imposition of unlimited personal liability for the debts of the company.[87] If the company is wound up within 12 months of the declarations being made it is presumed that the directors did not have reasonable grounds for the making of them and it falls to the directors to displace that presumption.[88]

Meetings of Directors

The meetings of directors can be a great deal more informal than the meetings of shareholders. The directors are given the powers to exclusively manage the day-to-day business of the company.[89] The Act states that they "may meet together for the dispatch of business, adjourn and

---

[84] *ibid*, s 207(1).
[85] *ibid*, s 202(6)(b).
[86] *ibid*, s 208(a) and (b).
[87] *ibid*, s 210.
[88] *ibid*, s 210(2).
[89] *ibid*, s 158.

otherwise regulate their meetings as they think fit".[90] Most of the rules relating to directors meetings — all of which can be displaced by a company's constitution—are found in s 160 and s 161. Some of the most notable are as follows:

- Questions arising at any such meeting shall be decided by a majority of votes and where there is an equality of votes, the chairperson shall have a second or casting vote;
- A director may, and the secretary on the requisition of a director shall, at any time summon a meeting of the directors;
- All directors are entitled to reasonable notice of any meeting of the directors but, if the directors so resolve, it shall not be necessary to give notice of a meeting of directors to any director who, being resident in the State, is for the time being absent from the State;
- No one but a director has the standing to object to the notice given for a directors' meeting;
- The quorum necessary for the transaction of the business of the directors may be fixed by the directors (if it's not fixed it shall stand at two but, where the company has a sole director, the quorum is one);
- The directors may establish one or more committees consisting in whole or in part of members of the board of directors;
- A resolution in writing signed by all the directors of a company who are for the time being entitled to receive notice of a meeting of the directors shall be as valid as if it had been passed at a meeting of the directors duly convened and held;
- Directors are obliged to keep minutes of their meetings.[91]

---

[90] *ibid*, s 160.
[91] *ibid*, s 166

CHAPTER TEN

MEMBERSHIP AND SHARES

Membership of a Company and the Register of Members

The subscribers to the constitution of a company are deemed to have agreed to become members of the company and, on the registration of the company, they are entered as members in its register of members.[1] The key attribute of membership is that a person's name is entered in the register of members.[2] The register of members must contain: the names and addresses of the members and a statement of the shares held by each member (distinguishing each share by its number so long as the share has a number); it must state the amount paid or agreed to be considered as paid on the shares of each member; it must state the date at which each person was entered in the register as a member[3]; it must state the date at which any person ceased to be a member. You will never find any notice of any trust (express, implied, constructive) entered on the register of members or on any CRO records: the company is not obliged to concern itself with any names but the names of the holders of the share.[4] The register is *prima facie* evidence of any matters contained within it.[5] Any *person*—i.e. persons who are not yet members, persons who may have bought shares but who were informed that the directors had declined to register the share transfer—who is "aggrieved" by their omission from the register of members may apply to court to have the register rectified. To succeed, they must particularise the argument that their name has been omitted "without sufficient cause."[6]

Shareholder Rights of Inspection

The following are statutory rights which accompany the purchase of a share. The books and records of the company are often kept either in the registered office of the company or in the offices of the company's accountants (referred to in the Act as "another person"). Where they are

---

[1] Companies Act 2014, s 168(1).

[2] *ibid*, s 168(2).

[3] *ibid*, s 169(1)(a) and (b); according to s 169(3) these particulars must be entered within 28 days after the date of conclusion of the agreement with the company to become a member or, in the case of a subscriber of the constitution, within 28 days after the date of registration of the company. It is a category 3 offence not to comply with this rule.

[4] Companies Act 2014, s 170, see also s 66(6) and (7).

[5] Companies Act 2014, s 171.

[6] *ibid*, s 173; the statute also allows for a person who is aggrieved by their *inclusion* in the register to make such an application.

kept by "another person" they must be kept in a place within the State.[7] The following registers or documents must be open to the inspection of any member of the company without charge, during business hours[8]:

(a) The copies of directors' service contracts and memoranda;
(b) The copies of instruments creating charges;
(c) The directors' and secretaries' register;
(d) The disclosable interests register;
(e) The members' register; and
(f) The minutes of meetings.

A member of the company may request a copy, or a copy of any part, of the directors' and secretaries' register; the disclosable interests register; the members' register; or the minutes of meetings.[9]

The following must be open to the inspection of any other person, (i.e. non-member) on payment of a small fee: the directors' and secretaries' register; the disclosable interests register; the members' register.[10] The fee is €10 where one register is inspected, and €15 where more than one is inspected (but the company can charge less if it chooses).[11] Non-members can also request, for a small fee, copies of those three categories of document.[12] As long as the required fee has been paid by the requester, the company must satisfy the request within ten days of it being made.[13] The court has powers to compel compliance with these rules.[14]

The copies of instruments creating charges must be open to inspection by any creditor of the company without charge.[15]

The Features of a Share

Shares do not come under the rubric of the Sale of Goods Act. Legally, they are not "goods", but are things called *"choses in action"*. This phrase,

---

[7] Companies Act 2014, s 216(4).
[8] *ibid*, s 216(7) and (8).
[9] *ibid*, s 216(11).
[10] *ibid*, s 216(9).
[11] *ibid*, s 217(1).
[12] *ibid*, s 216(12).
[13] *ibid*, s 216(13).
[14] *ibid*, s 217(4).
[15] *ibid*, s 216(10).

a blend of French and English, means that a share is a "thing" which has rights attaching to it which you can enforce by taking proceedings: the "action". Keane J described a share as "a bundle of proprietary rights which can be sold or exchanged for money or other valuable consideration".[16] Another judge described a share as an interest "measured by a sum of money", as well as being "a series of mutual covenants" that all the shareholders enter into with one another.[17] The extent of a shareholder's rights can only be ascertained when the company's constitution is examined.[18]

A share confers an *interest* in the company: it does not give the shareholder a proprietary interest in the assets of the company. The property of the company belongs to the company, not to its shareholders. A share creates a contract between the shareholder and the company, and between the shareholder and the other shareholders (the constitution, when registered, binds the company and the members of it to the same extent *as if it had been signed and sealed by each member*, and contained covenants by the company and each member to observe all the provisions of the constitution and any provision of this Act as to the governance of the company).[19] A share confers statutory rights and obligations, which will be discussed in this chapter (rights to information about the company, company documents, rights to petition for relief when oppressed, and so on). Ownership of shares is "one of the bundle of rights which constitute ownership of private property" and is recognised and protected by the Constitution.[20]

The Five Key Rights of Shareholders

There are five key rights which a share gives a shareholder. They are: (1) the right to a dividend (if it is declared); (2), the right to attend and vote

---

[16] *Re Sugar Distributors Ltd* [1995] 2 IR 194 at 207.

[17] *Per* Farwell J, *Borland's Trustee v Steel Bros and Co Ltd* [1901] 1 Ch 279 at 288.

[18] A share is "personal estate" and not real estate. Before modern company law took shape, it was thought that a share gave the holder a right to a portion of the company's property. From at least the beginning of the twentieth century this has not been the case (*Attorney General for Ireland v Jameson* [1904] 2 IR 644; *Kerry Co-operative Creameries Ltd v An Bord Bainne Co-op Ltd* [1990] ILRM 664 and [1991] ILRM 851). Shareholders do not "own" the company in the sense of owning parts of its property. For a definition of a chose in action see *Re Cuff Knox (deceased)* [1963] IR 263, *per* Kingsmill Moore at 291.

[19] Companies Act 2014, s 31.

[20] *Per* Carroll J, *PMPS v AG* [1983] IR 339 at 349, citing Kenny J at 84 of *Central Dublin Development Association v AG (1969) 109 ILTR 69*.

at general meetings; (3) the right to a return of capital and any surplus if the company is wound-up; (4) statutory rights to notices, information, and to seek relief against the company, which are conferred by the Companies Acts; (5) a member has a *prima facie* right to transfer his shares. Some of these are self-explanatory and some will be explained in more detail in the following paragraphs.

Share Capital of a Company

"Share capital", in relation to a company, means the aggregate amount or value of the nominal value of shares of the company.[21] Shares in the capital of a company must have a nominal value[22]; in many cases, a share will have a value of €1. Each share should be distinguished by a number.[23] A LTD cannot invite the public to subscribe for any shares of the company[24]: the listing of shares or securities on any market is a matter for PLCs, not LTDs, DACs, and so on. A company can allot shares of different nominal values or with different amounts payable on them if it wishes.[25] Allotments of shares can only take place if they are authorised, either by the general authority vested in the directors, by the constitution of the company, or by ordinary resolution of the company.[26] It is the directors who allot the shares, and they must do so "on such terms and conditions and at such times as they may consider to be in the best interests of the company and its shareholders".[27] Shares cannot be allotted at a discount to their nominal value: if they are, the allottee will be liable to pay the company an amount equal to the amount of the discount and interest at the appropriate rate.[28]

Pari Passu and Different Classes of Shares

All shares are equal, but some are more equal than others. The starting point is the principle that all shares rank *pari passu*, a Latin term means

---

[21] Companies Act 2014, s 64.

[22] *ibid*, s 66(1).

[23] *ibid*, s 67(1), unless all the issued shares in a company or all the issued shares in it of a particular class are fully paid up and rank *pari passu* for all purposes; in that case, none of those shares need thereafter have a distinguishing number, so long as it (a) remains fully paid up; and (b) ranks *pari passu* for all purposes with all shares of the same class for the time being issued and fully paid up.

[24] Companies Act 2014, s 68(1).

[25] *ibid*, s 66(2); it may allot shares of different currencies.

[26] Companies Act 2014, s 69(1).

[27] *ibid*, s 69(4)(b); knowing contravention of this rule is a category 3 offence, per s 69(5).

[28] Companies Act 2014, s 71(2) and (3).

that all shares are presumed to be equal. Unless it says so in the company's constitution, each share will carry the same rights to voting, to a dividend, and to a return of capital in a liquidation. More often than not, however, shares are weighted differently.

Any share in a company may be issued with whatever preferred, deferred or other special rights or restrictions which the company may specify in its constitution. Restrictions may cover the right to dividends, restrictions on voting rights, restrictions on the return of capital and so on.[29] A company may issue redeemable shares[30]: this means that when the share is issued, it is envisaged that the company will redeem it at a later point, a practice that allows for a short-term injection of capital in the company. Shares in a company are personal estate, not real estate[31] (this is relevant when it comes to paying tax on them; another example of personal estate is a leasehold).

The basic divide is between ordinary and preference shares. A preferential share might entitle the holder to receive a fixed dividend each year in priority to the ordinary shareholders. If there are not enough distributable profits that year, it could be that only the preferential shareholders receive a dividend. An example of this going spectacularly wrong for the preferential shareholders is *Re Williams Group Tullamore Ltd*[32] (see Chapter 12). The profits of the company were so consistently high that the dividend for ordinary shareholders was often over 100% of their capital, while the preferentials were stuck with the fixed return of 8% per year (which also took a knock because of inflation). Another feature of the case was the difference in voting power. The company had drafted its articles so that ordinary shareholders would not be entitled to receive notice, let alone attend or vote at, any general meetings, as long as there were any preference shareholders in existence.

A classic case on differently weighted shares is *Bushell v Faith*.[33] There were three shareholders, a brother, Geoffrey, and his two sisters, Constance and Kathleen. They each had 100 shares, and were each a director of the

---

[29] Companies Act 2014, s 66(3).
[30] *ibid*, s 66(4).
[31] *ibid*, s 66(5).
[32] [1985] IR 613.
[33] [1970] AC 1099.

company. The sisters were unhappy with their brother's conduct as director and called a meeting to remove him. The sisters voted in favour of the resolution and, unsurprisingly, Geoffrey voted against it. To the sisters' surprise, Geoffrey said the motion wasn't carried. His one hundred shares were worth 300 votes in this situation, he said, and their hundred shares were worth 100 votes each. Geoffrey was right. Article 9 of the company's articles stated that if a resolution to remove a director was proposed at a meeting, then any shares held by that director should be worth three times their usual voting weight. The aim was clearly that no sibling could ever be removed against his or her will, and the House of Lords upheld the right of companies to attach special weights to shares.

Preference shares might be payable out of the profits of the year (i.e. the dividend will represent a portion of profit for one given year) or they might be cumulative (i.e. the dividend for a number of years may be paid out at the one time.

Preference shares might also stipulate that there is a priority right to the repayment of capital in a winding up, and that its votes are weighted more favourably than the ordinary shares, as seen above in *Bushell v Faith*; in practice, this is rare enough, and with preference shares "often carry[ing] no voting rights whatsoever or perhaps only a limited entitlement to vote".[34]

Calls on Shares

The primary duty of a shareholder is to pay for his shares. Shares can be bought without the purchaser paying for them in full at the time of purchase. The directors of a company may from time to time make calls upon the members in respect of any monies unpaid on their shares.[35] Once a call is made, each member has at least 30 days to pay the amount called on his shares—the time by which the call should be paid should be stated by the directors in the call.[36] The directors can revoke or postpone

---

[34] MacCann and Courtney, *Annotated Companies Acts 1963–2006* (Bloomsbury Professional, 2006) at p 175.

[35] Companies Act 2014, s 77(2); this does not apply to shares where the conditions of allotment of them provide for the payment of moneys in respect of them at fixed times.

[36] Companies Act 2014, s 77(4).

a call.[37] They can stipulate that the call should be paid in instalments.[38] The directors might, on the issue of the shares, have differentiated between the holders of different classes as to the amount of calls to be paid and the times of payment.[39] Joint holders of a share are jointly and severally liable to pay any call made upon them. Failure to pay a call might lead to the directors deciding that interest on the sum must be paid, starting on the day appointed for payment of the call.[40] A member can offer at any time to pay all or any part of the moneys uncalled and unpaid upon any shares held by him, but it is up to the directors to accept this offer: they will do so "if they think fit".[41] The directors may pay a dividend in proportion to the amount paid up on each share, where a larger amount is paid up on some shares than on others.[42] The company has a "first and paramount lien" on every share which is not a fully paid share.[43] The lien on a share extends to all dividends payable on it.[44] The Companies Act 2014 makes provision for the sale of a shareholder's shares by the company, where the shareholder has not paid up an amount which he has been called on to pay.[45]

The Right to a Dividend

A company is not permitted to make a distribution except out of profits available for the purpose.[46] A company's profits available for distribution are its accumulated, realised profits, (so far as not previously utilised by distribution or capitalization), less its accumulated, realised losses, (so far as not previously written off in a reduction or reorganisation of capital duly made).[47] A "distribution" means every description of distribution of a company's assets to members of the company, whether in cash or otherwise.[48]

---

[37] ibid, s 77(5).
[38] ibid, s 77(6).
[39] ibid, s 78(3).
[40] ibid, s 77(8).
[41] ibid, s 78(4).
[42] ibid, s 79(c).
[43] ibid, s 80(2).
[44] ibid, s 80(4).
[45] ibid, s 80(5), (6) and (7) and s 81.
[46] Companies Act 2014, s 117(1).
[47] ibid, s 117(2).
[48] ibid, s 123(1); see 123(1)(a) to (d) for exceptions to this general rule (the issue of fully or partly paid bonus shares, the redemption of preference shares, for example).

A company may declare dividends by ordinary resolution, but no dividend can exceed the amount recommended by the directors of the company.[49] The ultimate decision to declare dividends, therefore, rests with the directors, and if they have made a decision not to declare them, they cannot be forced to do so (*Scott v Scott*[50]). A dividend is only payable when it is declared.[51] If the company goes into liquidation, the shareholders have no right to any dividends because the assets of the company can no longer be considered "profits".[52] The directors can decide to pay the members interim dividends, if this is justified by the profits of the company. They may decide to set aside a certain sum of money out of the profits of the company, in order to form a reserve which will be applicable for any purpose to which the profits of the company may be properly applied[53]: this reserve may be employed in the business of the company or be invested in such a way as the directors decide. The directors might simply carry forward any profits which they may think prudent not to distribute, without putting any company money into a reserve.[54] Whatever the course of action, it is a matter for the directors. The directors, depending on the wording of the constitution,[55] may have the power to deduct from any dividend payable to any member, all sums of money immediately payable that member to the company on account of unpaid calls.[56] No dividend bears interest against the company.[57]

Consequences of Making an Unlawful Distribution

There are serious consequences for directors and shareholders if a distribution is made unlawfully. Section 122(1) of Companies Act 2014 states:

> "Where a distribution or part of one, made by a company to one of its members, is made in contravention of any provision of this Part [of Companies Act 2014] and, at the time of the distribution, he or she *knows or has reasonable grounds for believing that it is so made*, he or she shall be liable to repay it or

---

[49] Companies Act 2014, s 124(2).
[50] [1943] 1 All ER 582.
[51] *Bowland v Earle* [1902] AC 83.
[52] *Wilson v Dunnes Stores Cork Ltd*, Unreported, High Court, Kenny J, 22 January 1976.
[53] Companies Act 2014, s 124(3)(b).
[54] *ibid*, s 124(3)(c).
[55] If the constitution is silent, the Companies Act 2014 will apply.
[56] Companies Act 2014, s 124(7).
[57] *ibid*, s 125(6).

that part, as the case may be, to the company or (in the case of a distribution made otherwise than in cash) to pay the company a sum equal to the value of the distribution or part at that time." [*emphasis added*]

The classic case in this area is *Flitcroft's Case*.[58] Directors paid out dividends under a false premise and the Court of Appeal held them liable to repay the company the money that had wrongly flowed out of its coffers. Ten years after that case, Lindley LJ said:

> "As soon as the conclusion is arrived at that the company's money has been applied by the directors for purposes which the company cannot sanction, it follows that the directors are liable to replace the money, however honestly they may have acted. Whether they can in turn get it back from those persons who receive it is another matter, but their own liability to restore it is now clearly settled."[59]

It might be recalled that another situation in which the honesty of the directors is irrelevant is where they make a profit by virtue of their position which they do not reveal to the shareholders; in such cases—as we saw in Chapter 6—directors simply have to "disgorge" the profits.[60] The principle has been repeated in more recent times in *Bairstow v Queens Moat Houses plc*,[61] where the Court stated:

> "The basic rules about lawful and unlawful dividends, developed from the earliest days of company law and now elaborated in accordance with Community legislation, exist not only for the protection of creditors, but also for the protection of shareholders ... If directors cause a company to pay a dividend which is *ultra vires* and unlawful because it infringes these rules, the fact that the company is still solvent should not be a defence to a claim against the directors to make good the unlawful distribution"[62]

---

[58] (1882) LR 21 Ch D 519.
[59] *Re Sharpe* [1892] 1 Ch 154 at 165–166.
[60] *Regal (Hastings) Ltd v Gulliver* [1967] 2 AC 134.
[61] [2001] 2 BCLC 531.
[62] *Per* Robert Walker LJ [2001] 2 BCLC 531 at 546. *For an example of* a distribution not made out of profits see *MacPherson v European Strategic Bureau Ltd* [2000] 2 BCLC 683. For an allegation that the declaration of a dividend by a subsidiary was ultra vires see *Re Cleveland Trust plc* [1991] BCLC 424.

Transfer of Shares

PART I

Introduction

A person who holds shares has a *prima facie* right to transfer them, but private companies are required to restrict this right. Why is this? The law recognises that private companies "from a business and personal point of view…are much more analogous to partnerships than to public corporations".[1] Most companies in Ireland are very small. Many are run by families or by friends. If something happens — a death or a departure — and shares suddenly become available, directors feel happier when they can either refuse to register a transfer of shares or when there is a provision which means that the existing shareholders must be offered the chance of buying the newly available shares before anyone else. Both of these options are possible.

Section 95 of Companies Act 2014 states that — unless the company's constitution provides otherwise — the directors of a company "may in their absolute discretion and without assigning any reason for doing so, decline to register the transfer of any share."[2] This power to decline to register a transfer of shares only lasts for two months; that is, it expires two months after the date of delivery to the company of the instrument of transfer of the share.[3] It is important that the directors communicate the decision to refuse registration by sending notice of the refusal to the transferee.[4]

Thus, a successful share transfer involves three different parties: the transferor, who executes the "instrument of transfer", the transferee, who purchases the share, and the directors, who agree to register the name of the new owner in the company's register of members. Crucially, the transferor remains the legal owner of the share until the name of the transferee is entered in the register in respect of it.[5] Until his name is registered, the transferee is only the beneficial owner of the share, and does not enjoy the rights that attach to it (the right to vote at meetings, for

---

[1] *Per* Lord Greene MR, *Re Smith and Fawcett Ltd* [1942] 1 Ch 304 at 306.
[2] Companies Act 2014, s 95(1)(a).
[3] *ibid*, s 95(1)(b).
[4] *ibid*, s 95(3).
[5] *ibid*, s 94(3).

example). The transferee is in limbo in such a situation.[6] He might have paid over money for the shares, but he is not yet the legal owner of them. The transferor is still the legal owner.[7]

One technical thing to look out for is that the share transfer takes place using a "proper instrument of transfer"[8]: this means a share certificate which has been stamped for Revenue purposes. Section 129(1) of the Stamp Duties Consolidation Act 1999 provides that if any person whose job it is to enrol or register (i.e. a company secretary) any instrument chargeable with duty (i.e. a stock transfer form), and that thing hasn't been stamped, then that person is liable to a fine. Does this mean that the stock transfer form which hasn't been stamped is invalid? No. While the document should be stamped, it isn't invalidated if it is not. The defects are "mere irregularities."[9] The section simply provides for a fine for the person who allowed it to slip through.

Directors' Power to Refuse a Share Transfer

Can directors really decline to register the transfer of any share "in their absolute discretion and without assigning any reason for doing so"? There is a good deal of case law which says that as long as they are acing bona fide and in the interests of the company, they may. Lindley LJ put it strongly in *Re Coalport China Co*[10]:

> "They [the directors] do refuse a transfer; they do not say why. The argument is...that it is for them to justify their conduct. Now, that appears to me to be wrong. It is for those who say that the directors have exercised their power improperly to give some evidence to that effect. Here there is absolutely none.

---

[6] See *Kinsella v Alliance and Dublin Consumers' Gas Company*, Unreported, High Court, Kenny J, 5 October 1982.

[7] A refusal to register you doesn't mean your contract with the transferor is void. It is still a binding contract (*Skinner v City of London Marine Insurance Corp* (1885) 14 QBD 882). What if the person who transferred you the shares was a director, who then voted against registering them in your name? He can't. If he transferred them to you, he must vote in favour of registering you (*Lee and Company v Egan*, Unreported, High Court, Kenny J, 27 April 1978). Does the transferor have to vote the way you, the transferee, tell him? Yes (*Musselwhite v CH Musselwhite & Son Ltd* [1962] Ch 964).

[8] Companies Act 2014, s 94(4).

[9] Per Leggatt LJ, *Nisbet v Shepherd* [1994] 1 BCLC 300 at 305, approved by Laffoy J in *Re Charles Kelly Ltd; Kelly v Kelly and Anor* [2010] IEHC 38.

[10] [1895] 2 Ch 404 at 407.

> Therefore, in common fairness, as a matter of justice between man and man, it strikes me that the decision [of the lower court] is based upon an erroneous principle."

The reason is that it is up to the person seeking the help of the court — in the form of rectification of the register — to prove why the court should use its power to intervene. In the absence of evidence, the court must presume the directors have acted properly. In *Re Dublin North City Milling Co Ltd*,[11] the directors refused to register a Mr Spicer, who sought to compel them to do so, but made no definite charge of impropriety against them. Meredith MR said:

> "I dislike mystery, but I think the law is wise in refusing to compel directors to disclose their reasons for accepting or declining a transfer. The directors have kept themselves within the rule, and the reasons operating on their minds are not disclosed, and I cannot speculate or guess as to what they were ... I am of opinion that the law allows the directors to hold their tongues. It allows the to say that everything was done honestly and *bona fide* in the interests of their Company; and they have unanimously decided that it is not for the interest or advantage of the Company that these shares should be transferred to Mr. Spicer: and according to my view I have no power to make them say more."[12]

The short English case *Re Smith and Fawcett Ltd*[13] made the same point. Mr Smith and Mr Fawcett incorporated a company to carry on their business. Some 4001 shares were issued to Smith and 4001 to Fawcett. There was the "absolute discretion" provision in the company's constitution regarding the transfer of shares. Fawcett died. His wife and his son, Edwin, were the executors of his will. He left 2000 shares to his daughter and 2001 shares to Edwin. Edwin, as executor, applied to Smith on his and his sister's behalf to become a shareholder in the company. Smith refused to register all the shares. Instead, he offered to register 2001 shares and buy the remaining ones himself. Smith appointed his solicitor, Mr Feather, as director of the company, and when Edwin renewed his request that he and his sister have all the 4001 shares registered, Smith

---

[11] [1909] 1 IR 179.
[12] *ibid*, at 184.
[13] [1942] 1 Ch 304.

and Feather refused. The question for the Court was whether they were allowed to. The answer was yes because there was no evidence that they were acting other than *bona fide* and in the interests of the company. Lord Greene MR stated that the Court would require evidence of *mala fides* or a collateral or improper purpose, and not merely allegations and affidavit evidence: a judge will want to see the deponent (the person who swears the affidavit) submit himself to cross-examination because judges, with good reason, "strongly dislike being asked on affidavit evidence alone to draw inferences as to the *bona fides* or *mala fides*" of the people involved.[14]

This is because

> "[i]t is a general rule of procedural fairness that if a court is to be invited to disbelieve a witness, the grounds upon which his evidence is to be disbelieved should be put to him in cross-examination so that he may have an opportunity to offer an explanation."[15]

In *Re Hafner*[16] a man whose uncle had built up a business was left 500 shares but the directors, Mr and Mrs Powderly, who were paying themselves "indefensible emoluments", refused to register him as a member. Black J recognised that continued payments of these "bloated emoluments would convert this flourishing company from a dividend-paying concern into a director-remunerating enterprise".[17] In that case it was held that where such allegations were made against directors and they remained silent, the Court was entitled to draw the inference that their refusal was not a *bona fide* exercise of their discretion. More recently, in *Banfi Ltd v Moran* Laffoy J found that directors had been refusing to register a transfer of shares in an effort to prevent the transferee bringing oppression proceedings against them, and in this they were "motivated by self interest, not the interest of the company as a whole".[18]

---

[14] *Per* Lord Greene MR, [1942] 1 Ch 304 at 308.
[15] *Per* Lord Hoffmann, [1998] 2 BCLC 327 at 338.
[16] [1943] IR 426.
[17] *ibid* at 443–444.
[18] [2006] IEHC 257 at 21.

Personal Feelings and the Decision to Refuse

A brilliant example of an attempt to impugn a decision not to register can be seen in *Popely v Planarrive Ltd*.[19] Laddie J recognised that Ronald Popely's attempt to have the Court rectify the register in his favour was "but one facet of a bitter feud".[20] The feud was between Ronald and the rest of his family, his wife, Linda, and their children and nephew. Litigation had flourished as a result of their hostility. Linda was the MD of Planarrive. The other directors were Ronald and Linda's son, daughter and daughter-in-law. "Shorn of all its technicalities," Laddie J said, "the application was "an attempt by Mr. Popely to wrest control of the company" from those directors. Ronald said that the reason the directors had refused to register him was because they had fallen out — there were feelings involved, and feelings should have no place in the decision to register. There certainly were feelings involved. Linda had discovered that Ronald had been having affairs with two women, and had fathered a child with each. The revelation had a "profound effect" on her, the judge recognised, and damaged her health. The rest of the family took her side. Had their refusal to register Ronald been made done *bona fide* and in the interests of the company, or was it rooted in merely "personal views"?

Laddie J had no hesitation in accepting that the refusal had been done *bona fide* and in the interests of the company. Mrs Popely submitted compelling evidence — compelling because it was not contradicted — that Mr Popely had speciously obtained a judgment against Planarrive and had used that judgment to try and wind the company up, which froze the company's bank accounts. If he gained control of the board he would use his control to prevent the company taking actions against him personally (for example, for the recovery of seven horses which he took, and from recovering money from companies he controlled). Taking all the evidence together Laddie J concluded that on the evidence before him, "any reasonable board would have been likely to have taken the same decision as Mrs Popely and her children took".[21] The lesson of the case is that if a party can show that personal feelings got in the way of a decision that was

---

[19] [1997] 1 BCLC 8.
[20] *ibid* at 9.
[21] *ibid* at 18.

bona fide and in the interests of the company, then the decision may be impeached, but that

> "directors will normally have private views as to the suitability of new shareholders. It would be unrealistic and unworkable in many cases to require the directors to disqualify themselves in relation to the issue of registration of shareholdings merely because such views exist".[22]

Uncertain Language and Doubtful Implications

Section 95 of Companies Act 2014 applies "save where the constitution of the company provides otherwise". Therefore it is open to companies to modify the wording of the rule. The key lesson is this: if you modify the wording, you will be held strictly to whatever that wording is. There should be no "uncertain language or doubtful implications" when companies purport to cut down the right of transfer.[23] In *Re Bede Steam Shipping Co Ltd,*[24] for example, the relevant article gave the directors the power to refuse to register a share transfer if they "did not approve" of the intended transferee, believing that to transfer shares to that person would be against the interests of the company. In that case, Warrington LJ said that the article "gives them one ground, and one ground only for refusing to register the transfer of a fully paid share".[25] Any "cutting down" of the right to transfer shares will be subject to the language used in the article and the general considerations outlined above (*bona fide* and in the interests of the company). If directors refuse for some other reason, then they will clearly have exceeded their powers. They can draft as wide ranging a clause as they wish, but they must stick to the words they used when drafting it, when they purport to refuse someone. In *Re Smith and Fawcett Ltd* Lord Greene MR said, and the courts have followed ever since, "I decline to write into that clear language any limitation other than" the limitation of having to act bona fide and in the interests of the company.[26]

---

[22] *ibid* at 15.

[23] Lord Greene MR said in *Greenhalgh v Mallard* [1943] 2 All ER 234 at 237: "if the right of transfer, which is inherent in property of this kind, is to be taken away or cut down, it seems to me that it should be done by language of sufficient clarity to make it apparent that that was the intention."

[24] [1917] 1 Ch 123.

[25] *ibid* at 136.

[26] For a more recent consideration of the law, see *Mactra Properties Ltd v Morshead Mansions Ltd* [2009] 1 BCLC 179.

In *Tangney v The Clarence Hotels Company Ltd*,[27] the company's constitution said

> "if the directors are of opinion that the proposed transferee is not a desirable person to admit to membership, they may decline to register the transfer of any such share."

The problem for the directors was that the plaintiff, Denis Tangney, had been a shareholder in the defendant company for many years, and the company had incorporated articles which said that if any shares were to be transferred, they would first be offered to existing members. Johnston J said that the directors' power to decide who was and who wasn't a desirable person "seems to be absolute and cannot be questioned, except by showing affirmatively that they are exercising their powers capriciously or wantonly", but it seemed to the judge that "that clause was intended to meet the case of a stranger proposing to come into the family, as it were".[28] The desirable person category, therefore, could only apply to outsiders, not to Mr Tangney.

Directors May Give Further Reasons at a Later Date

It was thought at one point that if the directors gave reasons at the time of the refusal, they should be bound by them,[29] but this is no longer the case. In *Village Cay Marine Ltd v Acland*,[30] a case which arose out of a joint venture to develop land on the island of Tortola for residential purposes, Mr Acland gave reasons for refusing to register a transfer of shares in a letter, and then gave further reasons at trial. It was argued that he couldn't do this, that he was stuck with the reasons he gave in the letter.[31] Lord Hoffmann said that the Privy Council did

> "not think that there is any rule of law by which the directors are confined to the reasons they have given. Of course as an evidential matter they may have difficulty in persuading a

---

[27] [1933] IR 51.
[28] *ibid* at 63.
[29] *Re Bede Steam Shipping Co Ltd* [1917] 1 Ch 123 was authority for this.
[30] [1998] 2 BCLC 327.
[31] This was argued because in *Re Bede Steam Shipping Co Ltd* [1917] 1 Ch 123 Lord Cozens-Hardy MR stated (at 135) "the directors ought not to be allowed to state their reason in the certificate itself to the transferee and then to say that it was not the only reason, but they had other and different reasons."

court that their refusal was based upon reasons which they did not mention, but the question for the judge in the end is whether at the time they believed in good faith that the refusal of registration was in the interests of the company."[32]

Notice of Refusal to Register a Share Transfer

If the directors refuse to register a transfer of shares they must communicate this to the transferee within two months or lose their right to decline the transfer.[33] This might seem straightforward, but the courts have had to deal with a number of "what if" scenarios. What happens if a decision to refuse is made but not communicated to the transferee? In *Re Hackney Pavilion Ltd*[34] there were three directors, Sunshine, Kramer and Rose. When Mr Sunshine died, his wife, who was the executrix of his estate, applied to be registered. Only Kramer and Rose were left on the board and they disagreed on whether to register her: so there was deadlock, and the proposal to register Mrs Sunshine couldn't be carried. The Court held that the refusal to register had to be *active*. Astbury J said that the board "did not and could not exercise its right to decline".[35] The failure to register which was brought about by the deadlock was passive, and the executrix's right to be registered was upheld (the company had to pay the costs of her application).

What if no decision is made during the two month window? In *Re Swaledale Cleaners Ltd*[36] the company was a dry-cleaners in Yorkshire, run by the Smart family. Two of the shareholders died and Leslie Smart applied for their shares. The only person left as director after those two deaths was Major Smart. When an AGM was held, Leslie presented the share transfer forms (the details of how he got them do not matter — it was all done properly). A board with one member was inquorate. It couldn't effectively do anything — so Leslie's request to have the shares registered in his name was not accepted or rejected. As Harman LJ put it, "[t]here the matter seems to have gone temporarily asleep".[37] Four months later Major

---

[32] [1998] 2 BCLC 327 at 337.
[33] Companies Act 2014, s 95(1)(b) and s 95(3).
[34] [1924] 1 Ch 276.
[35] *ibid* at 280.
[36] [1968] 1 WLR 1710.
[37] *ibid* at 1714.

Smart appointed his wife, Eunice, to the board, and the two formally refused to register the share transfer. The Court stated:

> "It seems to me that by that time the natural right of a shareholder to have his name put on the register must exist — must prevail — unless there is some valid reason in the contract between the parties (i.e., the articles) why that should not be done."

Harman J noted that there was a time period during which the directors had to make up their minds, and so "waiting four months without any decision at all was an unreasonable delay". That is not enough in itself. That delay has to destroy their right to refuse at a later date. There was no authority on this, but the trial judge, Pennycuick J, "firmly took the view that, if you delay too long, you lose your rights, and that seems to me," said Harman J, "to be consonant with good sense".[38] This meant that the right to register the transfer had become absolute.[39] In a very short and snappy judgment, Carnwath J, stated that the principle remained unchanged. The case was *Re Inverdeck Ltd*.[40] The failure to refuse revolved around one director, a Mr Hahn. Carnwath J noted that:

> "[a]s a director he had a duty, enforceable by penal sanctions, to register within two months or give notice of refusal. He failed to do that and on the authority of *Re Swaledale Cleaners Ltd*, it seems to me that as director he has lost the right to do so."[41]

Challenging a Refusal to Register: The Procedure

We have seen examples of challenges to refusals, but we have not looked at how a person goes about doing this. The procedure is set out in s 173 of Companies Act 2014. It says that if any name is entered or omitted "without sufficient cause" in the register of members, then the person who is "aggrieved", or any member of the company or the company itself, may apply to the court for rectification.[42] The court may order rectification, and also that the company pay the aggrieved person compensation for

---

[38] *ibid* at 1715.
[39] See also *Moodie v W & J Shepherd (Bookbinders) Ltd* [1949] 2 All ER 1044, where the failure to exercise the right to refuse also meant that the applicants were entitled to be registered.
[40] [1998] 2 BCLC 242.
[41] *ibid* at 244–255.
[42] Companies Act 2014, s 171 states that the register of members shall be *prima facie* evidence of the matters set out therein.

any loss they have sustained.[43] If, for example, a party has lost out on dividends because the directors wrongly refused to register him, then the court will measure his damages in terms of the sum he would have received through the dividends (plus interest).[44] As Laffoy J has said, it is a discretionary remedy.[45]

Shares on the Death of the Shareholder

If a shareholder dies his shares will be transferred to his personal representative. The shareholder is not actively transferring them. The process is passive, and so it is known as "transmission of shares by operation of law", rather than share *transfer*.[46] The same is true where a person becomes bankrupt: his shares are transmitted to the assignee in bankruptcy. In what follows, it will only be referred to when a shareholder dies, but the same process occurs when a shareholder becomes bankrupt (simply replace "personal representative" with "assignee in bankruptcy").

The personal representative steps into the shoes of the deceased member and although he is not himself a member of the company, any transfer the personal representative makes is "as valid as if he had been such a member at the time of the execution of the instrument of transfer".[47]

In the case of a member's death, the only person recognised by the company as having title to the share is the personal representative of the deceased.[48] If the deceased was a joint holder the survivor (or survivors) are the only persons recognised by the company as having title to the shares in question. The directors may ask for evidence of the death of a member (death certificate, grant of probate, for example). Once this is produced, the person who is entitled to the share can choose to either: (a) be registered himself or herself as holder of the share; or (b) to have some person nominated by him or her to be registered as the transferee of

---

[43] Companies Act 2014, s 173(2).
[44] *Sri Lanka Omnibus Co Ltd v Perera* [1952] AC 76.
[45] See *Re Olde Court Holiday Hostel Ltd; Trehy v Murtagh et al* [2006] IEHC 242.
[46] The other case of transmission is when a merger occurs. The transfer of shares in such cases happens by virtue of the merger, without an instrument of transfer.
[47] Companies Act 2014, s 94(6).
[48] *ibid*, s 96(2).

the share.[49] Importantly, the directors are in the same position, with regard to registering the entitled person or the nominated person, as they would have been in had the death not taken place: that is, they have the same right to decline or suspend registration, the same "absolute discretion".[50]

If the personal representative elects to be registered himself, he must give the company a notice in writing, signed by him, stating that he has chosen this course of action. Alternatively, he can execute a transfer of the share to the nominated person. A person becoming entitled to a share by reason of the death or bankruptcy of the holder is entitled to the same dividends and other advantages to which he or she would be entitled if he or she were the registered holder of the share.[51] But that is not the full story. The dividends will be held in trust until that person is registered. Such a person is not entitled to exercise any right conferred by membership in relation to meetings of the company, before being registered as a member in respect of the share.[52] Members can attend meetings, vote at meetings, have the right to speak at meetings. They may be counted as forming the quorum at meetings. A unregistered holder of a share has none of these rights until the directors register him or her. In *Arulchelvan and Wright v Wright*[53] Carroll J said that the regulations seemed "eminently clear" to her in that respect. The only right the person has in relation to meetings, until he or she is registered, is the right to notice of them.

It should be noted that, despite the fact that they are not members, personal representatives are given standing to take proceedings for oppressive conduct under s 212(8) of Companies Act 2014.

PART II

Pre-Emption Rights

A pre-emption right gives the existing shareholders a right of first refusal on any shares that come free. If someone decides to sell their shares, they cannot offer their shares to non-members immediately if there is a

---

[49] *ibid*, 96(4); that person will have to consent in writing to the nomination.
[50] *ibid*, 96(5).
[51] *ibid*, 96(8).
[52] *ibid*, s 96(9).
[53] Unreported, High Court, 7 February 1996 at 8 of the transcript.

pre-emption clause in place in the constitution of the company. The purpose of such a clause is the same as the purpose of a provision which gives the directors absolute discretion to refuse to register transferees: the owners of the company want to be able to regulate who becomes part of their group. There is no universal pre-emption clause. They differ, and whatever the wording, the courts approach them in the same way. They interpret them very strictly.

A basic pre-emption clause could look like this:

> "No share shall be transferred to a person who is not a member, so long as any member is willing to purchase the share at a fair value. In order to ascertain whether any member is willing to purchase such share, notice in writing shall be given to the company stating the desire of the holder thereof to transfer the same."[54]

An example of a slightly different pre-emption clause can be seen in *Cream Holdings v Davenport*.[55] Cream Holdings was a music and concert promoter. Mr Davenport was a director. The case was about how to value Mr Davenport's shares but it begins with the pre-emption clause, which came into play when Mr Davenport departed from the company. The relevant article of association said that when any employee who was also a shareholder left the company, he had to transfer his shares within fourteen days of leaving the company, and was obliged to offer his shares for sale to the remaining shareholders.[56]

Lee and Company v Egan[57] is a good example of a pre-emption clause at work. There were four shareholders in the company. Mr Roe had the largest shareholding. He wanted to retire so he hired an auctioneer to sell his shares. The auctioneer found a buyer, Mr Conroy, who was managing director of Lee and Company. Mr Roe — perhaps he forgot — was going to sell his shares to Mr Conway without offering them to the existing members first. He entered an unconditional contract. When

---

[54] Such was the clause in *Re Coalport China Co* [1895] 2 Ch 404.

[55] [2012] 1 BCLC 365.

[56] An epic battle between Irishman Patrick Killeen and the Barclay brothers for some of London's best known hotels, involved argument over pre-emption rights; see *Re Coroin* [2012] 2 BCLC 611; [2012] BCC 575.

[57] Unreported, High Court, Kenny J, 27 April 1978.

Mr Roe subsequently sought a higher price for his shareholding Mr Conroy sought specific performance of the contract. Kenny J gave specific performance, but it was a pyrrhic victory because the order was subject to the right of any other existing shareholder to choose to buy them first.

The *Safeguard Industrial Investments* case[58] is an example of the kind of highly technical, almost philosophical conundrum that can arise in company law. A man called Philip made a will and appointed a bank as his executor. In the will he left shares in a family company called Wright's to his god-daughter Georgina. Before he died he decided he wanted to leave his shares to Georgina and her brother Michael, divided equally. He died before he could change his will but Georgina gave effect to his wish and she executed what is called "a deed of family arrangement" to do this. As we know, most companies adopt the model regulations which say that transfers of shares by personal representatives (in this case it would be the bank) operate under the same rules as transfers would, had the deceased person been alive and performing them. The problem was that Wright's had specifically excluded that provision in its articles. As Oliver J explained, this meant that "the bank had a right to be registered as a member of the company without regard to the pre-emption provisions contained in the articles".[59] The bank did so. It was registered as the holder of Philip's 22,254 shares. The bank then regarded itself as holder of these shares on trust for Georgina and Michael. Now enter a company called Safeguard, which owned one-sixth of the shares in Wright's. It wanted to be given the opportunity to buy the shares. But to trigger the pre-emption clause which would allow them to buy the shares, a notice of transfer had to be given. Who was going to give it? Not the bank: and, perhaps because they didn't want Safeguard to gain more control of the family company, not Georgina and Michael. They were content to let the shares sit with the bank. Safeguard argued that the bank should be deemed to be "desirous of transferring" the shares, even though the beneficiaries weren't exercising their right to make the bank do so. Of course, the bank had no *desire* to make a transfer. Safeguard was forced to argue that it simply had a *duty* to start the transfer process. This "simple equation", that "duty equals desire", was not one which Oliver J

---

[58] *Safeguard Industrial Investments Ltd v National Westminster Bank Ltd* [1982] 1 All ER 449.
[59] [1982] 1 All ER 449 at 451.

found persuasive. What this case goes to show is that the wording of the articles is crucial where the courts are asked to enforce a pre-emption clause. In this case there had to be a "proposing transferor". Because the bank, and Georgina, and Michael, took a passive stance, there was no such party, and without such a party, the pre-emption mechanism could not be triggered, and Safeguard could never had an opportunity to buy the shares.[60] Thus, the lesson is: the wording of the pre-emption clause will be crucial.

---

[60] See also *McAuliffe v Lithographic Group Ltd* Unreported, Supreme Court, 2 November 1993, *ex tempore*, O'Flaherty J, where the wording of the pre-emption clause was crucial.

Protection of Minorities

Introduction

Protection of Minorities is a Corporate Governance issue, and as such is set out in Part 4 of Companies Act 2014. Under the heading "protection for minorities", s 212 sets out the remedy in case of oppression. The law is exactly as it was under s 205 of Companies Act 1963, with one exception: s 212 of Companies Act 2014 empowers the court to award compensation, something which was not permitted by the old statute (an omission which was sometimes circumventing by judges ordering the sale of the minority shareholder's shares at a slight overvalue[1]).

Who May Apply for Relief?

Section 212 states:

> "Any member of a company who complains that the affairs of the company are being conducted or that the powers of the directors of the company are being exercised—(a) in a manner oppressive to him or her or any of the members (including himself or herself), or (b) in disregard of his or her or their interests as members" may apply to the Court for relief.[2]

Apart from members of the company, the Act gives *locus standi* to two more categories of person: personal representatives (of a person who, at the date of his or her death, was a member of a company); and any trustees of (or persons beneficially interested in) the shares of a company by virtue of the will or intestacy of any member.[3] The phrase "affairs of the company" does not extend to acts of shareholders acting in a private capacity. For example, a dispute involving a shareholder's refusal to sell his shareholding is not "company affairs".[4] Nor does share dealing between the directors amount to the conduct of the company's affairs.[5]

---

[1] *Per* Barron J *Morgan v Murphy* [1997] 3 IR 23 at 28–29; the inability of the Court to award compensation under s 205 of Companies Act 1963 was articulated by the Supreme Court in *Irish Press v Ingersoll* [1995] 2 IR 175.

[2] Companies Act 2014, s 212(1).

[3] *ibid*, s 212(8)(a) and (b).

[4] *Re Legal Costs Negotiators Ltd* [1999] 2 BCLC 171 (Peter Goldsmith QC sitting as a Deputy Judge of the High Court).

[5] *Re New Ad Advertising Co Ltd* [2007] IEHC 436 (Smyth J), citing *Re Leeds United Holdings plc* [1996] 2 BCLC 545 (Rattee J) and *Re Saul D Harrison & Sons* [1995] 1 BCLC 14 (Hoffmann LJ).

The most technical *locus standi* issue was litigated in *Re Via Net Works (Ireland) Ltd.*[6] Via Net Works (Ireland) was a subsidiary of a Dutch parent. It was in an insolvent position and the parent was pouring money into it by way of loans, in order to keep it up and running. At a certain point shareholders contracted with the parent to sell their shares within a specified period if the Dutch parent gave them thirty days' notice. The parent was not obliged to buy the shares, but the shareholders were obliged to sell them if called on to do so. When the Dutch company gave notice that it would purchase the shares at the price of one penny per share the two petitioners sought the relief of the court. Keane CJ declined relief on the basis that the petitioners had no *locus standi* because at the date they presented their s 212 petition they were contractually bound to divest themselves of their rights as shareholders and to transfer them to the Dutch parent. The learned Chief Justice stated that

> "persons...who have voluntarily disposed of their entire shareholding in a company could not conceivably have been contemplated by the legislature as persons who would be entitled to relief under [s 212]."[7]

In Camera Proceedings

Section 212 proceedings will only be held *in camera* if the proceedings would involve the disclosure of information which would be seriously prejudicial to the legitimate interests of the company if published.[8] In *Re Skytours Travel Ltd*[9] the respondent sought an *in camera* hearing because he had appropriated monies belonging to the company for his own use and had informed the Revenue Commissioners of this fact: the respondent did not wish this information to be published in open court. The disclosure of this information was not seriously prejudicial to the legitimate interests of the company and the Court refused to hear the matter behind closed doors.

Orders Which the Court May Make

If the court is "is of opinion that the company's affairs are being conducted or the directors powers are being exercised" in a manner oppressive to the

---

[6] [2002] 2 IR 47.
[7] *ibid* at 55.
[8] Companies Act 2014, s 212(9).
[9] [2010] IEHC 531 (Laffoy J, 9 July 2010).

shareholders, or in disregard of their interests, the court may "with a view to bringing to an end the matters complained of, make such order or orders as it thinks fit".[10] A list of four possible orders is set out in the Act, but the phrasing of the foregoing sentence suggests that the court has a wide discretion and that the following list does not purport to be exhaustive. Section 212(3) states:

> The orders which a court may so make include an order—
>
> (a) directing or prohibiting any act or cancelling or varying any transaction;
> (b) for regulating the conduct of the company's affairs in future;
> (c) for the purchase of the shares of any members of the company by other members of the company or by the company and, in the case of a purchase by the company, for the reduction accordingly of the company's capital; and
> (d) for the payment of compensation.[11]

Section 212 proceedings often do not get to hearing: they are settled before the day of trial. This is well known and the Supreme Court has recognised that s 212 proceedings are most effective as a "weapon to be brandished to secure a settlement".[12] The most common order which is made, if the proceedings do come before a judge, is an order for the purchase of a member's shares, often the shares of the member who is being oppressed, thus "bringing to an end the matters complained of". The "proper" price is "the price which the court in its discretion determines to be proper having regard to all the circumstances of the case".[13]

Where the Court Orders an Amendment to the Company's Constitution

If the court makes an order amending the company's constitution, the order will have the same effect as if it had been made by a resolution of the

---

[10] Companies Act 2014, s 212(2).

[11] *ibid*, s 212(3).

[12] *Per* O'Donnell J in *Glynn v Owen et al* [2012] IESC 15 at 13.

[13] *Per* Oliver LJ, *Re Bird Precision Bellows Ltd* [1985] 3 AER 523 at 529; approved in Ireland by O'Hanlon J in *Re Clubman Shirts Ltd* [1991] ILRM 43 at 53; and *Bell v Rollville Ltd* [2011] IEHC 79 (High Court, Herbert J, 26 January 2011). For valuation of shares where there is divergence between two valuation reports, see *Kelly v Kelly & Anor* [2012] IEHC 330 (Laffoy J, 19 June 2012).

company.[14] The company will not have the power to make a subsequent amendment to the constitution which would be inconsistent with that court order, unless it has the leave of the court to do so.[15] Any order made under s 212 which amends — or grants leave to amend — the company's constitution must be delivered by the company to the CRO within 21 days after the date of the making of the order[16] (failure by the company to do this is a category 4 offence for company and any defaulting officer).[17]

Case Law on "Disregard of Interests"

The majority of s 212 applications are brought under the "oppression" heading, and there is only one Irish case where the applicants sought an order for "disregard of interests": it is *Re Williams Group Tullamore Ltd.*[18] The case turned on the distribution of profits from the sale of Irish Mist Liqueur. There were two categories of shareholder: ordinary and preference. The preference shares carried a right to a fixed 8% dividend and a right to vote. The ordinary shareholders had no voting rights. Primarily due to the success of the company, each year the ordinary shareholders were receiving greater dividends than the preference shareholders. The preference shareholders felt sore about this. At a certain point, a lump sum came to be distributed. The preference shareholders decided to distribute it among themselves, to the exclusion of the ordinary shareholders, thereby, in their minds, redressing the imbalance. This idea was put to a vote, and it was passed to great acclaim, because only the preference shareholders were able to vote. The ordinary shareholders took an action claiming that this proposed distribution was both oppressive and in disregards of their rights. The High Court found that an individual transaction could give rise to s 212 relief and that while the ordinary shareholders were not in general being treated in an oppressive manner (the proposal was put forward "in good faith"[19]), their interests were being disregarded and an implementation of the proposal would be oppressive to the ordinary shareholders.

---

[14] Companies Act 2014, s 212(5).
[15] *ibid*, s 212(4).
[16] *ibid*, s 212(6).
[17] *ibid*, s 212(7).
[18] [1985] IR 613.
[19] *ibid* at 622.

The English courts have a slightly different test to Ireland: they speak of "unfair prejudice". In *Re Bovey Hotel Ventures Ltd*[20] Slade J stated:

> "The test of unfairness must, I think, be an objective, not a subjective one. In other words it is not necessary for the petitioner to show that the persons who have had de facto control of the company have acted as they did in the conscious knowledge that this was unfair to the petitioner or that they were acting in bad faith; the test, I think, is whether a reasonable bystander observing the consequences of their conduct, would regard it as having unfairly prejudiced the petitioner's interests."

Case Law on "Oppression"

By far the most common complaint in s 212 proceedings is of oppressive conduct. *Scottish Cooperative Wholesale Society v Meyer*[21] is notable for two things: First, it is the only company law case where the respondents[22] had fled Nazi Germany. Second, and more importantly, it is the case where "oppression" was first defined by the courts. Viscount Simonds simply reached for the dictionary,[23] and it said that oppression meant "burdensome, harsh and wrongful". The majority shareholder treated the two respondents, who were shareholders and directors of the company, oppressively by deliberately setting out to destroy the company once it had "served its purpose".[24] The result was that the Court fixed a fair price at which the appellant had to purchase the shares of the respondents.

This dictionary definition was adopted in Ireland by Keane J in *Re Greenore Trading Company Ltd.*[25] Greenore was a Louth-based company which provided services to cattle exporters. It had three shareholder-directors, who will be referred to by their first names: Adolph, Omer and Sean. The oppression turned on one particular transaction. At the time it took place, Adolph had resigned as director but was still a shareholder. Omer agreed

---

[20] Unreported, 31 July 1981, quoted with approval by Nourse J in *Re R A Noble & Sons (Clothing) Ltd* [1983] BCLC 273 at 290–291 and approved by Peter Gibson J in *Re Sam Weller & Co* [1990] BCLC 80 at 85.

[21] [1959] AC 324.

[22] They were experts in the manufacture of a semi-synthetic material called rayon fabric and had a Europe-wide network of contacts in the business.

[23] *ibid* at 341.

[24] *ibid* at 342.

[25] [1980] ILRM 94.

to pay Sean £22,500 for his shares. He paid Sean £8,000 from his own funds and had the company pay him £14,500. Adolph petitioned the Court for relief under s 205 (as it then was). Keane J found that the transaction was unlawful because it was not disclosed to the other member of the company — Adolph — nor was it approved by the company in a general meeting. Furthermore, it wasn't specified in the company's accounts. These failures meant it fell foul of two provisions of the 1963 Act.[26] So, the conduct was oppressive of Adolph. The transaction "was not merely irregular, but grossly irregular", the learned judge calling it "the patent misapplication of the company's money for the purpose of giving [Omer] a dominant position" in the company's affairs. Keane J would have wound-up the company on just and equitable grounds, but because this wasn't in the interests of the shareholders he granted the petitioner relief under the previous incarnation of s 212 of Companies Act 2014, directing Omer to buy Adolph's shares at a fair price.

The definition of oppression adopted in *Scottish Cooperative* and *Re Greenore* is the definition today, and was approved by Laffoy J in *Re Charles Kelly Ltd*,[27] a bitterly fought case involving brothers who had fallen out. Two of the brothers had turned on one. The two purported to suspend the one and Laffoy J found that the purported suspension was "a sham, which had been contrived" and that it was designed "to annoy, harass and embarrass" the minority brother.

Re West Winds Holding Company Ltd[28] established that an isolated act of oppression will be enough to meet the requirements of s 212 (in that case, the company's lands were sold by one director, using fraudulent means, without the knowledge of the other director). A person can avail of s 212 in their capacity as a director (as long as they are also a shareholder).[29] In *Re Bird Precision Bellows Ltd*[30] two directors were excluded from participation

---

[26] s 186 (the non-disclosure to the other members) and s 191 (failure to specify the transaction in the company's accounts). Keane J said that if he viewed it another way, if the £14,500 was not paid as compensation to Sean for quitting the company, but as consideration for the shares, then the transaction fell foul of s 60 of 1963 Act, which we will come across in detail in the chapter on capital maintenance. s 60 prohibits companies from providing financial assistance for the purchase of their own shares.

[27] [2011] IEHC 349.

[28] Unreported, High Court, Kenny J, 21 May 1974.

[29] *Re Murph's Restaurants Ltd.* [1979] ILRM 141; *Re Charles Kelly Ltd* [2011] IEHC 349.

[30] [1984] 1 Ch 419.

in major decisions of the company and this exclusion was conduct that was unfairly prejudicial to them (a terminology which the English courts prefer to "oppressive"). In *Re Ghyll Beck Driving Range Ltd*[31] a joint venture between four men to turn ten acres of relatively useless farmland into a golf driving range turned sour, and when tensions came to a head over a disagreement about whether or not to finish plastering the toilets, the petitioner felt that he had been frozen out of the running of the business, which, together with the fact that the three respondents gave him notice of sham directors' meetings only for the purpose of being able to remove him for failure to attend, constituted oppressive behaviour: the Court found that the petitioner was justified in believing he could no longer trust his co-participators and ordered that the petitioner's shares be bought by them. It is quite open to a director to seek relief under s 212. *Re Murph's Restaurant Ltd*[32] is the seminal Irish case in which a director was frozen out of the day-to-day management of the company by his fellow directors. The business was set up by three friends, Kevin, Murph and Brian. Kevin and Murph were brothers and in time, despite the success of the business, they sought to exclude Brian from it. The brothers told the Court they were getting rid of Brian because his work was no longer acceptable. Gannon J didn't believe them, finding their conduct irregular and arrogant, and

> "a deliberate and calculated repudiation by both of them of that relationship of equality, mutuality, trust and confidence between the three of them which constituted the very essence of the company."[33]

Rather than grant relief under s 212, however, Gannon J wound the company up under s 569(e) (see Chapter 16).

The Test is Objective

When considering how to judge the behaviour of a director the test is an objective one. This was established in the first Irish case to deal with s 212 of Companies Act 2014 *Re Irish Visiting Motorists' Bureau Ltd*[34] where

---

[31] [1993] BCLC 1126.

[32] [1979] ILRM 141.

[33] The Court elected to wind-up the company on just and equitable grounds rather than grant relief under the minority protection heading

[34] *Re Irish Visiting Motorists' Bureau Ltd*, Unreported, High Court, 7 February 1972. (The case, of course, considered the previous incarnation of s 212 of Companies Act 2014, which was s 205 of Companies Act 1963).

Kenny J drew a parallel between oppressive directors and oppressive figures throughout history. The learned judge stated:

> "One of the most terrifying aspects of human history is that many of those who we now regard as having been oppressors had a fanatical belief in the rightness of what they were doing."[35]

This being the case, it wouldn't make any sense to judge them by their subjective belief.

Does Mismanagement Amount to Oppressive Conduct?

Would the failure to hold general meetings and to furnish important information to shareholders amount to oppressive conduct? *Re Clubman Shirts Ltd*[36] tells us that this will not amount to oppressive conduct: instead, the court will look for the higher threshold of *deliberate planning* to cause loss or damage or deprivation of rights to a shareholder. The petitioner said that the company had failed to hold AGMs or present audited accounts for a number of years, and so the board was preventing him from being informed of the financial affairs of the company while at the same time asking him to sell his shareholding at what he thought was a low price. He also complained that the directors had concluded a transaction which seemed to involve the handing over of the company's entire business to a newly formed company. O'Hanlon J said it was "extraordinary that the petitioner, who owns or controls about 20% of the equity of the company, had to wait until the case came into court before he learnt the details of this transaction"[37] and found that the petitioner's complaints "were borne out in large measure by the evidence" but he had "some reservations about putting it into the category of oppressive conduct towards a minority".[38] The reasons for his reservations are important. O'Hanlon J found that the evidence showed "a series of irregularities by the directors in complying with their obligations of the Companies Act, rather than a case of oppression in the sense of [s 212]". The learned judge stated that omission to comply with provisions relating to meetings and the provision of information

---

[35] *ibid*, Kenny J at 37.
[36] [1983] ILRM 323.
[37] *ibid* at 325.
[38] *ibid* at 327.

"were examples of negligence, carelessness, irregularity in the conduct of the affairs of the company, but the evidence does not suggest that these defaults or any of them formed part of a deliberate scheme to deprive the petitioner of his rights or to cause him loss or damage".[39]

It is important to view these comments in their context. O'Hanlon J accepted that the company had "reached the end of its tether" and the directors' actions — in particular the selling off of a large part of the company's assets — were *bona fide* and done to stave off receivership and the probable liquidation of the company. This latter action was enough to get the petitioner over the line. The Court ordered the majority shareholders to buy out the petitioner's shareholding based on the true value of the shares as they were when the business of Clubman Shirts was spirited away to the newly formed company. It is not, as a general rule, oppressive to decline to consult with shareholders, but it will be oppressive if the board is taking such drastic action as selling the entire of the company's undertaking without notice to minority shareholders.

In *McCormick v Cameo Investments Ltd*[40] McWilliam J stated:

"it is not oppression for the directors to make an unsatisfactory decision in the conduct of the business of a company."[41]

In *Re a Company, ex p Shooter*[42] the English Chancery Division held that a repeated failure to hold AGMs and to lay accounts before the members was conduct that went beyond mismanagement and into the realm of conduct that was unfairly prejudicial to the interests of the members. The company in that case ran a football club and the respondent was a Mr Noel Kelly who had acquired a controlling shareholding in the company in 1980 and from that time — a period of seven years until proceedings were brought – had run the company without observing any of the usual formalities as to meetings and accounts. In *Clubman Shirts* O'Hanlon J said that the failure to prepare proper accounts annually was due to the "completely cavalier attitude"[43] that had been adopted by the directors, an

---

[39] *ibid* at 327
[40] [1978] ILRM 191.
[41] *ibid* at 194.
[42] [1990] BCLC 384.
[43] *ibid* at 325.

attitude, he said, was unfortunately the case in many private companies. In *Re a Company, ex p Shooter* it seemed that Mr. Kelly's attitudes went beyond the cavalier and into the deliberate. When considering whether there is oppression, it would seem that the touchstone is deliberate damage. Thoughtlessness or stupidity may account for a cavalier attitude or for incompetence,[44] but neither would seem to constitute oppression. The need for "a deliberate plan to damage the interests of the company" was emphasised in *Scottish Cooperative Wholesale Society v Meyer* and that decision was relied on by Barron J in *Irish Press v Ingersoll*,[45] which is the most modern Irish statement of the deliberate damage requirement. This said, surely a case could be made that mismanagement by directors amounted to disregard of members' interests. Indeed, in *Re Elgindata Ltd*[46] the Court stated:

> "I do not doubt that in an appropriate case it is open to the court to find that serious mismanagement of a company's business constitutes conduct that is unfairly prejudicial to the interests of minority shareholders. But I share Peter Gibson J's view that the Court will normally be very reluctant to accept that managerial decisions can amount to prejudicial conduct."

Lastly, it should be noted that oppression doesn't have to take the most obvious form. It could be the case that there is a possibility to settle legal proceedings, and to reject the settlement would be "an improvident gamble" which the courts would consider oppressive and in disregard of the interests of other shareholders (so the Court held in *Crindle Investments v Wymes*[47]).

PART II

The Rule in *Foss v Harbottle*

Before s 212 of Companies Act 2014 provided protection and relief for minorities in company law, there was s 205 of Companies Act 1963, which, as we have mentioned, was identical to s 212 in all respects, other than the

---

[44] *Re Five Minute Car Wash Service Ltd* [1966] 1 AER 242.
[45] [1995] 2 IR 175.
[46] [1991] BCLC 959, *per* Warner J at 993; see also Ussher, *Company Law in Ireland* (Sweet & Maxwell, 1986) at 263.
[47] [1998] 4 IR 567.

ability of the court to award compensation to the oppressed party. Before 1963, however, there were no statutory rules which enabled a shareholder to seek redress for oppressive behaviour or disregard of interests. There was only a common law rule, and the exceptions to it, which provided for something slightly different. The rule was called "the rule in *Foss v Harbottle*", and it said that if a wrong was done to the company, the proper plaintiff was *the company itself*. The rationale was this: if the company takes a decision to pursue a course of action, it is not for a minority to question the majority. If the rule in *Foss v Harbottle* did not exist, crank shareholders could take actions which would paralyse the company.[48] If a shareholder takes an action on behalf of the company, it is known as a derivative action, and if the company succeeds, it is the company which is awarded damages, and not the shareholder who took the action on its behalf.

Exceptions to the Rule in *Foss*

This rule could not stand without exceptions, because what if the company was in the hands of a bad bunch, who were intent on doing improper things? In such a case, the fact that they were in the majority would prevent any minority shareholders from taking a case in the name of the company, to vindicate the wrong done to the company. So exceptions to the rule developed. They have been set out by Irvine J in *Fanning v Murtagh*.[49] An individual minority shareholder may sue on behalf of the other shareholders or the company if there is:

1. An act which is illegal or *ultra vires* the company[50];
2. An irregularity in the passing of a resolution which requires a qualified majority;[51]

---

[48] See the comments of O'Flaherty J in *O'Neill v Ryan* [1993] ILRM 557 and, for the "classic definition", see Jenkins LJ in *Edwards v Halliwell* [1950] 2 AER 1064 at 1067.

[49] [2009] 1 IR 551.

[50] It is strange that this ever was, and still is, considered to be an exception, because a shareholder has the ability to prevent a company from committing such an act as a personal right. It was also an idea enshrined in s 8(2) of the 1963 Act, which states that "the court may, on the application of any member or holder of debentures of a company, restrain such company from doing any act or thing which the company has no power to do."

[51] Where 75% is required to carry a resolution it is not permissible to deem it passed by simple majority of 51%. If a company purports to do this, it is a wrong done to the company and a member may take proceedings to vindicate the wrong.

3. An act purporting to abridge or abolish the individual rights of a member[52];

4. An act which constitutes a fraud against the minority and the wrongdoers are themselves in control of the company.

It has been said of the above, that only point number 4 — an act which constitutes a fraud on the minority — is a true exception to the rule in *Foss*. The arguments against the first three points being true exceptions to *Foss* are set out in the footnotes below. We will consider fraud when we look at *Connolly v Seskin Properties Ltd.*[53] Before then, we should not neglect a purported fifth exception to the rule, which also may not really be an exception. It has been said that individual minority shareholder may sue on behalf of the other shareholders if "the justice of the case so requires".[54] This is seen as a stateable exception because Wigram VC, in *Foss v Harbottle* itself, stated that in the face of technical rules "the claims of justice would be found superior". Finlay Geoghegan J considered this in *Glynn v Owen*[55] and concluded that because the rule in *Foss v Harbottle* is an exception to the "elementary principle" that the courts are reluctant to interfere in the internal management of the company, the proposed fifth exception "should not be broadly or liberally applied" and "a strong case would have to be made out" before an action would be allowed under it. *Glynn v Owen*[56] was appealed to the Supreme Court and O'Donnell J cast doubt on the fifth exception by prefacing his remarks with the phrase "assuming such a broad exception to the rule exists". He found that in *Glynn v Owen* the appellants had merely asserted it, rather than given it serious argument. If the court were to assume that such a justice of the case exception existed, "it would require some compelling facts" and any need for such a wide-ranging exception had been reduced by the introduction of the s.212 remedies and by "the development of more sophisticated shareholders' agreements".[57] So for a party to plead that the justice of the case requires it, the pleadings must be compelling.

---

[52] An exception which Courtney has said "is not an exception at all, but rather an example of a situation in which the rule has no application whatsoever". Courtney, *The Law of Companies*, (3rd ed, Bloomsbury Professional, Dublin, 2012) at para 11.128.

[53] [2012] IEHC 332.

[54] See the discussion in *Biala Pty Limited v Mallina Holdings Limited* [1993] ACSR 785.

[55] [2007] 1 IEHC 328.

[56] [2012] IESC 15.

[57] *Glynn v Owen* [2012] IESC 15 at para 22.

It should also be noted that it is exceptionally difficult for a party to convince a court that it should be allowed to bring a derivative action. Four cases — recent by the standards of *Foss* case law — demonstrate this, and three of them Irish. In *Glynn v Owen*[58] the applicants were rebuffed, the Supreme Court finding that their appeal grounds were implausible. The outcome was similar in *Connolly v Seskin Properties Ltd*,[59] which we will consider below. In *Kenny v Eden Music Ltd*[60] the High Court found that a derivative action would be overwhelmingly to the disadvantage of the company. In *Abouraya v Sigmund*[61] the Court held that the claimant had failed to establish a *prima facie* case that the proposed action fell within the exception to the rule in *Foss v Harbottle*.

Two Areas Not Touched by *Foss*

Two areas are not touched by the rule in *Foss v Harbottle* and they should be expressly stated for the avoidance of confusion. The first is that a member can always vindicate his personal rights in the company, which come about through the s 31 contract, for example the right to have his vote counted at a meeting (*Pender v Lushington*[62]). Secondly, a shareholder can never sue for something called reflective loss. What that means is if the value of a shareholder's shares falls while the company is trading, that shareholder has suffered a loss for which there is no remedy (*O'Neill v Ryan*[63]).

Preliminary Matters in a *Foss* Application

Before the court will consider whether an applicant has brought himself under one of the exceptions, the applicant must jump a preliminary hurdle. Peter Gibson LJ set out the principles the court should apply when considering a derivative action in *Barrett v Duckett*[64] and Kelly J has approved them in this jurisdiction.[65] There is an onus on the shareholder "to establish to the satisfaction of the court that he should be allowed to

---

[58] [2012] IESC 15 (O'Donnell J, 23 February 2012).
[59] [2012] IEHC 332 (Kelly J, 27 July 2012).
[60] [2013] IEHC 628 (White J (Michael), 6 November 2013).
[61] [2014] EWHC 277 (Ch) (Richards J, 13 February 2014).
[62] (1877) 6 Ch D 70.
[63] [1993] ILRM 557.
[64] [1995] 1 BCLC 243.
[65] *Connolly v Seskin Properties Ltd* [2012] IEHC 332 at para 53.

sue on behalf of the company" and the shareholder will only be allowed to sue on behalf on the company if he is bringing the action: 1 *bona fide* for the benefit of the company; 2 for wrongs to the company; *and* 3 for which no other remedy is available. All three of these boxes must be ticked. The Court of Appeal in that case held that it was a clear duty of the Court to decide this issue as a preliminary issue.

The English test in this regard is that the shareholder must establish a *prima facie* case before being allowed to proceed (*Prudential Assurance Company Limited v Newman Industries Ltd (No.2)*[66]). The test in Ireland is different: the courts have set a higher threshold, a "realistic prospect of success" test (*per* Irvine J in *Fanning v Murtagh*[67]).

It is not, therefore, easy to bring a derivative action. An applicant must first prove that he has a realistic prospect of success: that he ought to be allowed sue on behalf of the company; that no other remedy is available; and then that he falls within one or more of the exceptions to the rule in *Foss*. It is surprising anyone takes such an action. As noted above, the applicants in the four most recent *Foss* cases failed — *Glynn v Owen*,[68] *Connolly v Seskin Properties Ltd*,[69] *Kenny v Eden Music Ltd*[70] and *Abouraya v Sigmund*.[71] The practical advice to any client seeking to take a derivate action would have to be: there must be an alternative route.

Case Study: *Connolly v Seskin Properties Ltd*

It will be enough to look at one of them, *Connolly v Seskin Properties Ltd*,[72] for the practical difficulties to become apparent. There were three people and two companies involved. The people were Sean Connolly, the applicant, and his business partner and friend of thirty years, Michael Whelan and Michael's son, who were the respondents. The companies were Seskin Properties and Maplewood. The Whelans controlled Maplewood and were also, taken together, the owners of 51% of the shares in Seskin. The applicant owned 49% of the shares in Seskin and was its

---

[66] [1982] 1 Ch 204.
[67] [2009] 1 IR 551.
[68] [2012] IESC 15 (O'Donnell J, 23 February 2012).
[69] [2012] IEHC 332.
[70] [2013] IEHC 628 (High Court, White J (Michael), 6 November 2013).
[71] [2014] EWHC 277 (Ch),[2014] All ER (D) 208 (Feb) (David Richards J).
[72] [2012] IEHC 332.

managing director and moving spirit. The two companies used to work hand in glove, developing property. Maplewood provided the land and Seskin built the houses. The crux of the matter was that Mr Connolly said Maplewood owed Seskin €5m. Seskin should sue for it. But the Whelan's didn't want to because of their interest in Maplewood, so they were blocking Seskin from doing so. This was a wrong on Seskin.

The Whelans took a different view. They said there was no point in Seskin suing Maplewood, because the latter had no money, because it was only trading for the benefit of its secured creditors (NAMA and Ulster Bank), because a receiver had been appointed over its assets, and because if sued it would itself seek rectification of the written agreement which lay at the heart of the dispute and stood a good chance of succeeding. They said that if Maplewood lost and went into liquidation Seskin would be an unsecured creditor and would recover nothing. Seskin, on the other hand, was solvent, with assets of over €1.5m. In short, they believed that it didn't matter whether Mr Connolly won or lost: if he were allowed to take the action Seskin would be destroyed.

As you know from above, the rule in *Foss v Harbottle* prevented Mr Connolly from taking an action unless he came under one of its exceptions. Mr Connolly said he came under the fourth and fifth exceptions, fraud on the minority and the justice of the case.

Kelly J said that what united the cases where fraud had been found was a varying degree of "moral turpitude". The learned judge said that "given the ever changing circumstances of modern commercial life" it would be

> "unwise to identify what might or might not constitute fraud
> on a minority in any given case. What can be said, however,
> is that it usually involves some element of moral turpitude".[73]

The onus in such cases is only discharged where it is shown that a wrong was done to the company, when the company was controlled by the alleged wrongdoers, and that those wrongdoers benefitted from what they did.

---

[73] *Connolly v Seskin Properties Ltd* [2012] IEHC 332 at 27.

In the oldest authority on fraud, *Menier v Hooper's Telegraph Works Ltd*[74] a new company, the European and South American Telegraph Company Ltd, had a great dream: it was going to lay a transatlantic telegraph cable, a cable that would connect Portugal and São Roque, on the north-eastern tip of Brazil. The facts are colourful, but space will not permit us to go in to them. The essential part is that a company which held a majority shareholding in the telegraph company allowed a set of proceedings to be settled because it received a secret benefit, and then procured a resolution for the telegraph company's liquidation. Mr Menier, a minority shareholder, felt something was not right, took an action, and the question before the Court was whether he was entitled to do so. The case became the classic case on the fraud exception to *Foss v Harbottle*. James LJ stated that

> "the majority have put something into their pockets at the expense of the minority. If so, it appears to me that the minority have a right to have their share of those benefits ascertained for them in the best way the court can do it, and given to them."[75]

Another example of fraud was *Cooks v Deeks*,[76] where the directors of a company diverted a company contract to themselves.

These are the considerations you must apply to the facts in Seskin – but before you do, you must consider whether Mr Connolly's case had a realistic prospect of success. Kelly J found that his prospect of success was "poor". There was the evidence of the company's accountant, which all favoured Maplewood: there were contemporaneous documents which tended to confirm the accountant's version: there was the fact that Mr Connolly had delayed a long time in raising the matter; the fact that success against Maplewood was "likely to be hollow"[77]; that Maplewood stood a good chance of having the agreement rectified; that a court would find it difficult to conclude that the Whelans had breached their duties to Seskin (rather than simply taking a realistic, commercial view). So the applicant failed the threshold test. When asked to advise on this area, you must go through the same exercise as the judge, weighing up whether the

---

[74] (1874) 9 Ch App 350.
[75] (1874) LR. 9 Ch. App. 350 at 353.
[76] [1916] 1 AC 554.
[77] *Connolly v Seskin Properties Ltd* [2012] IEHC 332 at 31.

facts are such that will see your client pass the first threshold, and then considering the applicability of each of the exceptions to the rule in *Foss* in turn.

Kelly J briefly considered the exceptions to *Foss v Harbottle*, and found that the applicant failed to bring himself under the fraud rubric because there was no evidence that the decision not to pursue Maplewood was a wrong on Seskin and the Whelans obtained no fiscal benefit from declining to take action. There was no moral turpitude. There was nothing like what was found in the *Menier* case, or in *Cooks v Deeks*. That being so, it was impossible that a "justice of the case" argument could succeed.

CHAPTER THIRTEEN

Capital Maintenance

Financial Assistance for Acquisition of Shares

Company law prohibits a company from giving financial assistance for the purpose of buying its own shares, if the company giving the assistance does not first go through the Summary Approval Procedure.[1] Failure to observe the proper procedure leaves the transaction void and is a category 2 offence.

Section 82(2) of Companies Act 2014 states:

> "It shall not be lawful for a company to give any financial assistance for the purpose of an acquisition made or to be made by any person of any shares in the company, or, where the company is a subsidiary, in its holding company."

This is drawn from the old s 60 of Companies Act 1963. It sets out the rules in relation to the provision of financial assistance for the acquisition of a LTD's own shares, and outlines the exemptions. The meaning of "acquisition" is unchanged. It is the same wide definition (in relation to shares, it means "acquisition by subscription, purchase, exchange or otherwise"[2]). The prohibition applies whether the financial assistance is given: (a) directly or indirectly; or (b) by means of a loan or guarantee, the provision of security or otherwise.[3] This latter element reflects the diversity of ways in which financial assistance can be given. MacCann and Courtney say that

> "the law abounds with instances where the parties have channeled the assistance through a series of transactions involving shelf companies, trusts and other vehicles, rather than giving the assistance directly to the person who is acquiring the shares."[4]

The rule set out in s 82(2) is subject to the following qualifications. It does not prohibit the giving of financial assistance in relation to the acquisition of shares in a company or its holding company if:

---

[1] The Oireachtas was so serious about this rule that, prior to Companies Act 2014, it enacted it twice, in s 60 of Companies Act 1963 and in s 41(1) of Companies Act 1983.

[2] Companies Act 2014, s 82(1).

[3] *ibid*, 82(3).

[4] MacCann and Courtney, *Annotated Companies Acts 1963–2012*, Bloomsbury, 2012, at p 145

(a) the company's principal purpose in giving the assistance is not to give it for the purpose of any such acquisition; or

(b) the giving of the assistance for that purpose is only an incidental part of some larger purpose of the company,

and the assistance is given in good faith in the interests of the company.[5]

Further to this, the prohibition can be circumvented by a company using the Summary Approval Procedure.[6] Any transaction which contravenes s 82 of Companies Act 2014 shall be voidable at the instance of the company against any person (whether a party to the transaction or not) who had notice of the facts which constitute such contravention.[7] Contravention of the section is, as we have seen, a category 2 offence.[8] The following should be noted (the list is not exhaustive):

1. The company is not prohibited from paying a dividend or making, by way of dividend, any distribution out of profits of the company (which are available for distribution)[9];

2. The company is permitted to lend money in the ordinary course of business where the company's business (or part of it) is to loan money[10];

3. Financial assistance may be given to employees of a LTD in order to them to acquire shares in it[11];

4. The company is not prohibited from granting a loan to refinance a loan which has already been given by the company (as long as it was properly done, i.e. the SAP was used)[12];

5. The prohibition does not apply where the company's *principal purpose* in giving the assistance is not to give it for the purpose of any acquisition of shares, and the assistance is given in good faith and in the interests of the company[13];

---

[5] Companies Act 2014, s 82(5).
[6] ibid, 82(6)(a).
[7] ibid, 82(9).
[8] ibid, 82(11)
[9] Companies Act 2014, s 82(6)(b); see also s 82(6)(c)–(o), which reproduce s 60(12) of Companies Act 1963, as inserted by s 56(1) of the Investment Funds Companies Miscellaneous Provisions Act 2005.
[10] Companies Act 2014, s 82(6)(e).
[11] ibid, s 82(6)(f) and (g); see also 82(6)(o).
[12] ibid, s 82(6)(h).
[13] ibid, s 82(5)(a).

6. The prohibition does not apply where the giving of financial assistance is *incidental to some larger purpose* of the company, and the assistance is given in good faith and in the interests of the company.[14]

A private limited subsidiary is not allowed to give financial assistance in accordance with the Summary Approval Procedure in order to acquire shares in its parent public company,[15] though the Minister for Jobs, Enterprise and Innovation may make regulations allowing this in certain circumstances.

The Reasoning Behind Section 82 of Companies Act 2014

What is the reasoning behind this prohibition? In *Trevor v Whitworth*[16] Lord Macnaghten focused his mind in a particular direction. He was thinking that if a company had a "troublesome partner" and if the shareholders wanted to get rid of him they should "put their hands *in their own pockets* and buy him out" but they shouldn't be "drawing on a fund in which others as well as themselves are interested". By "others", he was referring to the company's creditors. The idea that the paid up share capital is a fund for creditors, which will be used to satisfy their claims in the event of a winding up, is and old one. Courtney has said that this is "largely illusory in practice" because, in many Irish companies the issued share capital may only be €1 or €2, making the idea that it is a creditors' fund "little more than a nonsense".[17]

This nonsense—the idea that the share capital is a creditors' fund—has always been, and still is, the rationale behind this area of the law. Speaking with this underlying assumption Cotton J said in 1882 that it followed logically

> "that whatever has been paid by a member cannot be returned to him…Capital is liable to be spent or lost in carrying on the business of the company, but no part of it can be returned

---

[14] *ibid*, s 82(5)(b).
[15] *ibid*, s 82(7).
[16] (1887) 12 App Cas 409 at 436.
[17] Courtney, *Law of Companies* (3rd ed, Bloomsbury, 2012) at pp 551–552.

to a member so as to take away from the fund to which the creditors have a right to look as the fund out of which they are to be paid."[18]

Returning to *Trevor v Whitworth*, Lord Watson said that:

"[p]aid-up capital may be diminished or lost in the course of the company's trading; that is a result which no legislation can prevent; but persons who deal with, and give credit to a limited company, naturally rely upon the fact that the company is trading with a certain amount of capital already paid, as well as upon the responsibility of its members for the capital remaining at call; and they are entitled to assume that no part of the capital which has been paid into the coffers of the company has been subsequently paid out, except in the legitimate course of its business."[19]

There is more to s 82 that simply this, however. It is designed to prevent people from buying a company with the company's own money. Lord Greene MR put this scenario in memorable terms in 1942:

"Those whose memories enable them to recall what had been happening after the last war for several years will remember that a very common form of transaction in connection with companies was one by which persons – call them financiers, speculators, or what you will – finding a company with a substantial cash balance or easily realisable assets such as [a] war loan, bought up the whole or the greater part of the shares of the company for cash and so arranged matters that the purchase money which they then became bound to provide was *advanced to them by the company whose shares they were acquiring*, either out of its cash balance or by realisation of its liquid investments. That type of transaction was a common one, and it gave rise to great dissatisfaction and, in some cases, great scandals (my emphasis)."[20]

---

[18] *Guinness v Land Corpn of Ireland* (1882) 22 Ch D 349.
[19] (1887) 12 App Cas 409 at 423–424.
[20] *Per* Lord Greene MR in *Re VGM Holdings Ltd* [1942] Ch. 235 at 239.

So, the main mischief is to prevent people buying things which they don't really pay for, acquiring companies and their assets by a sleight of hand. Speaking in the 1970s, Lord Denning MR said that since the 1940s:

> "financiers have used more sophisticated methods...Circular cheques come in very handy. So do puppet companies. The transactions are extremely complicated, but the end result is clear. You look to the company's money and see what has become of it. You look to the company's shares and see into whose hands they have got. You will then soon see if the company's money has been used to finance the purchase."[21]

What was alleged to have happened in Anglo Irish Bank is a variation of this prohibited sleight of hand: a company providing others with the funds to buy shares in it, so that, in the case of Anglo, it looked healthy to outsiders.[22] The essence of the Quinn family's defence against Anglo's claim against them for €2.3bn was that the transactions between them were designed to prop up the bank's share price, and the alleged debts are thus unenforceable because they are tainted by illegality.[23]

Let us take the example of a loan. Say you obtain a loan from your bank for the purpose of buying a majority shareholding in a company. On the day you buy the company, you, being now in control, will be able to arrange for the company to guarantee the loan you obtained for the bank. Alternatively, you could get the company to give the bank a charge on some or all of the company's assets. These transactions can take place almost simultaneously. If you are obtaining the loan from the bank on the understanding that moments later you will, as the new owner or controller of the company, cause it to execute a guarantee or a security in the bank's favour, then the company you are buying is doing all the running. *It is giving the assistance.*

---

[21] *Wallersteiner v Moir* [1974] 1 WLR 991 at 1014.

[22] According to the *Sunday Independent*, 23 June 2013, ('*Bondholders are f***ing us up the arse'* – *Anglo*), after Anglo's share price collapsed in March 2008, "IL&P gave €750m for a few days, Royal Bank of Scotland gave €570m for just one night, and AIG deposited €1.2bn on March 31 for days."

[23] See *The Irish Times*, "Tens of thousands of files under scrutiny by individuals and inquiries," by Colm Keena, 25 June 2013.

The equivalent of s 82 has been abolished in England and, as one commentator sees it, it

> "will not be mourned by the legions of junior lawyers and trainees who became very familiar with the vast amount of paperwork a whitewash generated with its bureaucratic and formalistic requirements."[24]

The Way Around Section 82(2)

The Summary Approval Procedure is set out in s 202 of Companies Act 2014. The declaration which must be made in the case of financial assistance for the acquisition of own shares is set out in s 203 of Companies Act 2014. The declaration must state:

(a) The circumstances in which the transaction or arrangement is to be entered into;

(b) The nature of the transaction or arrangement;

(c) The person or persons to or for whom the transaction or arrangement is to be made;

(d) The purpose for which the company is entering into the transaction or arrangement;

(e) The nature of the benefit which will accrue to the company directly or indirectly from entering into the transaction or arrangement; and

(f) That the declarants (i.e. the directors) have made a full inquiry into the affairs of the company and that, having done so, they have formed the opinion that the company, having entered into the transaction or arrangement (the "relevant act"), will be able to pay or discharge its debts and other liabilities in full as they fall due during the period of 12 months after the date of the relevant act.

A copy of the s 203 declaration must be delivered to the Registrar not later than 21 days after the date on which the carrying on of the restricted activity is commenced; if this is not complied with, the court may — on application to it by any "interested party" — declare that the carrying on of the restricted activity concerned shall be valid for all purposes if the

---

[24] "Financial Assistance for the acquisition of shares in private companies: finally laying the undead to rest," by David Ereira, *Journal of International Banking and Finance Law* (2008) 6 JIBFL 289.

court is satisfied that it would be just and equitable to do so.[25] Where a director makes this declaration without reasonable grounds for his opinion the court may make him personally liable for all the debts of the company.[26] The law presumes that there was no reasonable grounds for his opinion if the company is wound-up within twelve months of the declaration and the onus is on the director to prove otherwise.[27]

The Meaning of Financial Assistance

There is no one definition of "financial assistance". The courts have shied away from saying anything definitive, because the phrase is so broad as to include almost all kinds of transactions. To try and define it, might only to mistakenly limit the concept. It is enough, the courts have said, to look at the statute and use common sense. In *Charterhouse Investment Trust Ltd v Tempest Diesels Ltd*[28] Hoffmann J said that the phrase financial assistance had no technical meaning and had to be construed by reference to "the language of ordinary commerce." He said that we

> "must examine the commercial realities of the transaction and decide whether it can properly be described as the giving of financial assistance by the company, bearing in mind that the section is a penal one and should not be strained to cover transactions which are not fairly within it."[29]

This was echoed in the Irish High Court by Murphy J in *Eccles Hall Ltd v Bank of Nova Scotia*.[30] He said that because the legislation carries the threat of imprisonment and fines, the wording should not be strained to cover transactions which are not fairly caught by it. Having said this, though, he then acknowledged that the words of the section are "of wide import", potentially catching a great number of transactions; Murphy J gave as an example of financial assistance the purchase by one company of an asset at an inflated price from another company, where the purchasing company knows that vendor company intends to take it over.

---

[25] Companies Act 2014, s 203(4).
[26] *ibid*, s 210(1).
[27] *ibid*, s 210(2).
[28] [1986] BCLC 1.
[29] *ibid* at 10.
[30] Unreported, High Court, 3 February 1995.

The Trial of FitzPatrick, McAteer and Whelan

Financial assistance for the purpose of buying own shares was what was alleged to have taken place at Anglo Irish Bank in July 2008.[31] It was alleged that the CEO, the former finance director and the former managing director of lending gave financial assistance to sixteen people to enable them to buy shares in the bank, which had the temporary effect of artificially propping up the bank.[32] These facts gave rise to the trial of three former executives of Anglo Irish Bank.

Every officer who was in default of s 60(1) of Companies Act 1963 was capable of being made liable on conviction on indictment to imprisonment for a term not exceeding five years and/or to a fine not exceeding €6,348.70 (under s 82 of Companies Act 2014 breach of the rule is a category 2 offence). Given the penalties, the trial was heard in the Circuit Court.

The trial produced the country's first ever convictions for breaches of this section of company law.[33] As is the norm in criminal cases, a transcript of the trial is not in the public domain and the jury did not issue a written decision nor did it explain its reasons. The jury found two of the accused guilty and exonerated one. The indictment is not in the public domain (though it will have been read publicly at the arraignment, when the jury was charged and when the verdict was being announced). Without

---

[31] Anglo Irish Bank was nationalised in January 2009. Anglo merged with another toxic lending institution, Irish Nationwide Building Society, and was given a new name, the Irish Bank Resolution Corporation ("IBRC") in July 2011. The government made a sudden decision to liquidate IBRC in February 2013 and it was put into an unprecedented "special liquidation." The Governor of the Central Bank, Patrick Honohan, suggested in January 2015 that the eventual cost to the Irish taxpayer of rescuing the banks could be €40bn (*The Irish Times*, 16 January 2015). The gross cost of the bailout was €64bn. Prof Honohan said that the €40bn went "up in smoke" on "buildings nobody wanted to live in" and on the wages of those who built them. The Irish Government paid Merrill Lynch €7.3m for banking advice in 2008 and 2009, and Merrill Lynch advised the Government that the bank bailout would cost a maximum of €16.4bn—off target by €48bn (*Irish Independent*, 21 March 2014, reported by Joe Brennan).

[32] For a view of the trial before it began, see *The Irish Times*, 7 March 2013, *Judge warns of length of Anglo trial for jurors*. The trial was expected to last six months. In fact, it lasted 47 days.

[33] The judge was Martin Nolan. The men were convicted of illegal lending to the Maple 10, but not guilty of making illegal loans to six members of the Quinn family (The Maple 10 were each loaned €45m by the bank). At the end of July 2015 he imposed 240 hours community service on Patrick Whelan (53, former director of lending) and William McAteer (63, former finance director). "Mr Whelan...and Mr McAteer...nodded at the judge and smiled as they left the court room, with Mr Whelan adding "thank you" (*Irish Independent*, 31 July 2015, reported by Sarah Stack). CEO Sean FitzPatrick was acquitted on all charges.

speaking to jury members it is impossible, as in any criminal trial, to know why the jury reached its verdict. We can only speculate based on the matters put before them, which may be gleaned from the reported comments of the judge in the newspapers at the time, from reports of what was said at the trial, and so on, but these usually give an incomplete picture. Thus, we have an example of a complex trial, featuring three accused, and an important rule in company law which had not been before the courts before in criminal proceedings and we are unable to speak about it with any certainty.

It seems that the argument made on behalf of the non-executive director was that a very high threshold must be met before an NED can be found criminally liable for his actions or, as the case may be, omissions. This argument sits uneasily, in particular, with the Supreme Court's comments in *Re Mitek Holdings*.[34] It was argued by Counsel for Mr FitzPatrick that he was a mere non-executive director who was in France at the time of the transaction, and who was only in touch by telephone.[35] Counsel argued that it would put an "unreasonable burden" on a NED to expect him to "sniff…out" any "nefarious activity" and "play detective", and that FitzPatrick was "not a nanny", was in France at the time of the deal "going about his business" and "couldn't be expected to second guess the bank". However, it is *precisely* the role of a NED to second guess the board. The NED is on the board to offer his or her experience and advice. The NED is not a mere cipher. The position is not merely honorary. The exact contours of the duties of NEDs have yet to be clearly described by the Irish Courts but it is indisputable that, as a minimum, they must act honestly and responsibly. But Counsel for Mr Fitzpatrick was not making statements of law to the jury: he was engaging in advocacy for his client.

The case also appeared to introduce a novel principle. Some of Judge Martin Nolan's comments seemed to suggest that the Financial Regulator's incompetence could act to mitigate a director's duty to observe the Companies Acts ("It would be unjust to imprison these two gentlemen when a State agency has led them into error and illegality").[36] As a

---

[34] [2010] 3 IR 374.

[35] A phone call to the bank's chief executive David Drumm on 9 July 2008. Mr O'Higgins SC asserted that that phone call didn't amount to "a hill of beans".

[36] *The Irish Times*, 29 April 2009, reported by Fiona Gartland ("*McAteer and Whelan spared jail in Anglo case*").

proposition of civil law, this does not sit well with the principle that the court must have "tunnel vision" with regard to the conduct of the directors, and judge them on the basis of their actions.[37] The tunnel vision comments, however, were made in the context of judging a director's suitability for disqualification.

There is perhaps an argument to be made that such cases should be heard by a divisional court and not by a jury, and not at Circuit Court level. This would require an amendment to Article 38 of the Constitution which provides that "no person shall be tried on any criminal charge save in due course of law". It would require the creation of a special court, the justification of which would be "that the ordinary courts are inadequate to secure the effective administration of justice".[38] The argument in favour is that the subject matter involves the interpretation of a technical aspect of company law and the digestion of great quantities of finance-based argument. The argument against, of course, is that a person should be tried by his peers in criminal matters. This being a Circuit Court criminal law case, no precedent was ever going to arise from it, in the sense of a case law precedent, but in an informal way it offers guidance as to how prosecutions of this nature can be run, what the likely outcome of such prosecutions are, and so on. Given the gravity of the consequences of the breach, it is unfortunate that the matter is not heard by a higher court, which would set a precedent with its decision. As it is, if such a matter comes before the courts again, the case against FitzPatrick, McAteer and Whelan might as well not have happened.

Section 82 of 2014: Civil Case Law Examples

A good example of s 82 in action is *Lombard & Ulster Banking Ltd v Bank of Ireland*[39] The case turns on a private school on the outskirts of Bray. It was called Brook House School. A company had been set up to run it in the 1970s. When a decision to sell the school was taken, a group of parents came together to buy it. They formed a company to do this, but the company had no money. The parents agreed to ask a bank (the plaintiffs, Lombard and Ulster Banking) for a loan. They told the bank that the new company intended to buy 70% of the shares in the company that ran the

---

[37] Per Vinelott J said in *Re Pamstock Ltd* [1994] 1 BCLC 716 at 737.
[38] Constitution of Ireland, Article 38.3 1.
[39] Unreported, High Court, Costello J, 2 June 1987.

school. The bank agreed, as long as the company which ran the school would give a charge over the school buildings and execute a guarantee in favour of the bank. This is the classic scenario where s 82 is triggered. As the CLRG says in its First Report:

> "[a] typical example is where a bank…lends money to a person who uses the funds to purchase the shares of a company. As security for that loan, the company (being acquired) and its subsidiaries guarantee the repayment of the loan and, as security for their guarantee, create fixed and floating charges over their respective assets."[40]

Everybody was aware that this was indirect financial assistance for the purchase of own shares. The bank was assured that the SAP (formerly called the "whitewash procedure") had been gone through, but in fact it hadn't. The bank only discovered later. Costello J upheld the transaction because the bank hadn't had actual notice of the breach.[41] Another example of failure to observe the Summary Approval Procedure can be found in *Re Ravenshaw Ltd*,[42] a case which concerned the ownership of Barry's Hotel in Dublin.

It must be noted that the Summary Approval Procedure can't be used retrospectively. That is the lesson of *Re Northside Motor Company Ltd*.[43] In that case an attempt to remedy the failure to perform the SAP was made after the key transaction had occurred, and the language of the late resolution gave no hint that it was a retrospective attempt to go through the proper procedure. Costello J found that the resolution and statutory declaration were "materially inaccurate and misleading" and failed to comply with the s 82 requirements.

---

[40] CLRG, First Report, at para 5.3.4.

[41] When the parents' company went into liquidation the liquidator challenged the validity of the bank's guarantee and charge and the bank wasn't able to give satisfactory evidence that the resolution and the declaration had been passed at the appropriate times. The burden of proof rests on the person seeking to uphold the transaction. Costello J upheld the transaction, however, on the basis that the bank was not *actually* on notice of the invalidity and so the transaction was upheld.

[42] [2012] IEHC 37.

[43] *Re Northside Motor Company Ltd; Eddison v Allied Irish Banks*, Unreported, High Court, Costello J, 24 July 1985.

To give a final, and in some ways typical example—because many financial assistance cases involve convoluted series of transactions, which pass through subsidiaries—we turn to *CH (Ireland) Inc (in liq) v Credit Suisse Canada*.[44] The liquidator of the applicant company (which, for ease of reference, will be referred to as "the Irish company") was looking to prove that the transaction the applicant had entered into was void against the respondent bank. The Irish company was a subsidiary of a Canadian company. The Irish company was involved in the property market. The Canadian company had another subsidiary called Castor. Castor successfully applied to Credit Suisse Canada for a loan of £18.8m. Castor used the money to buy shares in its Canadian parent, and the Canadian parent company used that money to buy shares in the Irish company. The Irish company then deposited the money which the Canadian bank paid it for its shares with Credit Suisse Canada as ultimate security for the money that Credit Suisse Canada had advanced to Castor: the liquidator said that this was all quite circular, and that this last transaction must be void against Credit Suisse Canada (i.e. they had to give it back to the liquidator) because it breached s 82 of Companies Act 2014. McCracken J held that the only (or main) reason the Irish company deposited the money with the bank was to ensure that the bank would advance money to Castor, which would then convey money to its Canadian parent, which would then buy shares in the Irish company. McCracken J said that in his view "this was clearly the giving of financial assistance within the meaning of section [82]".[45] Without the Irish deposit, the Canadian company would never have been able to buy shares in the Irish company.

Acquisition of Own Shares

There are certain circumstances in which a LTD may buy its own shares without using the SAP. Section 102 of Companies Act 2014 sets these out; acquisition of own shares otherwise than in accordance with s 102 is a category 2 offence and the acquisition will be void.[46] Section 102 also forbids a LTD to buy shares in its parent public company, if it has one.[47]

---

[44] [1999] 4 IR 542.

[45] *ibid* at 555.

[46] The section is a mixture of s 41 of the C(A)A 1983 and an EU Regulation (SI No 67 of 1997). Certain subscriptions and allotments are not effected by these rules, and they are set out in s 103.

[47] Companies Act 2014, s 102(4).

The law as it stood prior to the enactment of Companies Act 2014 is reproduced, but what is new is the way it is phrased. Positive language is used ("a company *may* acquire …"). Incidental payments made in connection to own share purchase must be paid out of distributable profits.[48] If this rule is breached, either the purchase or the release (whichever applies in the situation) is void. Within 30 days of a LTD purchasing its own shares, it must notify the Registrar (using the H5 Form).[49]

Membership of Holding Company

A company cannot be a member of a company which is its holding company. Any allotment of transfer of shares in a company to its subsidiary is void.[50] This is a re-enactment of the rule designed to prevent undesirable forms of inter-company financing between holding companies and subsidiaries.

There are, however, certain conditions which would allow a subsidiary to acquire and hold shares in its holding company[51] (this, too, is a re-enactment of existing law). The most important aspects are as follows. First, if a subsidiary buys shares in its holding company it must use distributable profits to buy them. Second, the subsidiary is not allowed to exercise any voting rights in respect of those shares.

If an insolvent subsidiary is wound-up within six months of buying shares in its holding company the court may impose liability on the directors. The directors would be liable to repay to the company the total amount paid by the company for the shares. Such an application can be brought by a liquidator, creditor, employee or contributory of the company. The defence is that the director believed on reasonable grounds that the purchase was in the best interests of the company: if that defence is successful, the court may relieve the director of liability. The defence may only be partially successful, in which case the court will only relieve the director of a portion of the liability.[52]

---

[48] *ibid*, s 110.
[49] *ibid*, s 116.
[50] *ibid*, s 113.
[51] *ibid*, s 114.
[52] *ibid*, s 115.

Variation of Company Capital

Section 83 states that a company may vary its company capital from time to time by ordinary resolution.[53] Section 84 modifies the old rule about reduction of capital. Prior to Companies Act 2014 companies had to apply to the High Court to reduce their capital[54]: s 84 allows them to reduce it either by passing a special resolution or by using the Summary Approval Procedure (the Companies Act 2014 speaks of "company capital" rather than "share capital").[55]

Trading Loss EGMs

Under the old Companies Acts, directors were obliged to call an emergency general meeting within twenty-eight days if the net assets of the company fell below half of the company's called-up share capital.[56] This provision has been abolished on the recommendation of the Company Law Review Group, which considered the provision to be "in practice … meaningless" with regard to private companies. It said this for two reasons. First,

> "[t]here is no requirement to provide additional capital, for the very good reason that, particularly in the early stages, the company may simply be going through a development phase", and second, that "[i]f the members … decide to take no action in the face of a need to do so, a creditor will have no remedy against the members".[57]

The obligation is retained for PLCs.[58]

Miscellaneous Capital Maintenance Rules

- Any downward or upward alteration of share capital must be notified to the Registrar within 30 days and failure to notify render the company and defaulting officers guilty of a category 3 offence[59];

---

[53] *ibid*, s 83(1)(a)–(f).
[54] Under s 72(1) of Companies Act 1963.
[55] Companies Act 2014, s 64.
[56] Companies Act 1983, s 40.
[57] Company Law Review Group, First Report, at paras 5.5.3 and 5.5.4
[58] Companies Act 2014, s 1111.
[59] *ibid*, s 92 and 93.

- An LTD may alter or modify the rights attached to any class of shares, as long as certain conditions are met[60];
- Members holding a class of shares which has been varied can apply to court to have that variation cancelled[61];
- Section 87 sets out the consequences for shareholders where a LTD's capital has been reduced and it also deals with creditor protection in the wake of a capital reduction.[62]

---

[60] *ibid*, s 88. This section is a re-enactment of parts of s 38 of the C(A)A 1983.

[61] s 90 sets out the mechanism for this. This section comes from s 78 of the 1963 Act.

[62] This section is a re-enactment of ss 77 and 78 of the 1963 Act.

COMPANY BORROWING: CHARGES

PART I

Charges

A charge, in relation to a company, means "a mortgage or a charge, in an agreement (written or oral), that is created over an interest in any property of the company".[1] When a charge is created it must be registered with the CRO or it will be void against the liquidator and any creditor of the company.[2] The Registrar keeps a register of all charges relating to all registered companies, which states, among other things, the details of the properties charged, the persons entitled to the charge, and the registration procedure used.[3] There are two procedures which may be used. The "one-stage procedure" consists one of the parties to the transaction ensuring that the CRO receives the particulars of the charge not later than 21 days after the date of the charge's creation.[4] The "two-stage procedure" means that a party will: (a) send the CRO a notice stating the company's intention to create the charge; and (b) not later than 21 days after the date of the Registrar's receipt of this notice the CRO also receives a notice stating that the intention to create a charge has been acted on and the charge has been created. If this second step is taken, the date of the charge's creation is considered to be the date on which the Registrar received *notice of the intention to create it*, rather than the day it was actually created.[5] If the second step is not taken then the notice of the intention to create the charge is simply removed by the Registrar from the register.[6]

If a company borrows money from a lending institution and gives a charge in exchange for the loan, and if the charge is not registered and therefore becomes void, that does not in any way prejudice the loan agreement, and in fact the money secured by the charge "shall immediately become payable" in such a scenario.[7] The two-stage procedure can be used even if a charge comprises property outside the State, but practitioners should be aware that further proceedings may be necessary to make the

---

[1] Companies Act 2014, s 408(1)—the subsection sets out certain things which are excluded from this definition such as charges created over cash and charges over shares or debt instruments.

[2] Companies Act 2014, s 409.

[3] *ibid*, s 414.

[4] *ibid*, s 409(3).

[5] *ibid*, s 412(4)(b).

[6] *ibid*, s 409(5).

[7] *ibid*, s 409(6).

charge valid or effectual according to the law of the country in which the property is situate.[8]

It is up to the person sending the details of the charge into the Registrar to get everything right. The CRO is under no duty, and has no power, to examine any deed or any supplemental document to it.[9] The Companies Act 2014 states that it is the duty of the company that creates the charge to comply with the one or two-step procedures, but the Act goes on to modify this stance, stating that, in fact, "[a]ny person interested in the charge" may use the procedures, and if they do it "shall have the same effect as if the company had used that procedure".[10] The practical point being made is that it is in the interest of the lending institution to make sure that the charge is registered within the 21 days, so the chargee might feel more comfortable knowing that it has been taken care of. If the chargee takes care of the registration, it is entitled to recover from the company the costs of the registration.[11]

Priority of Charges

If the Registrar receives particulars relating to two or more charges which are the same, the one which will have priority is the one which arrived earlier.[12] If they arrived on the same day, the one which arrived earlier in the day will prevail. If the creditors have come to an agreement themselves in relation to the priority of charges[13] then these rules can be displaced.[14]

Negative Pledges and "Extraneous Material"

A negative pledge means any agreement entered into by the company and any other person or persons that provides that the company shall not, or shall not otherwise than in specified circumstances: (i) borrow moneys or otherwise obtain credit from any person other than that person or those persons; (ii) create or permit to subsist any charge, lien or other

---

[8] *ibid*, s 409(7).
[9] *ibid*, s 409(9).
[10] *ibid*, s 410(2).
[11] *ibid*, s 410(3).
[12] See *Re Fablehill Ltd* [1991] BCLC 830; and *Re HSS* [2011] IEHC 497 (High Court, Clarke J, 28 October 2011) where it was determined that the bank's charge took priority over the creditor in occupation. See also *AIB Finance Ltd v Bank of Scotland* [1995] 1 BCLC 185.
[13] For example, such as via an inter-lender agreement.
[14] Companies Act 2014, s 412(5).

encumbrance or any pledge over the whole or any part of the property of the company; or (iii) alienate or otherwise dispose of in any manner any of the property of the company. A negative pledge is also defined as something which contains a prohibition, either generally or in specified circumstances, on the doing by the company of one or more of the aforementioned things.[15]

The Registrar will not enter on the register any details of negative pledge clauses, events that may crystallize a charge, or any details about restrictions on the use of any charged asset. These kinds of particulars are known as "extraneous material".[16] A party might well send this kind of information into the Registrar, along with the other particulars, but doing so has no legal effect.[17]

Judgment Mortgages

If a judgment is recovered against a company, and that judgment is converted into a judgment mortgage affecting any property of the company, the judgment mortgage must be registered with the CRO within 21 days of the date on which the judgment creditor receives notification from the Property Registration Authority (PRA) that the judgment mortgage has been created. If this is not done, the judgment mortgage will be void against the liquidator.[18] There is a rebuttable presumption that the judgment creditor will have received the PRA notification by the third day after which the PRA sent the notification.[19]

Certificate of Registration

When the charge is registered by the Registrar, the Registrar issues a certificate of registration, which is conclusive evidence that the requirements of the 2014 Act in relation to the registration of the charge

---

[15] *ibid*, s 412(8).
[16] Companies Act 2014, s 412(6); the exception is a negative pledge clause included in particulars of a floating charge granted by the company to the Central Bank for the purposes of either providing or securing collateral.
[17] Companies Act 2014, s 412(6)(b).
[18] Companies Act 2014, s 413(1), (2) and (3). These rules only apply to judgment mortgages created after 1 June 2015. For the documents that must accompany the judgment mortgage to the CRO, see s 413(4) and (6).
[19] Companies Act 2014, s 413(5).

have been complied with.[20] Section 415 of Companies Act 2014 does not state to whom the certificate of registration must be sent: the company, or the party which registered the charge. It may be assumed that the certificate will be sent to the company because the Act obliges companies to keep copies of every instrument creating any charge.[21]

If a solicitor, for example, sends the CRO particulars of a charge, and some of the details are missing, the certificate of registration will reflect that, and that evidential deficit of the certificate "shall not extend to the particular property or properties in respect of which that omission occurs".[22]

Satisfaction and Release

If a loan was taken out and a charge over company property was given as part of the loan agreement, and that loan is repaid, the Registrar may enter a memorandum on the register of charges which states two things: that the debt in relation to which the charge was created has been paid, and the fact that the charged asset has been released from the charge.[23] If the debt is partially repaid, and the charged property partially released from the charge as a result, the memorandum will reflect this. When the Registrar enters this memorandum on the register, he must furnish the company with a copy of it.[24] The Registrar must, of course, be provided with evidence that satisfaction or release has taken place. This comes in the form of a statement by a director and secretary of the company (or by two directors of a company), which states that the satisfaction or release has taken place.[25] If a director or secretary signs this statement knowing it to be false it is a category 2 offence (on summary conviction, this could mean a €5,000 fine and/or maximum prison sentence of 12 months; it is submitted that the courts will not see any indictments on this issue). Signing such a statement when not having honestly believed on reasonable grounds that the statement is true can lead to the imposition of personal liability.[26]

---

[20] *ibid*, s 415(1) and (2).
[21] *ibid*, s 418; it is a category 3 offence not to do so.
[22] Companies Act 2014, s 415(3).
[23] *ibid*, s 416(1) and (2).
[24] *ibid*, s 416(3).
[25] *ibid*, s 416(4).
[26] *ibid*, s 416(6) and (7).

Extension of Time for Registration of Charges and Rectification of Register

If a charge is not registered within 21 days of its creation, or if some particular relating to it is omitted or misstated, the court may extend the time for registration or rectify the register. It will only do so where it is "just and equitable". It will only do so in cases where the omission or misstatement was "accidental or due to inadvertence or to some other sufficient cause" or if the late registration or the rectification "is not of a nature to prejudice the position of creditors or shareholders of the company".[27] The company or any person interested in the charge may make this application.

An example of inadvertence is where the bank's solicitors thought the company was registering the charge and the company thought the bank was doing it.[28] *Re Resnoid and Mica Products Ltd*[29] is an example of a company's unsuccessful attempt to register a charge late. A company called Bradley & Son Ltd sold a factory to Resinoid. Resnoid paid three fifths of the purchase price up front, and the balance was payable every six months over the course of the next two years. Resnoid gave Bradley's a registrable charge over the property to secure the amount. Bradley's didn't register it. Only the first installment was paid. The months went by and Bradley's still didn't register the charge. Twenty months later, Bradley's heard that a meeting of Resnoid had been called to put the company into creditors' voluntary winding-up. Bradley's woke up. They realised they had to register that charge and rushed to court, and were heard the day before the creditors' meeting. Their application was refused. They appealed and by the time of the appeal a liquidator had been appointed to Resnoid. The Court of Appeal stated that it was a long-established practice on these applications to ask whether the company in question was solvent, and whether a winding-up was on the horizon. The court will not make a late registration if the rights of creditors are affected by it. It is not for a party which has sat on its hands for a considerable time to come at the last

---

[27] *ibid*, s 417(1)(a) and (b); for a case of the court acceding to late registration where there was inadvertence see *Re Peleton Ltd (in receivership)* [2011] IEHC 479 (Laffoy J, 19 December 2011).

[28] *Barclays Bank plc v Stuart Landon Ltd* [2001] 2 BCLC 316 is a case where inadvertence was pleaded. See also *Re Chantry House Developments plc* [1990] BCLC 813 (the inadvertence was explained in an affidavit, the details of which Scott J. did not relate in the judgment).

[29] [1983] Ch 132.

minute and displace the other creditors, who dealt with the company in the meantime, in complete ignorance of the charge that had been created (see the comments of Kenny J in *Re International Retail Ltd*).[30]

In *Re Peleton Ltd*[31] the High Court allowed an extension of time for the registration of a charge which had been executed in 2004, but this was without prejudice to rights acquired between date of creation and date of registration.

Charges Pre 1 June 2015

Charges which were created before 1 June 2015 continue to be governed by the relevant provisions of the Companies Act 1963[32]: that is, ss 99 to 106, ss 108 to 110 and s 112 of that Act.

PART II

The Fixed and Floating Charge Introduced

There are two main kinds of charges: fixed charges and floating charges. A fixed charge can be given over something that is solid and immovable, like a piece of land, a business premises, a house, a factory, a set of machinery. In the early days of modern commercial life, when companies needed to raise capital they went to lending institutions, borrowed, and entered agreements that if they were unable to repay the loan the institution would have recourse to one or more of their fixed assets (these agreements were called "debentures" and "securities").

At a certain point in the nineteenth century the level of commercial and industrial expansion was so great that the demand for new capital outstripped the ability to provide security for it. It was time for a new concept. Why not offer lending institutions charges over assets that fluctuate, over "circulating assets, replaced in the normal course of

---

[30] Unreported, High Court, 26 July 1974. See also *Re Telford Motors Ltd* (Unreported, High Court, Hamilton J, 27 January 1978), though the point is not as well-illustrated here as in *Resnoid*. See also *Re Braemar Investments* [1988] BCLC 556 and, for another case on the effect of a long delay in making the application, *Re Telomatic Ltd* [1994] 1 BCLC 90.

[31] [2011] IEHC 479 (High Court, Laffoy J, 19 December 2011).

[32] Companies Act 2014, s 419(1).

business and constantly changing"?[33] In modern terms, this means, for example, that a forklift in a fruit and veg business or a fleet of trucks in a removals business, are things which a company could give a floating charge over. The floating charge means that the company is free to use the asset in question in the ordinary course of its business. In the case of a forklift or a truck, the company can replace the current model with a newer one without the permission of the debenture holder. If the asset were a fixed charge, the chargor company would need the express consent of the chargee bank before it could dispose of it. To give an example for illustrative purposes, a restaurant could create a fixed charge over its premises, and a floating charge over its knives and forks, which are "exactly equivalent to the loose plant and tools that one would find in a factory"[34]: they are items which it would be impossible to create a fixed charge over. The phrase "fixed plant and machinery" covers many kinds of things.[35] To take an example from a case where the company made cabinets, the fixed plant machinery over which a floating charge was given included typewriters, desks, woodworking machines, booths for spraying wood and a dust extraction system. If among the plant and machinery there were items which were properly part of the premises, and could not be unbolted with ease, or unscrewed and brought away, such items could be offered as a fixed charge.

Banks like fixed charges because they give them priority over almost all other creditors. Floating charges rank below fixed charges in priority, if the company goes into liquidation, and borrowers like floating charges because they can continue to deal with their assets in the day-to-day running of their business.

The Floating Charge Defined

This classic definition of the floating charge, which is still the starting point in contemporary judgments where the nature of the charge is at issue, is the three point test of Romer LJ in *Re Yorkshire Woolcombers Association Ltd*.[36] He stated:

---

[33] *Per* Lord Scott, [2005] 2 BCLC 269 at 304. Cf *Holroyd v Marshall* (1862) 10 HL Cas 191.
[34] *Per* Harman J in *Re Hi-Fi Equipment (Cabinets) Ltd* [1988] BCLC 65 at 73.
[35] See *Re Hi-Fi Equipment (Cabinets) Ltd* [1988] BCLC 65 for an in-depth treatment of the term.
[36] [1903] 2 Ch 284.

> "I certainly think that if a charge has the three characteristics that I am about to mention it is a floating charge. (1) If it is a charge on a class of assets of a company present and future; (2) if that class is one which, in the ordinary course of the business of the company, would be changing from time to time; and (3) if you find that by the charge it is contemplated that, until some further step is taken by or on behalf of those interested in the charge, the company may carry on its business in the ordinary way as far as concerns the particular class of assets I am dealing with."[37]

The Irish Supreme Court approved this test in *Re Holidair*.[38] It has been held that this third characteristic is the most important of all.[39] Romer LJ was careful to say that his was not an exhaustive definition, or that all three had to apply for a charge to be a floating one. Romer LJ made his remarks in the Court of Appeal. The following year the case came before the House of Lords (it was heard under the name *Illingworth v Houldsworth*[40]) where Lord Macnaughten set the fixed (or "specific" charge) and floating charge in contrast:

> "A specific charge, I think, is one that without more fastens on ascertained and definite property or property capable of being ascertained and defined; a floating charge, on the other hand, is ambulatory and shifting in its nature, hovering over and so to speak floating with the property which it is intended to affect until some event occurs or some act is done which causes it to settle and fasten on the subject of the charge within its reach and grasp."[41]

The courts still begin any analysis of this area with the *dicta* of Romer LJ ("a great authority on all chancery matters", according to Kenny J) and Lord Macnaughten ("that great Irish judge" known for his "lucidity").[42]

---

[37] *ibid* at 295.
[38] *Per* Blayney J [1994] 1 IR 416 at 445. See also Kenny J in *Re Interview Limited* [1975] IR 382 Kenny J, at 395, where he stated: "The charge floats over the assets of the company until some act is done which causes it to fasten on to the property and goods of the company."
[39] [2005] 2 BCLC 269 at 308–309, per Lord Scott, concurring with Lord Millett in *Agnew v IRC* [2001] 2 BCLC 188.
[40] [1904] AC 355.
[41] *ibid* at 358 (See also the similar comments of Buckley LJ in *Evans v Rival Granite Quarries Ltd* [1910] 2 KB 979 at 999).
[42] Both assessments are those of Kenny J, in *Welch v Bowmaker (Ireland) Ltd* [1980] IR 251 at 257–258

Finlay Geoghegan J observed in *Re JD Brian Ltd*[43] that a floating charge had not been defined anywhere in the Companies Acts and that "it appears there is no one definition of a floating charge". A floating charge does not fix on a particular asset right away: its operation is delayed; it operates on "a fluctuating body of assets which remain under the management and control of the chargor".[44] When the courts are asked to construe a charge, they will of course look at the wording of the debenture, but this will not necessarily be determinative[45]: they will look at the character of the charge, and at the mutual rights and obligations of the parties in relation to the charged asset.[46]

In the past, floating charges sometimes caused problems for the following reason: neither party recognised them as a floating charge. This happened in *Smith (Administrator of Cosslett (Contractors) Ltd) v Bridgend County Borough Council*,[47] where the Council didn't realise that a clause in the contract which allowed the Council to sell the contractor's plant and equipment and apply the proceeds in discharge of its obligations, if any one of a variety of situations of default by the contractor took place, *was actually a charge* (and a floating one, which required registration). The fact that it had not been registered meant it was void against the liquidator. Under the Companies Act 2014 all charges must now be registered. The key problem in *Cosslett* was the failure to recognise the arrangement was in fact the granting of a charge. With this in mind, the House of Lords in *Cosslett* provided some guidance on identifying charges. Lord Hoffmann stated:

> "I do not see how a right to sell an asset belonging to a debtor and appropriate the proceeds to payment of the debt can be anything other than a charge."

---

[43] [2011] IEHC 113 and [2011] IEHC 383; reported at [2012] 1 ILRM 27.
[44] *Halsbury's Laws of England*, 1269 ("Meanings of 'fixed charge' and 'floating charge'").
[45] Lord Templeman stated in *Street v Mountford* [1985] AC 809: "The manufacture of a five pronged instrument for manual digging results in a fork even if the manufacturer, unfamiliar with the English language, insists that he intended to make and has made a spade."
[46] For an example of a charge which was named a floating charge, but was found to be a fixed one, by its substance, see *Russell-Cooke Trust Co v Elliott* [2007] 2 BCLC 637; for an example of a charge named a fixed charge but found to be a floating one see *Re Spectrum Plus Ltd* [2005] 4 All ER 209 and *Re Lehman Bros International (Europe) (in administration) (No 5)* [2014] 2 BCLC 295.
[47] [2002] 1 BCLC 77.

Once that is understood, the question is whether it is a fixed or a floating charge. In *Cosslett*, the clause involved constructional plant, temporary works, goods and material on the site, i.e. a fluctuating body of assets which could be "consumed or...removed from the site in the ordinary course of the contractor's business" it was clearly a floating charge.[48]

The Crystallization of Floating Charges

A floating charge does not float on forever. The company either pays off the loan it owes to the bank, upon which the charge ceases to exist, or it fails to pay off the loan and the bank enforces its security. In the second scenario, company law speaks of a charge "crystallizing". Its ambulatory, shifting, circulating, freewheeling days are at an end. Finlay Geoghegan J stated that what happens is

> "the floating charge upon crystallization becomes a fixed charge. However, no new charge is created by the company. The existing charge, the floating charge created by the company, changes in nature and becomes a fixed charge."[49]

The charge in this circumstance is sometimes referred to as a "quasi-fixed charge", to distinguish it from a charge that began life as a fixed charge. Floating charges crystallize when a chargee appoints a receiver over the charge (see *Halpin v Cremin*[50]). If two or three creditors hold floating charges on different elements of a company, and one of the creditors appoints a receiver, then all the charges crystallize, not just the floating charge of the creditor which appointed him. A second scenario is where the company goes into liquidation. Charges can no longer float above the company when the liquidator is engaged in the exercise of examining claims and debts and making his tally of which creditors are paid what. A third scenario is where a company simply ceases to carry on business. In that case the cessation of business makes the charge crystallize (*Re Woodroffes (Musical Instruments) Ltd*[51]). Once a crystallising event occurs, is it possible for the charge to return to its floating, ethereal self, to "decrystallise"? The answer is yes, but only where a receiver has been appointed to a company—

---

[48] [2002] 1 BCLC 77 at 88–89.
[49] *Re JD Brian Ltd* [2012] 1 ILRM 27 at 34 (para 18).
[50] [1954] IR 19.
[51] [1986] Ch 366.

which causes the floating charge to crystallise—and shortly afterwards the company goes into examinership. That is because

> "once the examiner was appointed, the receivers could no longer act. It would accordingly have been pointless to keep the book debts frozen. The receivers would have had no right to collect them."[52]

A fourth example of crystallisation is where an automatic crystallisation clause has been inserted into the terms of the debenture: this allows the debenture holder to notify the chargor that it has decided to convert the floating charge into a fixed one.[53] This is relatively new development and a somewhat controversial one. The Supreme Court has called a situation where a debenture-holder under a floating charge can initiate an express crystallization by service of a Crystallization Notice "an unsatisfactory state of affairs",[54] because it allows the debenture-holder to leap-frog the preferential creditors: it can, however, only be rectified by amending legislation, Laffoy J stated, because the Court is obliged to read the plain meaning of the statutory words, found in s 621 of Companies Act 2014,[55] which refer to the status of charges as against preferential debts at the time of the commencement of the winding-up. Laffoy J, putting the matter simply, stated:

> "Once the floating charge crystallizes, the claims of the debenture holders are not claims under a floating charge; they are claims under a fixed charge."[56]

In overturning the High Court, the Supreme Court did quite clearly express its unease with its own conclusion and emphasised the need for legislative change.[57] In the High Court (*Re JD Brian Ltd*[58]), Finlay Geoghegan J had come to a different conclusion, following the reasoning of Barwick J in *Stein v Saywell*,[59] which emphasised the point that the

---

[52] *Per* Blayney J [1994] 1 IR 416 at 448.

[53] *Re JD Brian* [2015] (Laffoy J delivering judgment, with Clarke and Charleton JJ, 9 July 2015); (the written copy of the decision which I have does not bear a neutral citation). See particularly paras 75–78

[54] *Re JD Brian*, Unreported, Supreme Court, Laffoy J, 9 July 2015. at para 91.

[55] Previously s 285 of Companies Act 1963, *esp*, s 285(7) (and now, s 621(7) of the Companies Act 2014).

[56] *Re JD Brian* [2015] (Laffoy J, 9 July 2015) at para 93.

[57] *ibid* at para 96.

[58] [2012] 1 ILRM 27.

[59] [1969] 121 CLR 529.

efforts of the employees sometimes swells the assets of the company and it would not be fair, or in keeping with the intention of the legislature, to then allow their preferential claims for wages or accrued leave to be

"defeated by the circumstance that the floating charge had become crystallized before the time had arrived for determining and giving effect to that priority."[60]

This is an attractive argument, one which places an emphasis on potential unfairness to employees, but the Supreme Court was unable to affirm it because it does violence both to the clear wording of statute and to the clear wording of the automatic crystallization clause itself. The Supreme Court also stated the unilateral conversion of a floating charge to a fixed one in these circumstances is "the act of the company" and not the act of the debenture holder.[61]

Fixed Charges Over Book Debts

What are book debts? In *Response Engineering Ltd v Caherconlish Treatment Plant Ltd*[62] Hogan J gave the following colourful explanation:

"There is no doubt but that the phrase 'book debts' has, to the modern ear, something of a musty feel to it. The phrase conjures up images of Victorian bookkeeping and ledger entries, the tales in relation to which form many a sub-plot of the great novels of Dickens and Trollope. Yet the term refers to no more than future income which will accrue to the company by reason of the provision of goods and services to third parties by that company in the course of its trade or business."

The Irish courts have also accepted the following definition:

"Book debts mean all such debts accruing in the ordinary course of a man's trade as are usually entered in trade books, but to constitute a book debt it is not necessary that the debt should be entered in a book."[63]

---

[60] Hoffmann J also agreed. See *Re Permanent Houses (Holdings) Limited* [1988] BCLC 563.
[61] At para 92.
[62] [2011] IEHC 345; [2012] 2 ILRM 67.
[63] Lynch J in *Farrell v Equity Bank Ltd* [1990] 2 IR 549 at 553-4, approving the definition in Halsbury's Laws of England (4th ed.), Vol 3 at para 525.

In *Siebe Gorman*[64] Slade J stated that if the chargor of book debts, having collected the book debts,

> "had the unrestricted right to deal with the proceeds of any of the relevant book debts paid into its account, so long as that account remained in credit … the charge on such book debts could be no more than a floating charge."[65]

Hoffmann J in *Re Brightlife Ltd*[66] said that once the company's debts were in its bank account, they were outside the charge over debts and at the free disposal of the company and

> "[i]n my judgment a right to deal in this way with the charged assets for its own account is a badge of a floating charge and is inconsistent with a fixed charge".

This passage was cited with approval by Lord Millett in *Agnew v IRC*.[67] The Irish Supreme Court came to the same conclusion in *Re Keenan Bros Ltd*[68] and in New Zealand, Tompkins J came to the same conclusion in *Supercool Refrigeration and Air Conditioning (in receivership and liq) v Hoverd Industries Ltd.*[69] The consensus of the courts is that while the first two characteristics of the floating charge, as set out in Romer LJ's test, are typical of floating charges, they could also be said of fixed charges: what is key is the third characteristic in Romer LJ's test. The third point is "the hallmark of a floating charge and distinguished it from a fixed charge".[70] In *Agnew v IRC*[71] the Privy Council, applying the reasoning in *Brightlife* and *Supercool Refrigeration*, stated that:

> "[a] restriction on disposition [of book debts] which nevertheless allows collection and free use of the proceeds is inconsistent with the fixed nature of the charge; it allows the debt and its

---

[64] [1979] 2 Lloyd's Rep 142.
[65] *ibid* at 158.
[66] [1986] BCLC 418 at 422.
[67] [2001] 2 BCLC 188 at [24], [2001] 2 AC 710.
[68] [1986] BCLC 242; [1985] IR 401.
[69] [1994] 3 NZLR 300.
[70] *Per* Lord Millet in *Agnew v IRC* [2001] 2 BCLC 188, affirmed, *Re Spectrum Plus* [2005] 2 BCLC 269
[71] [2001] 2 BCLC 188 (also known as the *Brumark* case).

proceeds to be withdrawn from the security by the act of the company in collecting it."[72]

In all these cases, the courts said that banks needed to require the chargors to keep a special account, used only for the proceeds of the books debt, over which the bank had a commanding say. In *Re Keenan Brothers Ltd*[73] McCarthy J stated:

> "In my view, it is because it was described as a specific or fixed charge and was intended to be such that the requirement of a special bank account was necessary; if it were a floating charge payment into such an account would be entirely inappropriate and, indeed, would conflict with the ambulatory nature of the floating charge ..."[74]

The law in this area was definitely reviewed in *Re Spectrum Plus Ltd*[75] and each of the cases above was approved. Lord Scott offered his own definition of the essential characteristic of a floating charge. He said:

> "the characteristic that distinguishes it from a fixed charge, is that the asset subject to the charge is finally not appropriated as a security for the payment of the debt until the occurrence of some future event. In the meantime the chargor is left free to use the charged asset and to remove it from the security."[76]

When considering the question, the determinative issue will be, in the words of Blayney J in *Re Holidair*,[77]

> "whether the provisions in the debenture permitted the companies to carry on their business in the ordinary way in so far as concerned their book debts".[78]

---

[72] *Per* Lord Millett [2001] 2 BCLC 188 at 201.

[73] [1985] IR 401.

[74] *ibid* at 424. The charge in that case (found to be a fixed charge) stated: "The company shall pay into an account with the bank designated for that purpose all monies which it may receive in respect of the book debts and other debts hereby charged and shall not without the prior consent of the bank in writing make any withdrawals or direct any payment from the said account."

[75] [2005] 2 BCLC 269, *per* Lord Scott of Foscote, at 308.

[76] [2005] 2 BCLC 269 at 310.

[77] [1994] IR 416.

[78] *ibid* at 446.

If there is no restriction in the debenture on a company withdrawing money from the specified account then a purported fixed charge will be deemed to be a floating charge and will be void for want of registration. To conclude, we might observe a perfectly drafted fixed charge over book debts:

> "The company at all times during the continuance of this security shall pay all monies received by it from time to time in respect of book debts into an account with AIB Ltd at 36, Tullow Street, Carlow, designated for that purpose and shall not without the prior consent of the bank in writing make any withdrawal from the said account nor direct any payment to be made from the said account."[79]

Practitioners should note the one drawback of a fixed charge over book debts: it is the extraordinary power give to the Revenue Commissioners under s 1001 of the Taxes Consolidation Act 1997, which allows the Revenue to step into the shoes of the charge holder and take from the charged assets whatever amount of money is due and owing to them by the company.

Floating Charges Granted before Liquidation

Where a company is being wound-up, some of its floating charges may be called into question if they were created within 12 months before the date of the commencement of the winding-up. As a general rule, they will be deemed invalid unless it can be proved that the company was solvent immediately after the creation of the charge.[80] This general rule—found in s 597 of Companies Act 2014—does not apply if the company received "money actually advanced or paid" in exchange for the floating charge.[81] Nor does it apply if the actual price or value of the goods or services sold or supplied was obtained by the company. The value of goods or services sold or supplied to the company is the amount in money which could have reasonably have been expected to be obtained for them in the ordinary course of business, at the time of the sale or supply.[82] If a floating

---

[79] This was the clause in *Re Keenan Brothers Ltd* [1985] IR 401; see also *Re Rayford Homes Ltd; Ellis v Bank of Scotland PLC* [2011] BCC 715 for a contest over whether a charge was fixed or floating.

[80] Companies Act 2014, s 597(1).

[81] *ibid*, s 596(2)(a).

[82] *ibid*, s 597(3).

charge on the undertaking or property of a company is created in favour of a connected person, then the time period mentioned above is extended to two years: that it, if a connected person receives a floating charge from the company, it will be deemed invalid if it was granted within two years before the date of the commencement of the winding-up, unless any of the foregoing circumstances can be pleaded (see, for example, *Re Fairway Magazines Ltd, Fairbairn v Hartigan*[83]).

The law, in s 597 of Companies Act 2014, seeks to

> "prevent a company, which is on its last legs, from creating a floating charge to secure past debts or to secure moneys which do not go to swell its assets and become available for creditors."[84]

The court looks to the substance of the transaction. Did the company receive a benefit in exchange for the granting of the floating charge, or was the giving of the charge merely dressed up as such? In *Re Orleans Motor Co Ltd*[85] the Court found a "transparent subterfuge" in a circular transaction that relieved the company directors of their guarantee obligations. The directors had guaranteed the company's overdraft. They advanced money to the company which the company used to pay off the overdraft. In exchange for this cash advance, the company gave them a floating charge. Since this was a circular process, and the company received no actual value, the court invalidated the charge.

PART III

Registration of Title Clauses

The registration of title ("ROT") clause is an invention to ease the position of unsecured creditors, in case the company they supply goes into liquidation or receivership. In the commercial world there is always an element of uncertainty between two parties who engage in a course of dealing. A distributor might have a monthly agreement to provide stock for a convenience store. What if that store goes into liquidation? The

---

[83] [1993] BCLC 643.

[84] *Per* Mummery J [1993] BCLC 643 at 652, considering *Re Orleans Motor Co Ltd* [1911] 2 Ch 41, *Re Matthew Ellis Ltd* [1933] Ch 458 and *Re GT Whyte & Co Ltd* [1983] BCLC 311.

[85] [1911] 2 Ch 41.

distributor may have had no inkling that the store was in financial difficulty. What if, each month, the supplies he provides add up to €50,000? Is that money lost to him? Ordinarily, the distributor would be an unsecured creditor, ranking behind the preferential creditors, mortgagees and the holders of floating charges. By the time those parties get what they are owed (or portions of what they are owed), there will be nothing left for the unsecured creditor. As Templeman LJ said,

> "unsecured creditors ... receive a raw deal. It is therefore not surprising that this court looked with sympathy on an invention designed to provide some protection for one class of unsecured creditors, namely unpaid sellers of goods."[86]

If the distributor includes in his order forms a clause that says "we will provide you with the goods, but you will not have legal title to them until you pay us the purchase price in full", then that is an ROT clause in its simplest form, and is called a "simple ROT clause". The vendor has delivered *possession* of the goods but not legal *title*.[87] No charge is created: what is happening is simply the retention of title in the goods, until a condition—payment—is satisfied. A simple ROT clause is not a charge and it is not registrable under the Companies Act 2014. Unsecured creditors understood, however, that there would be situations where such a simple ROT clause may not suffice, and in some of these situations a charge *is* created, and this calls for wariness, because such charges must be registered. As a rule of thumb, a charge will be created where the ROT clause increases in complexity. For example:

(1) A vendor company sells goods to a purchaser company. The purchaser company sells them on without altering them in any way. The vendor company included in the ROT clause a provision that stated the vendor company would be able to trace its goods into the proceeds of sale. The clause means that the purchaser company is merely a fiduciary of the goods— and also of any money that arises from their sale—until the vendor company is paid in full for the goods. This ROT is a registrable charge.

---

[86] *Borden (UK) Ltd v Scottish Timber* [1981] 1 Ch 25 at 42.
[87] The statutory basis for an ROT clause is s 17 of the Sale of Goods Act 1893.

(2) The purchaser company might use the goods supplied by the vendor company in a manufacturing process, i.e. the goods supplied will become submerged in a new product. If the finished product is solely made up of the good supplied by the vendor company, then a simple ROT clause should be sufficient for the vendor company to protect its position. If the goods are incorporated into a larger product but are still identifiable, and can be removed at not too great a cost or effort, then a simple ROT clause should be sufficient for the vendor company to protect its position. If the goods lose their identity in the manufacturing process, if the process is non-reversible, the vendor company will not have any rights in the manufactured product or in any proceeds from the sale of the manufactured product simply because the vendor company sold the goods subject to a simple ROT clause.[88] In that situation, in seeking to incorporate a sufficiently complex ROT clause to cover the circumstance outlined, the vendor company would in effect be asking the purchaser company to create a charge in their favour over the manufactured goods. What sometimes happens is that vendor companies think their ROT clause is sufficient, and only learn when the purchaser company is in liquidation, that what they had was a charge, and that charge is void against the liquidator because it was not registered.

The earliest of the ROT cases is known as the *Romalpa* case.[89] Over the course of a year the plaintiffs sold aluminium foil to the defendant. At the point when a receiver was appointed to the defendant, it owed the plaintiff £122,239. A clause in the contract said "the ownership of the material to be delivered ... will only be transferred to the purchaser when he has met all that is owing to [the plaintiff]". A second part of the clause provided that if the purchaser used the aluminium in the manufacture of any new objects, then the seller would be given ownership of those objects until the purchaser had paid the seller everything it owed it. The defendant had sold some of the aluminium foil on to a third party. The receiver found that the proceeds of this sale, £35,152, were held in an account, and that there was still some aluminium foil on the premises. The plaintiffs sought a declaration that the foil was theirs and so was the £35,152. The plaintiffs

---

[88] *Clough Mill Ltd v Martin* [1984] 3 All ER 982; *Modelboard Ltd v Outer Box Ltd* [1993] BCLC 623.

[89] *Aluminium Industrie Vaasen B.V. v Romalpa Aluminium Ltd* [1976] 1 WLR 676.

were successful on both counts, the Court of Appeal finding that the ROT clause was part of the general terms and conditions and that the defendant had only a limited power to sell the aluminium to third parties, the power resting on the understanding that all such proceeds would be held in trust for the plaintiffs until the defendants discharged the purchase price of the original aluminium delivery.

The next case to come before the courts was *Re Bond Worth Ltd*,[90] an answered prayer for anyone who has longed to know the steps by which a carpet comes to be made. The product at issue was called "Acrilan", raw fibre that goes into carpets. The sellers included a clause that stated "equitable and beneficial ownership shall remain with us until full payment has been received", adding that if the Acrilan became incorporated into the carpets then they would have "equitable and beneficial ownership in such other products as if they were solely and simply the goods". Slade J commented that the drafting of the clauses had been "somewhat misleading and inadequate"[91] because the seller had transferred the legal title but purported to retain the "equitable and beneficial" title (properly drafted, the clause would have provided that the legal title in the raw fibre remained with the seller until the purchase price was paid). Because of this error of drafting Bond Worth could deal freely with the fibre, and even sell it, because they were the legal owners, and the sellers had only an equitable and beneficial title to it. Bond Worth, being the legal owners, had given the sellers an equitable floating charge (rather than the sellers, as usually happens in these cases, retaining legal title). Thus, it appeared to Slade J that what had been created was a floating charge. Once this was decided, the seller's claim was sunk, because they hadn't registered the charges and so they were void.

Borden (UK) Ltd v Scottish Timber Products[92] is famous because the good supplied became irreversibly mixed with a new good and the Court of Appeal held that in this circumstance the ROT right vanished. The defendants made chipboard. The plaintiffs supplied them with resin. Nothing in the contract prevented the defendants from using the resin before they paid for it. The problem was that the resin "became an inseparable component, or

---

[90] [1980] 1 Ch 228.
[91] *ibid* at 268.
[92] [1981] 1 Ch 25.

ingredient, of the chipboard".[93] A receiver was appointed to the defendants, at which point the plaintiffs were owed £318,321. Understandably distraught, the plaintiffs did their utmost to recover that sum. They argued that the chipboard, whether the resin was used in it wholly or partly, was charged with the payment of the £318,321, and so were the proceeds of any sale of chipboard. There were many unknown factors which the plaintiffs could only guess at, such as what the defendants had done with the proceeds—paid their taxes? Reduced their bank draft? Paid other creditors?—and whether the cost of the resin, of labour, of overheads, had fluctuated over time. Templeman LJ was quite scathing, stating:

> "At some distant date, when the court has unearthed the unearthable, traced the untraceable and calculated the incalculable, there will emerge the sum which it is said belongs to the plaintiffs in equity."[94]

There was no problem with the *idea* of the ROT clause. The plaintiffs could sell the resin to the defendants and retain legal title to it until it was paid for. The essential consideration was:

> "When the resin was incorporated in the chipboard, the resin ceased to exist, the plaintiffs' title to the resin became meaningless and their security vanished. There was no provision in the contract for the defendants to provide substituted or additional security. The chipboard belonged to the defendants."[95]

Thus, *Borden (UK)* is the key case whenever a product which is subject to an ROT clause has become "irreversibly mixed".

In *Re Peachdart*[96] a company called Freudenbergs were leather suppliers. Peachdart made handbags. The supply contract between them stated the usual simple ROT provision and added

> "[i]f such payment is overdue ... the seller may ... recover or resell the products or any of them and may enter upon the buyer's premises by its servants or agents for that purpose."

---

[93] *ibid* at 43.
[94] [1981] 1 Ch 25 at 44.
[95] *ibid*.
[96] [1983] WLR 878; [1983] 3 All ER 204.

The clause stated that "the property in the whole of such other goods shall be and remain with the seller" until the outstanding sums were paid and "all the seller's rights...shall extend to those other goods." The Court stated:

> "It may be that, as counsel for Freudenbergs asserts, an expert in the leather trade could identify each handbag, whether partly or completely manufactured, as made from a skin comprised in a particular parcel of leather. But after a handbag had been sold it would be impossible to do so. There is nothing in the conditions of sale which requires the company to keep a record of handbags sold so as to identify [them later]. No such records were in fact kept and there is nothing in the evidence which suggests that the parties contemplated that they would be. So, on the facts of this case it would be impossible for Freudenbergs now to prove that the handbags sold by the company but not paid for when the receiver was appointed were in fact made out of leather comprised in any of the parcels to which the unpaid invoices relied on by Freudenbergs relate. It seems to me that the parties must have intended that at least after a piece of leather had been appropriated to be manufactured into a handbag and work had started on it...the leather would cease to be the exclusive property of Freudenbergs...and that Freudenbergs would thereafter have a charge on handbags in the course of manufacture and on the distinctive products which would come into existence at the end of the process of manufacture... The charge would in due course shift to the proceeds of sale."[97]

As no charge was registered, Freudenberg's charge was void for want of registration.

In *Carroll Group Distributors Ltd v G & F Bourke Ltd*[98] the plaintiff tobacco company sought a declaration that the proceeds of the cigarettes it had supplied to the defendant, a retail business in Limerick, were held on trust for them. Carroll's were owed £54,517. Carrolls had incorporated the usual simple ROT clause into the supply contract, and added the proceeds of sale clause. The course of dealing was simple. Carrolls provided

---

[97] *Per* Vinelott, [1983] 3 All ER 204 at 210.
[98] [1990] 1 IR 481

Bourkes with cigarettes. Bourkes sold them on. The ROT clause said that in this regard, Bourkes acted "on their own account and not as agent for Carrolls".[99] Carrolls had sought to argue that when they were selling the cigarettes, Bourkes were obliged to keep the proceeds of the sale for them on trust until the price of the cigarettes had been paid. Since Bourkes were selling "on their own account" there could be no question of there being a fiduciary relationship between the two, and no question of a right to trace the money into a mixed bank account, which Bourkes used for its general business. Murphy J said that this agreement meant that

> "effectively Bourke's were creating or conferring a charge on the proceeds of sale in substitution for the right of property which Carrolls had previously enjoyed."

Carroll's hadn't realised this, so hadn't registered any charge, and therefore, the charge was void.

The Four Kinds of ROT Clauses Classified

At this point, the essence and pitfalls of ROT clauses should be clear. It remains to categorize the four main kinds and state which are registrable. The first kind is the simple ROT. The essence of what is happening is that the seller is retaining title in specified goods until the buyer pays the purchase price. Carroll J explained that in this situation, if the buyer were to go into liquidation, the buyer's creditors could not seize the goods because they are merely "in the apparent possession of the buyer".[100] The simple ROT clause does not require registration.

The second type of ROT clause which doesn't require to be registered is known as the "current account clause" or "all sums due" clause. They differ from the simple ROT clause only to the extent that they provide the title in the goods shall not pass until all sums due to the seller have been paid—not only the sums due arising from the particular contract at hand.

---

[99] *ibid* at 484. The supply agreement stipulated that Bourkes should keep a separate account for the proceeds of cigarette sales. Bourke's didn't do so. Murphy J thought it "probable" that Carrolls knew no separate account had not been opened, and nothing seems to have been made of this point.

[100] The buyer "is not the maker or giver of the bill of sale. He is the holder or grantee under the bill." See *Re Charles Dougherty* [1985] 1 IR 346. If title passes to the buyer and only equitable and beneficial ownership remains with the seller, as it did in *Re Bond Worth* [1979] 3 AER 919, then legal title will have passed to the purchaser, and the purchaser will be the one creating a charge over the goods in favour of the seller.

These clauses were upheld in Ireland as non-registrable charges (see *Re Stokes & McKiernan*[101]) and, after some doubt that they might be found to be otherwise in England, were upheld there too as non-registrable charges, in *Armour v Thyssen Edelstahlwerke AG*.[102] Thyssen and a Scottish company called Carron engaged in a course of dealing for some time before Carron got into trouble. Thyssen would sell steel strip to Carron. The contracts of sale were subject to Thyssen's general conditions. When Mr Armour was appointed receiver there was 67,000 kilograms of steel strip lying in Carron's premises at Falkirk. Part of it had been cut into sheets. Another part of it was in the process of being cut into sheets. Most of it was just as it had been when it arrived from Germany. This amount of steel cost £71,000 and none of that sum had been paid. The ROT clause was an "all sums due clause" and so the House of Lords found that ownership of the steel had not passed to Carron.[103]

The next two kinds of ROT clauses do need to be registered. The first of these is called an "aggregation clause". It begins with the usual ROT stipulation and adds that if the relevant goods are manufactured or processed into some other products, then title in those new products rests with the seller too. It is the safest course of action to assume that this type of clause is a charge that requires registration. Such a clause might fail if the goods are irreversibly mixed with something, as the resin was with the chipboard in *Borden (UK)*, or the leather with the handbags in *Peachdart*, but another scenario is where the relevant goods are sold, incorporated with something else (such as a diesel engine in a diesel generating set), but can be separated at a later stage with a little time and skill (as was the case in *Hendy Lennox Ltd v Grahame Puttick Ltd*[104]). Carroll J in the *Charles Dougherty* case said that

> "… a seller can make an effective reservation of title clause to goods prior to manufacture, but if he requires security over the

---

[101] [1978] ILRM 240.

[102] [1991] BCLC 28.

[103] See also *Clough Mill v Martin* [1984] 3 All E.R. 982, where the disputed yarn was "identifiable, unused and unpaid for".

[104] [1984] 1 WLR 485; for a case where the nature of rubble was discussed, as to whether or not it was firmly affixed to the land on which it was spread, and the meaning of "substantially attached to the realty" was canvassed, see *Ardfert Quarry Products v Moormac Developments Ltd* [2013] IEHC 572 (Laffoy J, 13 December 2013).

manufactured goods the buyer *will have to grant him this* and this would require registration as a Bill of Sale."[105]

The second registrable clause is the "proceeds of sale clause", which we saw in the *Carroll Group Distributors* case. It might be noted that Barron J suggested in *Re WJ Hickey Ltd*[106] that these clauses did not need to be registered, but Courtney has suggested that Murphy J's decision in *Carroll Group* will prevail, and "sounded the death-knell for proceeds of sale clauses".[107] This may not be the case, as Peart J, in *Unitherm Heating Systems*, has said of this apparent conflict: "I do not see any conflict in fact. Each [judge] was dealing with different facts and can be distinguished". He went on to say that they "co-exist comfortably".[108] In *Unitherm Heating Systems Ltd v Wallace*,[109] a liquidator argued that the applicant had no right to the €93,907.65 it sought on foot of a proceeds of sale clause because the clause was not registered but the court decided the matter in Unitherm's favour on equitable principles. The clause stated:

"pending the payment of all sums aforesaid and the passing of property in the said goods:

- a *fiduciary relationship* shall exist between the buyer and the company and the buyer shall hold the said goods *as trustee for* and on behalf of the company and shall return the same to the company on demand. [...]
- *(iv)* the buyer shall *store the goods separately* from goods belonging to the buyer or third parties so as to be clearly identifiable as being the goods of the company. [...]
- *(v)* the buyer shall *be entitled to sell the goods* to third parties ... in the *normal course of the buyer's business* (but not otherwise) *but the proceeds of any such sale shall be held by the buyer on trust* for the company *(to be lodged in a separate account by the buyer)* and the buyer is hereby *deemed to have assigned* to the company absolutely the *benefit of any claim* (including the right to trace the

---

[105] [1984] ILRM 437 at 441; *Kruppstahl AG v Quitman Products Ltd* [1982] ILRM 551 showed this, she said.

[106] [1988] IR 126 (also known as *Uniacke v Cassidy Electrical Supply*).

[107] Courtney, *Law of Companies* (3rd ed, Bloomsbury, 2012) at p 1275.

[108] *Unitherm Heating Systems Ltd* [2014] IEHC 177, at para 29 and 44.

[109] [2014] IEHC 177 (Peart J, 2 April 2014).

said goods or the proceeds thereof) which the buyer has *against any such third party* arising from such sale."

Peart J stated that the answer to the question before him depended on whether the applicant and the company were fiduciaries by reason of a relationship of principal and agent; if they were not the proceeds of sale clause was a registrable charge.[110] He cited Murphy J in the Carroll case, where Murphy J stated:

> "... it seems to me that the question must be asked how does a party come to sell property of which he is not the owner? Is he selling as a trustee in pursuance of a power of sale? Is he selling as the agent of the true owner? Does the sale constitute a wrongful conversion? If any of those questions were answered in the affirmative it seems to me that the law would impose a trust on the proceeds of sale which would confer on the true owner the right to recover those proceeds from the actual seller or, if the proceeds were no longer in the seller's hands, to trace them into any other property acquired with them."[111]

While not determinative of an agency relationship, Peart J noted in *Unitherm* that certain features of the ROT under consideration—the requirement to store the goods separately, to hold the sale proceeds in trust and in a separate bank account of the retention clause—were consistent with an agency relationship.[112] These, however, would not be sufficient for a court to conclude that an agency relationship pertained, when in fact a charge was created. The decisive factor was that "the amount of the company's profit on any transaction was set by the applicant"[113] and this, combined with the requirement to lodge all the proceeds of a re-sale into a separate account created a fiduciary relationship by virtue of this course of dealing. Therefore in this case, the proceeds of sale clause was not a charge requiring registration under the Companies Act but a trust, resulting from the fiduciary relationship between the two companies, which the liquidator was obliged to honour.

---

[110] [2014] IEHC 177 (Peart J, 2 April 2014), at para 26.
[111] [1990] 1 IR 481 at 484; see also *Tatung (UK) Ltd v Galex Telesure Ltd* [1989] 5 BCC 325; *Compaq Computer Ltd v Abercorn Group Ltd* [1993] BCLC 602 and *Re Andrabell Ltd (in liq.)* [1984] 2 All ER 407 which Peart J says "has a helpful clarity about it for anybody having difficulty understanding the vagaries of the various decisions in this area, and reconciling them."
[112] [2014] IEHC 177 at para 42.
[113] *ibid*, at para 45.

RECEIVERS

Appointing a Receiver

A receiver can be appointed by the court or on foot of a debenture: the latter is more common. To avoid any challenge to the validity of his appointment it is vital that the creditor follow to the letter the terms of the debenture on foot of which it appoints its receiver.[1] Banks are entitled to appoint a receiver where they have demanded repayment of the loan and that demand has gone unsatisfied. Banks may appoint receivers if they think that the assets over which they have security are in jeopardy, but the power to do so must be expressly stated. The courts will not imply such a power, especially where other provisions are expressly stated (this was the case in *Cryne v Barclays Bank plc*[2]). The decision to appoint a receiver is a purely commercial one. The bank does not have to consider the consequences for the defaulting company and its directors.[3] It may well take these into account in the stages before appointment, but appointment may be a result of frustrated attempts to negotiate a settlement. All the banker must consider it whether the bank's interests will be furthered by the appointment of a receiver. There is no reported decision of a successful application to have a receiver removed on the grounds that he was appointed in bad faith. The receiver's appointment means that all floating charges crystallize, the directors' power over the charged asset(s) are ceded to him, and the receiver may dispose of the entire undertaking of the company, if he considers that the interests of the creditor who appointed him require this.

The Receiver Manager

There is a second type of receiver called a "receiver manager": he may carry on the business as a going concern with a view to selling it in the near future. This happened, for example, in the case of a waste company, *Mr Binman*, which failed in its application to have an examiner appointed.[4]

---

[1] *Ferris v Ward; Ward's Wholesale Meats Ltd v Ferris* [1998] 2 IR 194.

[2] [1987] BCLC 548.

[3] Lending institutions will be familiar with the kind of letter that was sent by the first defendant in *Standard Chartered Bank v Walker* [1982] 2 All ER 938 at 941: "To put a receiver in at the moment, when the company has done so well in streamlining itself … and preparing to combat the recession, would mean, literally economic suicide … If commonsense prevails and we are allowed to continue to trade, which I may add now is profitably so, it will not be long before we can reduce down [our overdraft] but it is going to take a little longer in time." The bank appointed a receiver.

[4] *Re Mr. Binman and Ors* [2011] IEHC 401.

Bank of Scotland then appointed receivers, who carried on the trade. The company served more than 65,000 customers in Munster and employed 330 people. Receivers were appointed in October 2011. By March 2012 they had received three offers to buy the business. In April they sold the business to a consortium led by the Managing Director of a waste and recycling company.[5]

Who Pays the Receiver's Fees?

The receiver is paid out of the assets of the company. Statute also provides that he "may retain out of any money received, for remuneration and in satisfaction of all costs incurred as receiver, a commission at the prescribed rate".[6]

Time Between Demand and Appointment

How long must a bank wait between the time it makes the demand and the time it appoints a receiver? This question has come before the courts as another way of challenging the appointment of the receiver, with plaintiffs alleging that they were not given sufficient time once demand was made.[7] While the courts have said that people are not expected to keep the money in a box under the bed,[8] a bank must wait no longer than the time it takes for the reasonable mechanics of payment to take their course. In *Sheppard Cooper Ltd v TSB Bank plc*[9] the plaintiff company, which traded in antique and ancient glass, came to owe their bankers £618,083. The two directors were called in to an early morning meeting, during the course of which a letter of demand was given to them. One of the directors said that the company couldn't pay, but, depending on how certain sales went in New York, the company might be able to reduce the excess on the overdraft by half. Shortly after the directors left the meeting the bank appointed receivers. Was sixty minutes between demand and appointment sufficient? Harman J at first instance said that it was because "if the debtor admits that [he] cannot pay, it is clearly unnecessary for the creditor to allow time for the mechanics of payment which he knows cannot have any point".[10]

---

[5] See *Limerick Leader*, 19 April 2012 (*"Limerick waste company, Mr Binman, is sold by receivers"*).
[6] Land Reform and Conveyancing Act 2009, s 108(7).
[7] See *Treasury Holdings v NAMA* [2012] IEHC 237.
[8] Per Walton J in *Bank of Baroda v Panessar* [1986] 3 AER 751 at 759–760.
[9] [1996] 2 All ER 654.
[10] [1996] 2 AER 654 at 663.

Blackburne J agreed and dismissed the appeal. The courts do allow for a "mechanics of payment" test: all this means is that if the debtor has the money, he must be afforded a reasonable time to process its transfer through the banking system. It is a matter of "practical common sense". A bank could not appoint a receiver at 4.15pm on a Friday afternoon, if the debtor had made it known that it had the money and simply needed time on Monday to convey it. As Walton J said in the *Hawtin* case,

> "in practice, in 99 cases out of 100, this is completely academic, because the debtor has not got the money available anyway and the demand is only a step towards some other end, for example … appointing a receiver."[11]

Notification that a Receiver has been Appointed

Where a receiver of the property of a company has been appointed, every invoice, order for goods or business letter issued by or on behalf of the company or the receiver, being a document on or in which the name of the company appears, must contain a statement that a receiver has been appointed.[12] Failure to do this is a category 4 offence for which the company, any company officer who is in default, and any liquidator or receiver who "knowingly and intentionally authorises or permits the default" may be held liable.[13] When a receiver is in situ, any website of the company, and any e-mails sent to a third party by, or on behalf of, the company, must contain a statement that a receiver has been appointed: the statement on the website must be in a prominent and easily accessible place on it.[14]

Form E8

If a debenture-holder appoints a receiver it must fill out the CRO's E8 Form within seven days after the date of the order or of the appointment, and deliver the E8 to the CRO and ensure it is published in *Iris Oifigiúil*.[15]

---

[11] [1987] Ch 335 at 348.
[12] Companies Act 2014, s 429(1); if a receiver has been appointed and a winding up of the company is taking place (whether that winding up has commenced before or after that appointment), those documents must state that as well as being in receivership, the company is being wound-up.
[13] Companies Act 2014, s 429(6).
[14] Companies Act 2014, s 429(3); failure here is also a category 4 offence, see s 429(8).
[15] Companies Act 2014, s 436; if the receiver ceases to act the Form E11 must be filled out *by the receiver*. Default in either matter is a category 4 offence.

Forms E9 and E10

Where he has been appointed on foot of a debenture the receiver must notify the company of his appointment. The following paragraph outlines a number of rules which must be complied with by the receiver.[16] Within 14 days of the company receiving this notice a statement as to the affairs of the company must be made out to the receiver, using the CRO's E10 Form. The E10 must contain a number of matters, which are set out at s 431 of Companies Act 2014 (for example, particulars of the company's assets, debts and liabilities; the names and residences of its creditors, the securities they hold and the dates when they were given). The E10 must be verified on affidavit by at least one of the persons who is a director at the date of the receiver's appointment, if the receiver is court appointed. If the receiver is appointed on foot of a debenture, then instead of an affidavit a statutory declaration must be made.[17] Failure to comply is a category 3 offence (a director might find himself having to prove "to the satisfaction of the court" that it was "not possible" for him to comply with the requirements of this section, having been brought to court by the receiver or any creditor of the company[18]). Within two months of the receiver receiving the E10 he must send a copy of the statement and of any comments he or she sees fit to make on it to the following parties:

(i) The Registrar of Companies (who will inform the DCE of the receiver's appointment[19]);

(ii) The court (only if the receiver is court appointed)[20];

(iii) The company;

(iv) Any trustees for the debenture holders on whose behalf he or she was appointed; and

(v) So far as he or she is aware of their addresses, all such debenture holders.[21]

---

[16] Default in any of them will render the receiver guilty of a category 4 offence

[17] Companies Act 2014, s 431(2) and (4).

[18] ibid, s 432.

[19] ibid, s 430(9).

[20] ibid, s 430(5); these steps do not have to be taken by a second receiver who is appointed to act with an existing receiver, or by a receiver who is put in place to replace a receiver who has died or ceased to act (s 430(6)).

[21] Companies Act 2014, s 430(1)(c).

The receiver must then send to the CRO an abstract — the CRO's E9 Form — which shows the following three things:

(i) The assets of the company of which he or she has taken possession since his or her appointment, their estimated value and the proceeds of sale of any such assets since his or her appointment,

(ii) His or her receipts and payments during that period of six months (or, where he or she ceases to act, during the period from the end of the period to which the last preceding abstract related up to the date of his or her so ceasing), and

(iii) The aggregate amounts of his or her receipts and of his or her payments during all preceding periods since his or her appointment.

The receiver must send the E9 within 30 days of the expiration of the initial period of six months, and must send a new E9 every six months thereafter. He must send a final E9 within 30 days after the date on which he ceases to act as receiver of the property of the company.[22] This final abstract must be accompanied by a statement from the receiver which outlines his opinion as to whether or not the company is solvent. When this is received in the CRO, it is forwarded on to the DCE.[23]

Persons Who May Not Act as Receivers

A receiver will usually be an accountant or an experienced insolvency practitioner. The following persons may not act as a receiver:

(a) An undischarged bankrupt;

(b) A person who is, or who has, within the period of 12 months before the date of commencement of the receivership been, an officer or employee of the company (this includes a statutory auditor of the company);

(c) A parent, spouse, civil partner, brother, sister or child[24] of an officer of the company;

---

[22] *ibid*, s 430(3).

[23] *ibid*, s 430(4).

[24] This includes a child of the officer's civil partner who is ordinarily resident with the officer and the civil partner (s 433(2)(a)).

(d) A person who is a partner of, or in the employment of, an officer or employee of the company;

(e) A person who is not qualified by virtue of this subsection for appointment as receiver of the property of any other body corporate which is that company's subsidiary or holding company or a subsidiary of that company's holding company, or would be so disqualified if the body corporate were a company;

(f) A body corporate.

It is a category 2 offence for a person who is disqualified by s 433 to act as a receiver.[25] If a person who is a receiver of a company becomes disqualified by virtue of the section, he must immediately vacate his office and give notice in writing within 14 days after the date of vacation to the company, the CRO, and the person who appointed him (court or debenture-holder).[26] Normal resignation is provided for in s 434 of Companies Act 2014. The court may remove a receiver if an applicant can "show cause": a broad phrase that would have to be particularised thoroughly, and be made on substantial grounds, for an application to succeed.[27]

Powers of Receiver

Section 437(1) of Companies Act 2014 states that, as a general rule, a receiver of the property of a company

> "has power to do, in the State and elsewhere, all things necessary or convenient to be done for or in connection with, or as incidental to, the attainment of the objectives for which the receiver was appointed."

Those powers are stated in s 437(3)(a) to (t).[28] This list is not intended to be exhaustive but it is intended to provide clarity. Among the receiver's powers are:

---

[25] Companies Act 2014, s 433(6).

[26] *ibid*, s 433(3).

[27] *ibid*, s 435.

[28] The receiver's powers are subject to any provision of the order of the court by which limits the receivers powers, or the instrument under which the receiver was appointed, which gave him more limited powers. This list is new in Irish law and is modelled on the Australian Corporations law.

- To enter into possession and take control of property of the company;
- To lease, let on hire or dispose of property of the company;
- To borrow money on the security of property of the company;
- To repair, renew or enlarge property of the company;
- To convert property of the company into money;
- To carry on any business of the company;
- To execute any document, bring or defend any proceedings or do any other act or thing in the name of and on behalf of the company;
- To engage or discharge employees on behalf of the company;
- To appoint a solicitor, accountant or other professionally qualified person to assist the receiver;
- To appoint an agent to do any business that the receiver is unable to do, or that it is unreasonable to expect the receiver to do, in person;
- To make or defend an application for the winding-up of the company.

A Receiver May Apply to the Court for Directions

The receiver may apply to court for directions if any questions arise in the course of the receivership.[29] Other parties may also apply, where the receiver is appointed on foot of a debenture: they are an officer, member, employee or creditor[30] of the company, and a liquidator or contributory. In *Re HSS*[31] Clarke J stated that the section did "not give the court some general jurisdiction to consider whether things are fair or unfair".[32]

The Receiver's Agency is Exceptional

The most basic mistake people make about receivers arises out of their status as agent of the company. A director will often say: If the receiver is the agent of the company then he must have certain duties to me. From this proposition a wide-ranging series of duties are imagined. In fact, any duties are quite limited, and the agency in this situation is a totally

---

[29] Companies Act 2014, s 438(1); previously s 316 of the Companies Act 1963.
[30] The definition of creditor has been modified by Companies Act 2014; a creditor now means one or more creditors to whom the company is indebted by more than €13,000 (in aggregate).
[31] [2011] IEHC 497. The equivalent power for liquidators is s 280 of the Companies Act 1963.
[32] [2011] IEHC 497 at 9.

exceptional kind. It has nothing to do with the ordinary law of agency. It is correct law to say that the receiver is the agent of the company, but this is only a device to protect the debenture holder. The first reported misapprehension of the agency point in Irish law can be seen in *Irish Oil and Cake Mills Ltd v Donnelly*,[33] where the directors of the company were seeking financial management accounts, the latest balance sheets, details of purchases and sales made by the receiver, details of refinery programmes, information on staff, and so on. "The agency here is of course very different from the ordinary agency arising every day in commercial transactions," said Costello J, adding that the receiver had an "exceptional status".[34] Any rights the company had were equitable rights, not contractual ones. The orders sought were "entirely novel and wholly exceptional".[35] The directors were entitled to the same information as every other prospective purchaser, but not to more, and the receiver was "entitled to make a commercial judgment ... and decide that it would not be conducive to procuring an enhanced price to give these directors any more information".[36] The idea that there was a duty to keep the company appraised of how the business was going while under the management of the receiver was "a very far-reaching proposition, unsupported by any authority" and Costello J rejected it.[37]

Duties to Sell at Best Price Reasonably Obtainable

Receivers are subject to equitable duties. This means there is no general duty of care in negligence. One of the most important duties on receivers is the duty to sell assets at the best possible price reasonably obtainable (s 439 of Companies Act 2014[38]). *Ruby Property Co Ltd v Kilty*[39] considered this duty at length. It is a sad, messy case, and the second and third

---

[33] *Irish Oil and Cake Mills Ltd v Donnelly*, Unreported, High Court, Costello J, 27 March 1983.
[34] *ibid*, at 6.
[35] *ibid* at 11.
[36] *ibid* at 12.
[37] The UK Court of Appeal made similar statements in *Gomba Holdings UK v Minories Finance Ltd* [1989] BCLC 115. Fox LJ highlighted three aspects which made the receiver different from other agents. First, he becomes the mortgagor's (i.e. the borrower's) agent whether he likes it or not. Second, the mortgagor cannot dismiss him (the debenture holder has that power). And third, the mortgagor can't give the receiver instructions about how to act in the receivership. All this, he stated, is "far removed from the ordinary principal and agent situation." *Gomba Holdings UK v Minories Finance Ltd* [1989] BCLC 115 at 117.
[38] Previously s 316A of Companies Act 1964.
[39] Unreported, High Court, McKechnie J, 31 January 2003.

plaintiffs, a married couple, both died before it came to be heard. The dispute centred on a property in Sutton, which was beside a Superquinn. The plaintiffs complained that the property hadn't been sold by public tender, hadn't been advertised in the press, that no billboard had been placed outside, that there was no bargaining with third parties and that the market hadn't been tested. McKechnie J had been invited to find that the receiver was in breach of his duty to the company. The receiver sold the property to Superquinn and the Court found that, in fact, the price obtained by the receiver was even better than what the open market value was at the time: the supermarket had paid a premium because of its adjacent location. McKechnie J distilled a number of principles over the course of his judgment[40]:

1. The receiver is not required to postpone, defer or cancel a sale in the hope of the market improving. (A receiver has no obligation to exercise his power of sale,[41] unless perhaps the presence of perishable goods would mean a failure to sell would cause loss to both lender and company);

2. The duty to guarantors does not extend to unsecured creditors;

3. "There is no contractual relationship or duty owed in tort by the receiver to the mortgagor".[42] A duty is not owed to the mortgagor "individually but to him as one of the persons interested in the equity of redemption", which means the correct action to be taken is one to make the receiver liable to account for money lost as a result of his default, and not common law damages[43];

4. A receiver is not bound in any preset way to adopt a specified approach in how he particularises the property or asset in sale and there are no predetermined, fixed or rigid rules by which such disposal of property must take place. (Receivers do not have to spend money repairing a property before selling it[44] or to refurbish a property before selling it.[45]);

---

[40] The following list, part quotation, part paraphrase, is not exhaustive. See pages 14–19 of the judgment.
[41] *Routestone Ltd v Minories Finance Ltd* [1997] BCC 180 at 187.
[42] *Silven Properties Ltd v Royal Bank of Scotland plc* [2004] 1 BCLC 359.
[43] *ibid* at 370.
[44] *Meftah v Lloyds TSB Bank plc* [2001] 2 All ER (Comm) 741 at 744.
[45] *Routestone Ltd v Minories Finance Ltd* [1997] 1 EGLR 123 at 130 *per* Jacob J.

5. The duty imposed upon a receiver to take reasonable care is a duty personal to him, which is not necessarily discharged by the mere exercise of reasonable care in engaging competent experts to act on his behalf, though this is not intended to diminish in any way the very important role which advice from experts play in receiverships;

6. In determining a case of negligence against a receiver, the court of trial must judge the conduct in question at the time of and in the light of the facts and circumstances as these previously existed. Hindsight should not be used;

7. Whether "the best price" reasonably obtainable was in fact obtained, is a matter of historical fact to be established through admissible evidence;

8. The onus of proving a breach of s 439 rests on he who asserts it.

Examples of Failed Actions against Receivers

In *Lambert Jones Estates Limited v Donnelly*[46] the asset which the receiver was putting up for sale was a site by Stephen's Green. The receiver was going to sell it as one piece. The plaintiffs approached him and said that if he divided it into smaller units, applied for and obtained planning permission for the units, and created schemes of development for each of them, then he could sell each unit off and realize more money overall. The receiver didn't dispute that a better price could be obtained that way, but he decided not to pursue their plan. O'Hanlon J found that he was justified because the plaintiffs' plan was contingent on various factors: the planning aspect alone could take a long time and would certainly cost a lot of money. The receiver said that over such a period the interest on the sum owed would continue to run and the debt already stood at £1m. Finally, he had taken advice from a prominent firm of estate agents. In these circumstances the Court held it would be "perverse" to find that the receiver was being negligent or breaching his duty.

In *Re Bula Ltd*[47] the receiver sought court approval for a sale of ore in a mine for £27.5m. The directors of Bula opposed the application, stating that the price was a gross undervalue, and the ore in question was capable

---

[46] Unreported, High Court, O'Hanlon J, 5 November 1982.
[47] Unreported, High Court, Murphy J, 20 June 2002.

of fetching £60m. Murphy J approved the sale, primarily because the bid, which came from the neighbouring company, was the only realistic one.

Could a bank be found negligent for replacing a local selling agent with a provincial one? This was the argument advanced in *Anglo Irish Bank Corporation Ltd v Collins*,[48] where it was alleged that an estate agent whose practice ranged over Munster should not have replaced a local agent who had knowledge of the Kenmare market. If this argument were to have a hope of success it would need strong evidence, and even then it might not succeed. Dunne J held that there was no evidence that the replacement of the local with the provincial expert was "in any way inappropriate".[49]

Could a bank be found negligent for failing to adequately fund a receivership, where the secured asset is deteriorating through lack of use and is subject to vandalism? In *AIB plc v Heagney*[50] the defendant may have thought he was in a better position to resist the bank's claim — for summary judgment in the sum of €2.4m on foot of personal guarantees — because after the receiver was appointed the Revenue Commissioners put the defendant's company into liquidation. The legal effect of this was that the receiver ceased to be the agent of the company and the bank instead became mortgagees in possession of the hotel in question. The defendant may have thought that this strengthened his claim against the bank and the receiver for alleged acts of negligence and breach of duty to him as guarantor. Kearns P accepted that the bank became mortgagees in possession and that this gave rise to "an equitable duty to give back the property uninjured on redemption".[51] No such duty attached to the lender where a normal receivership takes place. Kearns P held that the test was reasonable man test set out by O'Dalaigh CJ in *Holohan v Friends Provident and Century Life*.[52] What had happened in *AIB plc v Heagney* was that the receiver took charge of the premises, arranged for an inventory, retained an auctioneer of thirty years' experience, explored the problems surrounding

---

[48] [2011] IEHC 385.

[49] *ibid* at 36.

[50] [2012] IEHC 138.

[51] *AIB plc v Heagney* [2012] IEHC 138 at 23; Kearns P cited Fisher and Lightwood's *Law of Mortgage* (Butterworths, 11th ed, 2002) at 737, where the following examples are given: "… the mortgagee in possession … will be liable if mortgaged mines are flood by improper working; if water pipes are negligently allowed to freeze; if mortgaged chattels are injured by negligent removal … ".

[52] [1966] IR 1.

the liquor licences in the hotel, and later, when incidents of trespass occurred, responded swiftly. Kearns P found that he had therefore "carried out his duties in a responsible fashion". The defendant had contended that when he had left the hotel with the receiver it had been in perfect condition, with all the beds made, and by the time the matter came on for hearing it was a dilapidated wreck. The Court found that the premises were in fact "in less than good condition" when the receivership began, that the receiver could not be "faulted because the state of the market combined with the ... condition of the hotel made a sale virtually impossible" and that the bank had not failed to adequately fund the receivership, as alleged. The bank had put aside €20,000 for the receivership. A year and a half into it the process had consumed €125,000 in the receiver's fees, security fees, repairs to the roof of the hotel, and so on. "Against a backdrop where the bank was already out of pocket to the tune of €7m," stated Kearns P,

> "I do not believe it can seriously be suggested that they had an obligation to continue clocking up expenses under these various headings in the clear knowledge that they would never recover them."[53]

Conditional Offers to Purchase

In *AIB plc v Heagney* one offer was made to buy the hotel. The bank rejected it, even though the receiver thought that it was better to accept it. The offer was a bid of €1.4m. The bank took the view that it was better to wait it out until the site could be sold as a site for development, rather than as a going concern hotel or bar. The Court stated that because the offer was conditional — on compliance with fire and licence issues — neither the bank nor the receiver could be found negligent in declining it. The Supreme Court in *Re Edenfell Holdings Limited*[54] held that, where a receiver is faced with two offers (one of €1.5m and another of €1.6m in this case), he is free to reject the higher bid if it comes with conditions, because the fulfilment of conditions can be a time-consuming and uncertain process.

---

[53] *AIB plc v Heagney* [2012] IEHC 138 at 27.
[54] [1999] 1 IR 443.

Duty of "Reasonable Competence" in Running a Business

In *Medforth v Blake*[55] it was argued on behalf of the receivers that they owed a duty of good faith and no more to a farmer whose farm they had taken over and managed. The farmer argued that they owed him an equitable duty to manage his farm with competence — and that they had managed it incompetently. Sir Richard Scott VC stated that because the receiver was not obliged to carry on the business — he could sell it off — then if he did decide to carry it on he is required to do so with "reasonable competence".[56] If only a duty of good faith were owed, then the receivers could decide, through good natured but incompetent management, that Mr Medforth's pigs only needed to be fed once a week, or that they didn't need to be inoculated. If the receivers' submissions were correct, they could ruin the business of the mortgagor through incompetence, but not be liable to him for any loss.[57]

Successful Actions by Guarantors

Receivers do owe a duty to guarantors. In *Standard Chartered Bank Ltd v Walker*[58] the defendant husband and wife owned a business that bought huge secondhand metal presses and moulding machines, which they resold to buyers all over the world. Their company took a loan from the plaintiff. They personally guaranteed the loan up to £75,000. Business was hit by a slump. Things went from bad to worse and the loan was called in. The overdraft came to £80,000. The bank appointed a receiver in November. He said he would auction the company's goods on 21 January. The plaintiffs asked him to wait, so he organised the auction on 4 February. At a conservative professional valuation, the company's goods should have raised around £90,000. The plaintiffs felt that the auction was being held at a bad time of the year and hadn't been advertised enough. The viewing arrangements weren't up to scratch and attendance was poor at them. The receiver didn't use the company's mailing list to alert international clients. Lord Denning MR memorably described the auction:

---

[55] [2000] 1 Ch 86.
[56] *Medforth v Blake* [2000] 1 Ch 86 at 93.
[57] Sir Richard Scott VC relied on *McHugh v Union Bank of Canada* [1913] AC 299.
[58] [1982] 3 All ER 938.

"It was a bitterly cold day. [The auctioneers] had a few heating stoves, but these made such a noise that the auctioneer could not make himself heard. So they were turned off; and many prospective buyers left."[59]

The Court held that the receiver had not used reasonable care to realise the assets to their best advantage, and that when this is the case,

"then the mortgagor, the company and the guarantor are entitled in equity to an allowance. They should be given credit for the amount which the sale should have realised if reasonable care had been used."[60]

Cuckmere Brick Co Ltd v Mutual Finance Ltd[61] is not a case involving a receiver, but it is often cited in this context because it concerned a mistake made by a mortgagee in possession, and this is to some extent analogous. The plaintiff, Mr Fawke, was a solicitor and property developer. The defendant bank loaned £50,000 to the plaintiff company, which Mr Fawke controlled, and Mr Fawke personally guaranteed it. The loan was bridging finance for a site which had obtained planning permission for 100 flats, and which later obtained permission for 35 houses. Either the flats or the houses, or some mixture of both, could be built on the land, but when the loan was defaulted on and the bank entered into possession it conducted an auction, the ads for which mentioned the permission for 35 houses, but said nothing of the permission for the 100 flats. The omission of this information caused the land to be sold for £65,000 less than it would have sold for, had all the information been available to the prospective purchasers. Salmon LJ stated that there was a duty on a mortgagee to take reasonable precautions when preparing a sale, that in deciding

"whether he has fallen short of that duty the facts must be looked at broadly, and he will not be adjudged to be in default unless he is plainly on the wrong side of the line".[62]

The bank had fallen short here, and was liable to account for the £65,000 loss that resulted from its negligence.

---

[59] [1982] 3 All ER 938 at 941.
[60] ibid at 942; see also *China and South Sea Bank v Tan* [1990] 1 AC 536.
[61] [1971] 1 Ch 949.
[62] ibid, *per* Salmon LJ at 969.

In *American Express International Banking Corp v Hurley*[63] the bank loaned money to a company called Egopath and received a floating charge over its equipment as security. The company provided lighting and sound to pop concerts. The defendant personally guaranteed the loan to the extent of £50,000. When a receiver was appointed he (through his team) did a terrible job of selling the company's equipment. He was told by the firm of valuers that he should get specialists to look at the equipment. He didn't. He did little more, at first, than ask a professional acquaintance if he had a client who would be interested in buying it. The acquaintance didn't. He didn't advertise in two important specialist magazines. His exchanges with one bidder evinced "no attitude of negotiation … at all". The most he did was send a stock list to four companies which had contacted him. Only one of those companies followed up. For these reasons Mann J held that he was liable in negligence to the guarantor. The way to assess the sum is to ask "how much would the equipment have realised had it been properly marketed?"[64] The Court took the conservative estimate that the equipment would have sold for £60,000. The receiver sold it for £34,500. He was "liable under a term to be implied in the contract of employment to indemnify the mortgagee against any loss caused by his negligence".[65]

The Duty Owed to Creditors

Receivers owe no duty to unsecured creditors, unless it can be shown that they did not act *bona fide*, or that they acted outside the scope of their authority. In *Lathia v Dronsfield Brothers Ltd*[66] the plaintiff alleged that the receivers had induced the breach of contract which it had entered into with the defendant to buy a roll grinding machine. The receivers asked the Court to strike the proceedings out because they disclosed no cause of action and the Court did so because receivers have no duty to unsecured creditors. Their duties are to the company and the debenture holder, not to the creditors of the company.[67]

What, then, is their duty to secured creditors? If there are two debentures granted to two different mortgagees, and both appoint receivers, what

---

[63] [1985] 3 All ER 564.
[64] *ibid* at 574.
[65] *ibid* at 575.
[66] [1987] BCLC 321.
[67] See also *Barclays Bank plc v Kingston* [2006] EWHC 533 (QB) in which *Burgess v Auger* [1998] 2 BCLC 478 was disapproved.

duty does the first debenture holder owe to the second? The answer is none, apart from his general duties. If the second debenture holder is unhappy, it can seek to have the first debenture assigned to it, put the company into liquidation, or, if it acts quickly, apply to have the company put into examinership.

> "If a receiver and manager decides at his discretion to manage and is allowed to manage and does manage in good faith with the object of preserving and realising the assets for the benefit of the debenture holder, he is subject to no further or greater liability."[68]

In *Downsview Nominees Ltd v First City Corporation*[69] the receiver who was first in time acted to frustrate the receiver who was second in time, causing loss to the mortgagor car dealers and breaching the duty of good faith he had to the subsequent encumbrancer. In such a case both he and the company which appointed him were liable to the plaintiffs for an award in equitable damages.

Prosecution of Offences Committed by Officers and Members of the Company

If, in the course of the receivership, it appears to the receiver that any past or present officer, or any member, of the company has been guilty of any offence in relation to the company, the receiver must "forthwith" report the matter to the Director of Public Prosecutions.[70] The second duty is to report it to the DCE. In both cases, the receiver must provide all relevant and necessary information. If either the DPP or the DCE decide there is a case to answer, every officer of the company (past and present) has "a duty" to give assistance in connection with the prosecution (the only person exempted from this duty is the person being prosecuted). That duty to give assistance extends to the bankers and solicitors of the company as well as any financial advisers (auditors, accountants, book-keepers, tax advisors, etc, etc).

[68] *Per* Lord Templeman, *Downsview Nominees Ltd v First City Corporation* [1993] 2 WLR 86.
[69] [1993] 2 WLR 86.
[70] Companies Act 2014, s 447.

CHAPTER SIXTEEN

Liquidators and Liquidations

PART I: LIQUIDATORS

Introduction

The liquidator is tasked with the administration of the property of the company to which he is appointed.[1] This involves ascertaining the extent of the property of the company and, as appropriate: (a) the collection and gathering of the company's property; (b) the realisation of such property; and (c) the distribution of such property in accordance with the Companies Act.[2] The acts of a liquidator will be deemed valid notwithstanding any defects that may afterwards be discovered in his appointment or qualification.[3] A court-appointed liquidator is known as the "official liquidator". Every liquidator must consent to be appointed as liquidator of a company, otherwise the appointment will have no effect.[4] If more than one liquidator is appointed to a company, the court — or the meeting — which appointed them must decide whether certain acts are to be done by one or all of the liquidators.[5] For the first time in Irish law, a person must be qualified to act as the liquidator of a company. This is not something that should cause insolvency practitioners who are not qualified any concern as anybody who has "practical experience of windings-up and knowledge of the relevant law" may simply pay a fee to the Irish Auditing and Accounting Supervisory Authority which will issue a certificate deeming them qualified.[6] Depending on the form of the liquidation, the liquidator, having furnished particulars of costs, will agree his fees with the committee of inspection, the creditors (in a creditors' voluntary winding-up where there is no committee of inspection), the members in a general meeting (in a members' voluntary winding-up).

---

[1] Companies Act 2014, s 624(1).

[2] *ibid*, s 624(2).

[3] *ibid*, s 625(2); this is subject to s 621, which deals with the preferential payments in a winding-up.

[4] Companies Act 2014 s 639; also note that it is a category 2 offence for a person to bribe a member or creditor of the company to secure appointment as a liquidator (*per* s 642).

[5] Companies Act 2014, s 640.

[6] *ibid*, s 633(5); the new rule does not affect any liquidator or liquidation commenced prior to 1 June 2015 (the commencement date of Companies Act 2014). s 634 sets out the indemnity cover requirements. s 635 states the prohibition on officers of the company acting as the company's liquidators, and the rule that no connected person may act as the company's liquidator without the leave of the court.

Provisional Liquidators

The duties of a *provisional* liquidator will be set out in the court order appointing him, which is a change from the old regime, where the provisional liquidator's powers were the same as a liquidator's, except where qualified or curtailed by the court.[7] The new position is that the provisional liquidator should have as little impact as possible on the running of the company. It is quite possible that a court could make the order that the provisional liquidator's powers are the same as a liquidator's, thus retaining the status quo. Section 262(2) gives the court power to limit or restrict the powers of any officers of the company upon the appointment of a provisional liquidator. An application to appoint a provisional liquidator can be made at any time after the presentation of the winding-up petition. The usual reason for appointing one is fear that between the presentation of the petition and the appointment of the official liquidator the assets of the company may be spirited away, or an unfair preference made to one creditor. A provisional liquidator is usually only appointed where the danger is quite clear, because the appointment of a provisional liquidator is "intrinsically detrimental".[8] This being the case, the applicant has to swear up to his version of events on affidavit.[9] The remuneration of the provisional liquidator is fixed by the court.[10]

---

[7] Companies Act 2014, s 624(3); see also s 559(3) to (5) which states that references to "liquidator" in the winding-up part of Companies Act 2014 may be read as references to a provisional liquidator. See also s 626.

[8] This is the phrase used in *Re a company (No 002180 of 1996)* [1996] 2 BCLC 409. In that case the two shareholders swore on oath that the company was suffering detriment as a result of the appointment and Knox J said, at p. 415, "that does seem to me to be an intrinsically probable state of affairs." A provisional liquidator may also be appointed to a solvent company where there is deadlock between the shareholders and a winding up petition is in view (*Re Tradalco Ltd* [2001] IEHC 89).

[9] For an unusual situation, where a construction company sought permission to keep a provisional liquidator in place, and never have him converted into an official liquidator, but instead have him act like an open-ended examiner, see *Re Coolfadda Developers Ltd* [2009] IEHC 263 & [2009] IESC 54. For circumstances that were deemed exceptional – i.e. where the provisional liquidator would be allowed to remain in place – see *MHMH Ltd v Carwood Barker Holdings Ltd* [2006] 1 BCLC 279.

[10] Companies Act 2014, s 645.

Liquidator's Powers

While the liquidator may apply to court for directions concerning the exercise of his powers,[11] the liquidator's powers are set out with clarity in s 627 of Companies Act 2014. Among the most notable are powers:

1. To take into his or her custody or under his or her control all the property to which the company is or appears to be entitled;
2. To dispose of perishable goods and other goods the value of which is likely to diminish if they are not immediately disposed of;
3. To "do all such other things as may be necessary" for the protection of the company's property;
4. To bring and defend any legal proceedings in the name of the company (including the power to give security for costs in any proceedings);
5. To recommence and carry on the business of the company "so far as may be necessary for the beneficial winding up thereof";
6. To obtain credit, whether on the security of the property of the company or otherwise;
7. To make any compromise or arrangement with creditors of the company;
8. To sell the property of the company by public auction or private contract.[12]

The liquidator may summon meetings — general meetings, meeting of the creditors, meetings of the committee of inspection, if there is one — for the purpose of obtaining any necessary resolutions.[13] No person is entitled to claims a lien of any of the books or documents belonging to the company.[14] The liquidator has the power to compel the company's banker to "pay, deliver, convey, surrender or transfer to or into the hands of" the liquidator any money, property, books or papers which happen to be in its hands and to which the company is *prima facie* entitled.[15]

---

[11] Companies Act 2014, s 631; so too may any creditor, any contributory, and the Director of Corporate Enforcement (DCE).

[12] For the notice periods that attach to the use of some of these powers, see s 629.

[13] Companies Act 2014, s 628.

[14] *ibid*, s 632.

[15] *ibid*, s 673(1).

A liquidator is prohibited from selling non-cash assets of the company to any person who was an officer of the company within three years prior to the winding-up, unless the liquidator gives at least 14 days' notice of his intention to do so to all creditors of the company who are known to the liquidator or who have been intimated to the liquidator.[16] This rule does not apply in the case of a members' voluntary winding-up, if the proposed transaction receives the assent of a majority in number and value of the members of the company: it does not apply in the case of a winding-up by the court or a creditors' voluntary winding up if the committee of inspection gives its assent, or if there is no committee, if a majority in number and value of the creditors of the company give their assent.[17]

What Happens in Practice?

When a liquidator is appointed, the directors cease to be directors (they are *functus officio*). What happens to the employees? They are automatically dismissed.[18] The official liquidator can choose to keep all or some of them on, but the legal position is automatic dismissal.[19] The following is representative of the steps in a liquidation which is court-supervised. The matter will appear in the chancery list. When the court makes the winding-up order it is adjourned to the list known as the examiner's list. It will keep appearing in this list until the final orders are made and the liquidation is finished. Unless there are no assets in the liquidation, the court will ask the liquidator to give a form of security, the purpose of this being the protection of the creditors.[20] The court may at that point also fix his remuneration, which ranks as a cost in the liquidation,[21] but what is usually done is the liquidator makes interim applications for fees. There is no set scale for fees, though the court will be conscious of the economic

---

[16] *ibid*, s 629(3) and (4); for the meaning of non-cash asset and "requisite value" see s 238 (Chapter 6).

[17] Companies Act 2014, s 629(9); for a case concerning a conflict between potential bidders for assets in a liquidation, see *Re Buzreel Ltd* [2014] IESC 45 (Clarke J, 16 July 2014), citing *Re Hibernian Transport Companies Ltd* [1972] 1 IR 190 and *Van Hool McArdle Ltd v Rohan Industrial Estates Ltd* [1980] 1 IR 237.

[18] This doesn't happen automatically when a provisional liquidator is appointed: it is only automatic upon the appointment of an official liquidator.

[19] See *Evan Henry Ltd*, Unreported, High Court, Murphy J, 15 May 1996.

[20] The court orders an indemnity in the form of a bond.

[21] Rules of the Superior Courts, Ord 74, r 46.

climate.[22] The liquidator may apply to court for directions at any point (this is a way of saying that he has come up against some unusual or unexpected legal issue, and needs the court to rule on it so he can continue with the liquidation[23]). The liquidator must draw up a preliminary report. It will go through all the basics: what the assets and liabilities of the company are, why things went wrong, if he thinks there was reckless and fraudulent trading, and so on. Once he is appointed, the liquidator must publish a notice to this effect in the CRO Gazette within 21 days.[24]

The liquidator may fix a time (or times) within which creditors must prove their debts or claims, failing which they will be excluded from the benefit of any distribution made before those debts or claims are proved.[25] The liquidator must write to the creditors, notifying them of this and the time cannot be earlier than 28 days after the day on which the creditors are notified of the fixed time. Creditors may apply to court seeking an extension of the time period.[26]

Removal of Liquidator

A liquidator may resign from his office at any time, and if he does so, must give notice to the CRO and the DCE and other relevant parties.[27] If it is a question of *removing* a liquidator, the following procedures apply. Where the liquidator is court appointed the court may remove him and appoint a replacement "on cause shown".[28] The court can do this of its own motion, or on the application of a member, creditor, liquidator or the DCE.

Where the liquidation is a members' voluntary winding-up the company may remove the liquidator at a general meeting convened for that purpose.[29] This meeting may be convened by any member with the written

---

[22] The reasoning of a number of remuneration rulings in examinerships is thought to apply: see *Re Missford Ltd* [2010] 3 IR 756; *Re Sharmane Ltd* [2009] 4 IR 285, *Re ESG Reinsurance Ireland Ltd* [2010] IEHC 365; and *Re Marino Ltd* [2010] IEHC 394.

[23] See *Re JD Brian Ltd* [2012] 1 ILRM 27 as an example of this.

[24] For a case where a foreign liquidator — appointed by the Eastern Caribbean Supreme Court — to a company was recognised in Ireland, see *Fairfield Sentry Ltd v Citco Bank Nederland NV* [2012] IEHC 81 (Finlay Geoghegan J).

[25] Companies Act 2014, s 674(1).

[26] Companies Act 2014, s 674(4); this must be done on notice to the liquidator.

[27] As set out in Companies Act 2014, s 641.

[28] Companies Act 2014, s 638(1).

[29] *ibid*, s 636(2).

authority of not less than one-tenth in number of the members, and a minimum of 10 days' notice should be given to the other members.

Where the liquidation is a creditors' voluntary winding-up the creditors may remove the liquidator at a meeting convened for that purpose, if the majority (in value only) of the creditors pass a resolution to do so. Any creditor of the company with the written authority of not less than one-tenth in value of the creditors may convene such a meeting and a minimum of 10 days' notice should be given to the other creditors.[30]

PART II: LIQUIDATIONS

Introduction to the Winding-up of Companies

The winding-up of a company may be done voluntarily or may be done by the court.[31] In contrast to the old system, the Companies Act 2014 seeks to move the emphasis away from court-ordered liquidations, to place them on the same footing as creditors' voluntary windings-up once the order for the winding-up has been made. The idea is to increase the involvement of creditors and reduce the involvement of the court. The voluntary winding-up of a company may be done in accordance with the Summary Approval Procedure. It may be done by the members[32] or, if there is a bar to the members doing it, by the creditors.[33] There are three possible obstacles to the members voluntarily winding the company up. They are: (1) where there is default in making the declaration required by the SAP; (2) if, on the basis that the creditor believes the company will be unable to pay its debts within the period stated in the SAP declaration, a creditor successfully applies to court to convert a members' voluntary winding-up to a creditors voluntary winding up[34]; (3) if the liquidator believes the company will be unable to pay its debts within the period stated in the SAP declaration and he summons a creditors meeting, and the winding-up becomes a creditors' voluntary winding-up.

[30] *ibid*, s 637.
[31] Companies Act 2014, s 561; practitioners should now refer to the new Ord 74 in the Rules of the Superior Courts, which came into being on 1 July 2015 by virtue of SI No 255 of 2015.
[32] Companies Act 2014, s 579.
[33] The three bars are set out in s 562(1)(a).
[34] See Companies Act 2014, s 582(2).

Winding-Up by Court

Section 569 states that a company may be wound-up by the court:

(a) If the company has by special resolution resolved that the company be wound up by the court;

(b) If the company does not commence its business within a year after the date of its incorporation or suspends its business for a continuous period of 12 months;

(c) If the members of the company are all deceased or no longer exist;

(d) If the company is unable to pay its debts;

(e) If the court is of the opinion that it is just and equitable that the company should be wound-up;

(f) If the court is satisfied that the company's affairs are being conducted, or the powers of the directors are being exercised, in a manner oppressive to any member or in disregard of his or her interests as a member and that, despite the existence of an alternative remedy, winding-up would be justified in the general circumstances of the case[35] (but this rule is subject to the court having the opinion that s 212 proceedings would be more appropriate);

(g) If the court is satisfied, on a petition of the Director of Corporate Enforcement, that it is in the public interest that the company should be wound up (this is new); or

(h) If an examiner is not able to secure agreement or formulate proposals for compromise or scheme of arrangement[36]; if a court refuses to confirm proposals of a scheme of arrangement; or if an examiner's report states that it hasn't been possible to reach agreement on a compromise or scheme of arrangement.[37]

Winding-Up under Section 569(d) — Inability to Pay Debts

Of the above, s 569(d) is the most common. Section 570 of Companies Act 2014 provides that a company is deemed to be unable to pay its debts:

---

[35] A petition on this ground can be brought by a member of the company or the personal representative of a deceased member.

[36] See Companies Act 2014, s 535.

[37] Winding up provided for by s 542(5).

(a) if— (i) a creditor...to whom the company is indebted in a sum exceeding €10,000 then due,[38] has served on the company (by leaving it at the registered office of the company) a demand in writing requiring the company to pay the sum so due, and (ii) the company has, for 21 days after the date of the service of that demand, neglected to pay the sum or to secure or compound for it to the reasonable satisfaction of the creditor,

or

(b) if— (i) 2 or more creditors...to whom, in aggregate, the company is indebted in a sum exceeding €20,000 then due, have served on the company (by leaving it at the registered office of the company[39]) a demand in writing requiring the company to pay the sum so due, and (ii) the company has, for 21 days after the date of the service of that demand, neglected to pay the sum or to secure or compound for it to the reasonable satisfaction of each of the creditors,

or

(c) if execution or other process issued on a judgment, decree or order of any court in favour of a creditor of the company is returned unsatisfied in whole or in part, or

(d) if it is proved to the satisfaction of the court that the company is unable to pay its debts, and in determining whether a company is unable to pay its debts, the court shall take into account the contingent and prospective liabilities of the company.

Once the sum owed exceeds €10,000, there is no point arguing that, for example, with regard to an alleged debt of €1m only €20,000 is in fact owed: this was the scenario in *Meridian Communications v Eircell Ltd*[40] and McGuinness J said

"it seems extremely unlikely that what purports to be a debt of some millions of pounds could be reduced below the

---

[38] Note that Companies Act 2014 increased the old minimum indebtedness threshold from €1,269.74 to €10,000.

[39] For an unsuccessful challenge to a petition on the grounds that it was not received at he company's registered office, see *Re BCON Communications Ltd* [2012] IEHC 362 (Laffoy J, 22 August 2012).

[40] Unreported, Supreme Court, McGuinness J, 10 May 2001., The Supreme Court endorsed the headnote in *Truck and Machinery Sales Limited v Marubeni Komatsu* [1996] 1 IR 12, a High Court decision of Keane J, and that is still an extremely helpful starting point for the principles relevant to these applications.

[minimum threshold as set out in statute][41]…or even anything near that figure."

Unsurprisingly, given the gravity of the remedy, a demand for money owing must be made with the utmost clarity, and without conditions. The debt should be absolutely clear. It would not be enough, for example, to say that a debt will fall due on the happening of some event which probably will occur soon. If a debt is disputed, the court will have to be concerned that there is a possibility it is not actually owed at all.[42]

The process cannot be used for an ulterior motive. In *Re A Company*[43] the real object of the petition was to force an agreement on costs: this was found to be an abuse of process. In *Re Goode Concrete*[44] the ulterior motive was a desire to stymie an action the company intended to take against the petitioner. The first thing the court will ask, when a petitioner comes looking for relief, and no one appears for the company, is whether the company was properly served with the letter. Older decisions said that a demand by fax or by telex was not proper service.[45] There doesn't seem to be a case on whether or not a demand letter sent by email could constitute good service. The statute is clear, if old-fashioned in this regard, that the letter should be "left at the registered office of the company". If there is any dispute about the debt then the presentation of a petition to wind-up is not appropriate: the right thing to do is litigate the debt in plenary proceedings. The presentation of a petition involves advertising it at least seven days before the hearing.[46] This can have the most serious consequences for a company and to protect companies there is the tort of "malicious presentation of a winding-up petition".[47] If a petition is presented where it is known that there is a genuine dispute over the debt the petitioner will be committing an abuse of process and costs will be awarded accordingly. In normal circumstances, the costs of the petitioner are payable ahead of all the other costs in the liquidation.

---

[41] The minimum threshold of indebtedness is now €10,000.

[42] See, for example, *Re Forrest Lennon Business Support Services* [2011] IEHC 523.

[43] [1998] 2 BCLC 111.

[44] [2012] IEHC 439.

[45] *Re a Company* [1985] BCLC 37, approved by Murphy J in *Re WMG (Toughening) Ltd* [2001] 3 IR 113.

[46] Once in Iris Ofigiuil and once at least in two Dublin daily morning newspapers; see Ord 74, r 7 of the Rules of the Superior Courts.

[47] See *Partizan Ltd v OJ Kilkenny and Co Ltd* [1998] 1 BCLC 451.

The test to be applied in winding-up applications under s 569(d) is well settled.[48] The court will not make an order where the debt in question is *bona fide* disputed (this can lead companies convincing themselves that their debt over the debt is *bona fide*, where the court may simply conclude that such contentions are no more than "smoke and mirrors"; see *Re R.E.P. Ltd*[49]) The court will ask whether the company's claim is in good faith and on substantial grounds. O'Hanlon J said in *Re Pageboy Couriers Ltd*[50]:

> "if the company in good faith and on substantial grounds disputes any liability in respect of the alleged debt, the petition will be dismissed, or if the matter is brought before a court before the petition is issued, its presentation will in normal circumstances be restrained. That is because a winding up petition is not a legitimate means of seeking to enforce payment of a debt which is bona fide disputed."[51]

The court does not ask itself whether the petitioner

> "will succeed in its claim, but whether it is a *bona fide* dispute which should be determined by the courts in the normal way without putting the company's existence at risk."[52]

These issues of fact usually fall to be determined by a court on affidavit evidence, something which Laffoy J has said is "almost invariably…not an easy task, and…frequently…an impossible task".[53] It appears to be the case in many of these applications that the affidavits are replete with "statements which are more akin to advocacy than proven fact".[54] This tends to be of very little assistance to the court and the advice in Odgers — which could be mistaken for Hemingway — should be borne in mind:

---

[48] Previously s 213(e) of Companies Act 1963.

[49] [2012] IEHC 392; for an example of an argument against winding up which failed, because it what was being sought was really an examinership, see *Re Heatsolve Ltd* [2013] IEHC 399 (Hogan J, 9 September 2013).

[50] [1983] ILRM 510.

[51] *Re Pageboy Couriers Ltd* [1983] ILRM 510 at 512; O'Hanlon J expressly adopted *Stonegate Securities v Gregory* [1980] Ch 576 and *Mann v Goldstein* [1968] 1 WLR 1091. Clarke J approved *Pageboy Couriers* in *Re Emerald Portable Building Systems* [2005] IEHC 301.

[52] Per McCracken J, *Re WGM (Toughening) Ltd (No 2)* [2003] 1 IR 389 at 392.

[53] *Re Kasam Investments Ireland* [2012] IEHC 553 at para 5.

[54] For example, see *Re Forrest Lennon Business Support Services* [2011] IEHC 523 at para 2.12.

"Facts should be alleged as facts. Terse, short, curt, blunt
sentences, all in the indicative mood, should be used."[55]

A question follows from the above: what is a court to do when faced with
diametrically opposed affidavits, when no one is asked to give oral
evidence? The effect is they cancel each other out when allegations are
"credibly denied".[56] McCarthy J stated in *Re Bula Ltd*[57] that the statute
"gives to the court a true discretion which should be exercised in a
principled manner that is fair and just".[58] The court is not compelled to
accede to a petition, even in the face of the proofs, though it will only
refrain from doing so where the debtor company shows good cause.

In *Re Kasam* Laffoy stated that the two versions of what had been agreed
were "diametrically opposed": "however, it has to be acknowledged that
there is nothing implausible about the company's version."[59] She had no
doubt that the company had met the *Pageboy Couriers/ WGM (Toughening)*[60]
test (that is that the company was disputing the time the money became
payable "in good faith and on substantial grounds"). The parties all agreed
there had been an oral agreement, but there simply was not enough
evidence before the court with regard to the circumstances of repayment,
and so the petition had to be dismissed.

If a petitioner brings a winding-up petition for an ulterior motive the
petition will be dismissed and costs may be awarded against the
petitioner.[61] The court's discretion to refuse an order to wind the company

---

[55] *Odgers on Civil Court Actions* (24th ed, by Simon Goulding, London Sweet & Maxwell, 1996)
at para 7.52.
[56] Per Lord Templeman, *Tay Bok Choon v Tahansan* [1987] BCLC 472 at 476: "If allegations are
made in affidavits by the petitioner and those allegations are credibly denied by the respondent's affidavits, then in the absence of oral evidence or cross-examination, the judge
must ignore the disputed allegations."
[57] [1990] IR 440.
[58] *Re Bula Ltd* [1990] 1 IR 440 at 448; approved in *Re Genport Ltd,* Unreported, High Court,
McCracken J, 21 November 1996.
[59] *Re Kasam Investments Ireland* [2012] IEHC 553 at para 27.
[60] [2001] 3 IR 113.
[61] See *Re Genport Ltd,* Unreported, High Court, McCracken J, 21 November 1996,); McCracken
J did not dismiss the petition. He put a stay on it pending the outcome of the litigation
between the parties. See also *Re Bula Ltd* [1990] IR 440. In *Re US Ltd* [2012] IEHC 600
(Murphy J, 29 November 2012) it was argued that the Revenue had "essentially bullied"
the company into making a settlement, but the court found that there was no substance to
this and wound the company up.

up, where the proofs are in order and there is no improper conduct, will only be exercised "sparingly and where good cause is shown".[62]

Section 569(d) and Cross-Claims

A cross-claim "must be genuine and serious or if you prefer, one of substance…it must be…in an amount exceeding the amount of the petitioner's debt".[63] Secondly, it must be "closely related to the petition debt. If it is, the Court will allow one to be set off against the other…[this] may have the practical effect of eliminating the petition debt".[64] For example, in *Re Goode Concrete*[65] the cross-claim was genuine and serious, was on substantial grounds and was "unquestionably closely related to the petition debt", which it dwarfed: in those circumstances it was a just a fair exercise of the court's discretion to dismiss the petition.[66]

Winding-Up under Section 569(e) — Just and Equitable Grounds

The courts have stated that s 569(e) "should only be engaged in the most intractable of situations".[67] The most common scenario which presents under the "just and equitable" grounds is the breakdown of a quasi-partnership type company. The idea of a "quasi-partnership" is a strange one because we are talking about a company and not a partnership. Why should it matter that a company has the look and feel of a partnership? At law, it is not a partnership. No judge has given a satisfactory answer to this question,[68] other than to say that where the qualities of "equality, mutuality, trust and confidence"[69] are present in a company, and have

---

[62] *Re La Plagne Ltd* [2012] 1 ILRM 203.

[63] *Per* Nourse LJ in *Re Bayoil SA* [1999] 1 All ER 374 approved by Clarke J in *Re Emerald Portable Building Systems Ltd* [2005] IEHC 301.

[64] *Per* Laddie J, *Re VP Developments Ltd* [2005] 2 BCLC 607 at 616.

[65] [2012] IEHC 439.

[66] *Re Goode Concrete* [2012] IEHC 439 at para 31; for a contrast, see *Re Mi-Zone Technology Ireland* [2013] IEHC 97.

[67] *Per* Charleton J, in *Re Fuerta Ltd* [2014] IEHC 12 at para 7.

[68] See the comments of Murphy J in *Crindle Investments v Wymes*[1998] 4 IR 567 at 576; Lord Wilberforce stated in *Ebrahimi*: "there is room in company law for recognition of the fact that behind [the legal entity], or amongst it, there are individuals, with rights, expectations and obligations inter se which are not necessarily submerged in the company structure." But he also said, (at 380b): "one should not press the quasi partnership analogy too far: a company, however small, however domestic, is a company not a partnership or even a quasi partnership."

[69] See the comments of Keane J in *McGilligan v O'Grady* [1999] 1 ILRM 303 at 343.

been lost: that is a situation where it is just and equitable for the courts to wind the company up. The jurisprudence begins in the 1970s: as usual the reasoning in an English case (*Ebrahimi v Westbourne Galleries Ltd*[70]) is wholly adopted in an Irish case (*Re Murph's Restaurants Ltd*[71]). In Ebrahimi the petitioner had gone into business on equal terms with a Mr Nazar but, after Mr Nazar's son became a shareholding director, Ebrahimi was excluded from the business. This entitlement to participation in the management was "an obligation so basic that, if broken, the conclusion must be that the association must be dissolved".[72] The relationship of equality, mutuality, trust and confidence, present from the beginning, had been repudiated, and this provided just grounds for winding-up the company. The same conclusion was reached in *Re Murph's Restaurants*, where two brothers combined against a former friend who was their business partner; the conduct of the brothers was, Gannon J found, "a deliberate and calculated repudiation" of the underlying relationship of trust and confidence. It is important that the business relationship should have been entered into on this equal basis from the start, that, for example,

> "two entrepreneurs [are] setting off to pursue a dream using the vehicle of a company as an expedience to secure limited liability or tax advantages, where the real nature of the relationship [is] more in the nature of a partnership."[73]

Further grounds for winding-up under s 569(e) are the so-called deadlock cases. *Re Yenidje Tobacco Co*[74] is an early example of this: two tobacco kings combined their businesses but soon fell out to the extent that communication between them had to take place through the company secretary. The English Court of Appeal, in winding-up the company, stated that it was not necessary

> "in order to induce the Court to interfere, to show personal rudeness on the part of one partner to the other, or even any gross misconduct as a partner. All that is necessary is to satisfy the Court that it is impossible for the partners to place that confidence in each other which each has a right to expect, and

---

[70] [1973] AC 360.
[71] [1979] ILRM 141.
[72] [1973] AC 360.
[73] Per Binchy J, *Hamill v Vantage Resources Ltd & Martin* [2015] IEHC 195, at para 74.
[74] [1916] 2 Ch 426.

that such impossibility has not been caused by the person seeking to take advantage of it."[75]

This was approved by Murphy J in *Re Vehicle Buildings and Insulations Ltd*,[76] who stated that where there was "equality of shareholding and equality of management and a complete unwillingness of each party to co-operate with each other" the onus shifted to the respondent to show some way of resolving the situation.[77] In *Vehicle Buildings* the only thing the two parties could agree on was that the dispute between them was "both comprehensive and irreversible" and so it was just and equitable to wind-up the company.[78]

Breakdown of a quasi-partnership company or deadlock are not the only "just and equitable grounds", but they are the most common.[79] In *Re Fuerta Ltd* Charleton J noted that "the notion of serious irregularity within a company can serve as fertile ground for the expansion of the traditional categories for the use of the just and equitable ground to wind up a company"[80] and wound a company up for persistent failure to file annual returns, and where there was total "stasis" in the company which made it impossible for the creditor to realise its security.

Locus Standi and Section 569

The following parties have *locus standi* to apply for the winding-up of a company: the company itself, any creditor, any contributory[81] (or all of

---

[75] *Re Yenidje Tobacco Co* [1916] 2 Ch 426 at 430.

[76] [1986] ILRM 239.

[77] In *Re Vehicle Buildings and Insulations Ltd* [1986] ILRM 239 at 242.

[78] See also *Re Tradalco Ltd*, Unreported, High Court, 9 May 2001, where Lavan J cited *Re Yenidje Tobacco Co* [1916] 2 Ch 426, and said that principle was applied by Kenny J in *Re Irish Tourist Promotions*, Unreported, High Court, 22 April 1974) and Murphy J in *Re Vehicle Buildings*. In the UK case law see *Re Internet Investment Corp Ltd* [2010] 1 BCLC 458, *Re Worldhams Park Golf Course Ltd* [1998] 1 BCLC 554 and *Tay Bok Choon v Tahansan* [1987] BCLC 472.

[79] In *Re Fuerta Ltd* [2014] IEHC 12 Charleton J notes that other grounds are cases in which the company was promoted fraudulently; cases in which the company's substratum has gone; cases in which there is a constitutional and administrative vacuum; cases in which the management and conduct of the company are such that it is unjust and inequitable to require the petitioner to continue as a member.

[80] [2014] IEHC 12 at para 3, citing *Dublin & Eastern Regional Tourism Organisation Ltd* [1990] 1 IR 579.

[81] The court will not hear a winding-up petition presented by a contingent or prospective creditor until such security for costs has been given as the court thinks reasonable, and

these together or separately). On the hearing of the petition the court may make any order it thinks fit.[82] It will be no defence to a petition to say that the company should not be wound-up because it has no assets, or to say that the assets of the company have been mortgaged to an amount equal to or in excess of its assets.[83] If a petitioner decides not to go ahead with the petition, that may not be the end of the matter for the company: the court has the power to substitute as petitioner any person who would have a right to present a petition in relation to the company, and who wishes to proceed with the petition.[84] If the petition is brought on the grounds of s 569(1)(a), (b), (c), (e) or (f) then the court may order that the company be wound-up as if it were a members' voluntary winding-up.[85] In terms of changes to the winding-up regime brought about by Companies Act 2014, this is one of the biggest. The role of the court is pared back: once the order to wind-up has been made, the process becomes more like that of a creditors' voluntary winding-up. The balance of involvement is altered: the court's is reduced, the creditors' is increased. This may become the standard practice in all cases other that those where the DCE is petitioning under s 569(g), where the petition arises out of a failed bid for examinership, under s 569(h), or where a creditor has sought to wind-up a company on the grounds of inability to pay debts, under s 569(d).

In court-supervised liquidations, the court may have regard to the wishes of the creditors of the company[86]: when considered the case of a creditor, it will have regard to the value of the creditor's debt. An order for the winding-up of a company operates in favour of all the creditors and of all the contributories of the company, as if it had been made on the joint petition of a creditor and of a contributory.[87]

---

until a *prima facie* case for winding up has been established to the satisfaction of the court (s 571(2)); see also s 571(5). For a case where a fully paid-up shareholder sought to petition see *Re Connemara Mining Co* [2013] 1 IR 661 (Laffoy J).

[82] 572(1); for its discretion to restrain the proceedings *after* the petition has been presented, see s 574; for an example of the court reading the sections of this part of the Act together, see *Re Dublin Cinema Group Ltd* [2013] IEHC 147 (High Court, Charleton J, 25 March 2013).

[83] Companies Act 2014, s 572(1).

[84] *ibid*, s 572(5).

[85] *ibid*, s 572(4).

[86] Companies Act 2014, s 566(1); in the case of contributories, the court will have regard to the number of votes conferred on each contributory by the constitution of the company.

[87] Companies Act 2014, s 576.

Members' Voluntary Winding-Up

A company may be wound up voluntarily as a members' voluntary winding-up.[88] As a general rule, a members' voluntary winding-up must be commenced using the Summary Approval Procedure (the CRO's "E1 SAP" Form must be used). The exceptions to this general rule are in cases where a company's constitution fixes a date for the company's expiry, or where the company's constitution provides that the company should dissolve upon the occurrence of some specific event: in those two cases there is an alternative to the SAP, though the alternative bears similarities to the SAP.[89] Where a company has passed a resolution for its voluntary winding-up it must give notice of the resolution by advertisement in *Iris Oifigiúil* within 14 days after the date of the passing of the resolution (and failure to do so is a category 3 offence for the company and any defaulting officer, including the liquidator).[90] The company, in a general meeting, appoints one or more liquidators to wind-up the affairs and distribute the assets of the company.[91] The Companies Act 2014 seeks to protect creditors where a company has passed a resolution to wind up voluntarily. The danger is that declarations as to the company's solvency will be made falsely or irresponsibly and the creditors would be left in difficulty. Section 582 allows creditors to apply to court to have the winding-up converted to a creditors' voluntary winding-up, provided the application is made within 30 days after the date on which the resolution for voluntary winding-up of the company has been advertised.[92] Further to this, s 584 imposes a duty on the liquidator to call a creditors' meeting if he is of the opinion that the company will not be able to pay its debts in full within the period stated in the s 207 declaration. Section 210 of Companies Act 2014 imposes civil sanctions for persons who, without reasonable grounds, express a positive opinion as to the solvency of the company in the required declaration.

---

[88] *ibid*, s 579(1).
[89] *ibid*, s 597(2) and (3), which lead to the procedure outlined in s 580; the *E1 (41)* Form should be used.
[90] Companies Act 2014, s 581(1).
[91] *ibid*, s 583.
[92] *ibid*, s 582(3).

Creditors' Voluntary Winding-Up

A company may be wound-up voluntarily as a creditors' voluntary winding-up.[93] This can be initiated by the company in a general meeting: the company passes a resolution stating that it cannot continue its business by reason of its liabilities, and that it be wound-up as a creditors' voluntary winding-up. In such cases, the company must give notice of the resolution by advertisement in *Iris Oifigiúil* within 14 days after the date of the passing of the resolution (failure to do so is a category 3 offence for the company, any defaulting officer, and the liquidator).[94] Alternatively, a members' voluntary winding-up can be converted to a creditors' voluntary winding-up, either upon the application of a creditor to court (under s 582(2)) or as the result of a meeting called by the liquidator who doubts the solvency of the company to which he has been appointed by the members (s 584).[95]

If the company is resolving to wind-up as a creditors voluntary liquidation it must call a creditors' meeting for either the day where the resolution to wind up is to be proposed, or for the day after that.[96] Each creditor should receive notice of the creditors' meeting at least 10 days in advance. The notice should be in writing, sent by the company.[97] The company must advertise the notice of this meeting at least once in two daily newspapers circulating in the district where the registered office or principal place of business of the company is situate: this must be done at least 10 days before the date of the meeting but does not have to include the list of the company's creditors.[98] At the creditors' meeting the directors of the company must ensure that a full statement of the position of the company's affairs is laid before the meeting, together with a list of the creditors and

---

[93] *ibid*, s 586(1).

[94] *ibid*, s 586(4) and (5).

[95] Further to this, in cases where the special SAP resolution or the ordinary s 580 resolution are purportedly passed but the required declaration is not made correctly, the winding up may be converted to a creditors' winding up)s 586 (3)(c)).

[96] Companies Act 2014, s 587(1); it is essential that the company first resolves to put the company into creditors' voluntary liquidation, otherwise the creditors' meeting can not be properly convened, as the applicants found out in *Bergin v Lost Weekend Ltd* [2012] IEHC 552 (Laffoy J, 18 December 2012).

[97] Companies Act 2014, s 587(2); see also 587(3) for the information which should be included in the notice. The notice requirements are the only new elements; the rest derives from s 266 of Companies Act 1963.

[98] Companies Act 2014, s 587(6).

the estimated amount of their claims. The board must appoint one director to preside at the creditors' meeting and it is his duty to attend the creditors' meeting and preside at it.[99]

The creditors will nominate a liquidator at the creditors' meeting.[100] The resolution proposing a liquidator shall be deemed to be passed when a majority (in value only) of the creditors present (personally or by proxy, and voting on the resolution) have voted in favour of the resolution.[101] If the creditors and the company nominate different persons, the person nominated by the creditors prevails.[102] If the liquidator nominated by the company has already taken office by the time the creditors' nominate a liquidator, the company's liquidator must vacate that office.[103] In case of a conflict over who will be liquidator, which cannot be resolved amicably, the Companies Act 2014 provides that any director, member or creditor of the company may, within 14 days after the date on which the nomination was made by the creditors, apply to the court for an order either: (a) directing that the person nominated as liquidator by the company shall be liquidator instead of or jointly with the person nominated by the creditors; or (b) appointing some other person to be liquidator instead of the person nominated by the creditors.[104] Further to this, the voluntary winding-up of a company does not bar the right of any creditor or contributory to have it wound-up by the court.[105]

---

[99] Companies Act 2014, s 587(7); if the company has one sole director, he is obliged to attend the creditors' meeting. Default in compliance with any of the requirements in s 587 is a category 3 offence.

[100] Companies Act 2014, s 588(1); strict compliance with all notice requirements, and the requirements relating to proxies should, should be made, to strengthen the appointment of the creditor's liquidator against later attack (Re Hayes Homes Ltd [2004] IEHC 253), but the court will sometimes exercise its discretion to protect the creditors, as it did in Re Managh International Transport Ltd [2012] IEHC 444 (Ryan J, 30 October 2012).

[101] Companies Act 2014, s 588(6).

[102] ibid, s 588(2)(a); also, the liquidator may have regard to the wishes of the creditors and the contributories, in administering the company's property, but if there is any conflict between the two the directions given by the creditors override those of the contributories and the directions (see s 687(2)).

[103] Companies Act 2014, s 588(3).

[104] ibid, s 588(4) and (5).

[105] ibid, s 577.

Conduct of Winding-Up

A court-ordered winding-up commences at the time of the presentation of the winding-up petition in respect of the company.[106] The effect of this rule is that any transactions that took place after the petition was presented, and before the order was made by the court, will be avoided. If the company passes a resolution to wind the company up voluntary, the winding-up is deemed to have commenced from the date of that resolution even if a petition to wind the company up is subsequently presented to the court.[107] A voluntary winding-up is deemed to commence at the time of the passing of the resolution for voluntary winding-up.[108]

When a winding-up order is made by the court, the court will direct an officer of the court — e.g. the liquidator — to furnish the CRO with the particulars of the order (the CRO's E2 Form should be used).[109] When a liquidator is appointed by the court, one or more of the directors[110] must cause a statement of the company's affairs to be created and swear to its accuracy on affidavit.[111] This must be filed within 21 days (of the making of the winding-up order) unless there are "special reasons" why the court might allow longer. The Companies Act 2014 imposes a duty on the directors — and other persons — who are involved in drawing up the statement of the company's affairs to provide the liquidator will all such information as he may "reasonably require" and give him all such assistance "as they are in a position to give" for the purpose of the liquidator's examining the company's affairs following his or her receipt of the statement.[112] Any person who is required to make or concur in making any statement of affairs must apply to the liquidator for the expenses which he believes he will incur in the helping to prepare the statement.[113] Only when the liquidator sanctions it, will such expenses be paid out of the assets of the company.[114]

---

[106] *ibid*, s 589(1).
[107] *ibid*, s 589(2).
[108] *ibid*, s 590.
[109] *ibid*, s 591(1); the notice requirements are set out in full in ss 591 and 592.
[110] The directors are the most likely candidates for this task, but s 593(4) lists alternatives.
[111] Companies Act 2014, s 593(1); what information must be contained in the statement of affairs is set out at s 593(2).
[112] Companies Act 2014, s 594(3); this duty does not extend to giving assistance, etc, to a provisional liquidator.
[113] Companies Act 2014, s 594(6).
[114] *ibid*, s 594(7).

Every invoice, order for goods or business letter issued by or on behalf of a company that is being wound up, or a liquidator of such a company, must contain a statement that the company is being wound-up.[115] The same applies to the company's website and e-mails.[116]

Winding-Up Not Irreversible

The commencement of a winding-up does not set in train an irreversible process. The court has the power, at any time after an order for winding-up is made, to annul the order for winding-up on such terms and conditions as it thinks fit.[117] Alternatively, the court has the power to make an order staying the proceedings, either altogether or for a limited time.[118]

Court's Power to Examine Persons

The court has the power to summon persons before it and examine them on oath as to matters relating to the company which is being wound-up.[119] Usually the liquidator makes such an application (the DCE and provisional liquidators are given standing, too). The person summoned does not have to have been an officer of the company. It can be "any person known or suspected to have in his or her possession any property of the company or supposed to be indebted to the company" or any person "whom the court deems capable of giving information relating to the (i) promotion or formation, (ii) trade or dealings, or (iii) affairs or property, of the company".[120] If it is just and equitable to do so, the court may direct that the costs of the examination be paid by the person examined. The court has extensive powers to require written statements to be made by the proposed examinee prior to his appearance in court. A person who is examined under s 671 is not entitled to refuse to answer any question put to him on the ground that his or her answer might incriminate him: any answer by the person to such a question may be used against that person in any proceedings (except proceedings for the prosecution of that person

---

[115] *ibid*, s 595(1).

[116] *ibid*, s 595(4); it is a category 3 offence not to comply with these rules.

[117] Companies Act 2014, s 669; this may be done following the application of the liquidator or any creditor or contributory, who proves to the court's satisfaction that to annul the order would be appropriate.

[118] Companies Act 2014, s 669(3).

[119] *ibid*, s 671.

[120] *ibid*, s 671(2).

for an offence other than perjury).[121] Failure to attend one's examination without reasonable excuse amounts to contempt of court.[122] If it appears to the court, in the course of an examination, that the person being examined is indebted to the company, or has in his or her possession or control any money, property or books and papers of the company, the court can order that person to pay to the liquidator the amount of the debt (or any part of it), or to convey whatever property of the company he has in his possession to the liquidator.[123]

Committee of Inspection

When a winding-up order is made by the court the liquidator has the option of calling a creditors meeting to determine whether or not a committee of inspection is to be appointed, and who the members will be if it is. This is a new option for the liquidator; he is obliged to do it, however, if directed to do so by a creditor or creditors representing not less than one-tenth in value of the creditors of the company.[124] Notice of the meeting should indicate who the proposed committee members are. The committee should consist of no more than five persons: a maximum of three can be added later (by being voted onto the committee at a general meeting — the maximum number on the committee should never exceed eight). Under the old system the liquidator had to make two applications to the court in order to appoint a committee of inspection.[125] These requirements have been abandoned in the interest of reducing the role of the court.

In the case of a creditors' voluntary winding-up the creditors should appoint the five at the creditors' meeting. Just as with the court-supervised winding-up, there is the option to appoint a further three members of the committee.[126]

---

[121] *ibid*, s 671(7).
[122] *ibid*, s 671(8).
[123] *ibid*, s 672(1); further to this the court can make search and seizure orders (s 672(2)). See also s 675, for arrest powers of officers, et al, who may be about to leave the jurisdiction.
[124] Companies Act 2014, s 666(1).
[125] Companies Act 1963, s 232.
[126] *ibid*, s 667(2).

A committee of inspection chooses when to meet (though the liquidator can call meetings of the committee "when he thinks necessary").[127] The committee may act by a majority of their members present at a meeting but must not act unless a majority of the committee is present. A member of the committee may resign by notice, in writing, signed by him or her and delivered to the liquidator. A person's office as member of the committee becomes vacant if the person is absent from two consecutive meetings of the committee without the leave of the other members.[128] The Companies Act 2014 makes provision for the removal of committee members by either the creditors or the company (depending on who appointed the committee): seven days' notice of the meeting must be given and a resolution must be passed removing the member.[129]

Distribution

Section 617(1) of Companies Act 2014 states that:

> All costs, charges and expenses properly incurred in the winding-up of a company, including the remuneration of the liquidator, remaining after payment of:
>
> (a)   the fees and expenses properly incurred in preserving, realising or getting in the assets, and
> (b)   where the company has previously commenced to be wound up voluntarily, such remuneration, costs and expenses as the court may allow to a liquidator appointed in such voluntary winding up,
>
> shall be payable out of the property of the company in priority to all other claims, and shall be paid or discharged in the order of priority [set out as follows]:
>
> (a)   First — In the case of a winding-up by the court, the costs of the petition, including the costs of any person appearing on the petition whose costs are allowed by the court;

---

[127] *ibid*, s 668(1).
[128] *ibid*, s 668(4)(b).
[129] *ibid*, s 668(5); for the purposes of s 668, at a meeting of creditors a resolution shall be deemed to be passed when *a majority in number* of the creditors present personally or by proxy and voting on the resolution have voted in favour of the resolution.

(b) Next — Any costs and expenses necessarily incurred in connection with the summoning, advertisement and holding of a creditors' meeting[130];

(c) Next — The costs and expenses necessarily incurred in the preparation and making of (or concurring in the making of) the statement of the company's affairs and the accompanying list of creditors and the amounts due to them[131];

(d) Next — The necessary disbursements of the liquidator (other than expenses properly incurred in preserving, realising or getting in the assets as provided [for in s 617(1) above]);

(e) Next — The costs payable to the solicitor for the liquidator;

(f) Next — The remuneration of the liquidator;

(g) Next — The out-of-pocket expenses necessarily incurred by the committee of inspection (if any).

Subject to the rules governing preferential payments, the property of a company on its winding-up must be applied in satisfaction of its liabilities *pari passu*.[132] Section 621 sets out the order of priority for preferential payments. All of the following debts rank equally among themselves and should be paid in full, unless the assets are insufficient to meet them, in which case they abate in equal proportions.[133] They have priority over the holders of floating charges, and can be paid out of any property comprised in or subject to that floating charge.[134] The preferential debts are as follows:

(a) Certain rates and taxes, such as local rates due from the company with the 12 months period of the commencement; certain taxes under the Taxes Consolidation Act 1997 and certain local property taxes;

---

[130] The creditors' meeting as provided for in s 587.
[131] See s 587(7).
[132] Companies Act 2014, s 618(1); s 619 re-enacts s 284 of Companies Act 1963, which provides that the bankruptcy rules apply in the winding up of insolvent companies in respect of (a) the respective rights of secured and unsecured creditors; (b) debts provable; (c) the valuation of annuities and future contingent liabilities (only the bankruptcy rules in relation to these three areas are imported into the Companies Act). On secured creditors, see the Bankruptcy Act 1988, Sch 1 para 24.
[133] Companies Act 2014, s 618(7)(a).
[134] *ibid*, s 618(7)(b).

(b) All wages or salary of any employee in respect of services rendered to the company during the period of four months before the commencement of the winding-up (though no claimant's claim may exceed €10,000, unless they are a "farm labourer", in which case they may be paid all the money due to them, if he entered into a contract for payment of a portion of his or her wages in a lump sum at the end of the year of hiring)[135];

(c) All accrued holiday remuneration becoming payable to any employee on the termination of the employee's employment before or by the effect of the winding-up order or resolution,

(d) Unless the company is being wound up voluntarily merely for the purposes of reconstruction or of amalgamation with another company—(i) all amounts due in respect of contributions which are payable during the 12 months before the relevant date by the company as the employer of any persons under the Social Welfare Acts [...];

(e) Unless the company is being wound up voluntarily merely for the purposes of reconstruction or of amalgamation with another company, all amounts due from the company in respect of damages and costs or liability for damages and costs, payable to a person employed by it in connection with an accident, being an accident occurring (i) before the commencement of the winding-up and (ii) in the course of the person's employment with the company, save to the extent that the company is not effectively indemnified by insurers against such damages and costs;

(f) All sums due to any employee pursuant to any scheme or arrangement for the provision of payments to the employee while he or she is absent from employment due to ill health;

(g) Any payments due at any time by the company pursuant to any scheme or arrangement for the provision of superannuation benefits to or in respect of employees of the company whether such payments are due (i) in respect of the company's contribution to that scheme or under that arrangement, or (ii) in respect of such contributions payable by the employees to the company under that scheme or arrangement which have been deducted from the wages or salaries of employees.[136]

---

[135] *ibid*, s 618(4).
[136] *ibid*, s 621(2).

To summarise the above: the legislature has intervened to displace the *pari passu* principle in certain cases, mainly in the case of money owed to the Revenue Commissioners and the company's employees, who are known as the preferential creditors. Sums deducted by the employer in respect of PRSI form, what is called, a super-preferential debt and rank ahead of all other preferential debts. Fixed charges stand outside the liquidation. The preferential creditors, however, rank ahead of the holders of floating charges (but not if the floating charge crystallized before the commencement of the winding-up[137]).

Effect of Winding-Up on the Business of a Company

From the commencement of the winding-up the company ceases to carry on its business, except so far as may be required for its beneficial winding-up.[138] The company is not dissolved upon the commencement of the winding-up: the company's corporate state and its corporate powers live on until the company is dissolved.[139] On the appointment of a liquidator all the powers of the directors of the company cease (this is not true of the appointment of a provisional liquidator): the only way the directors' powers may continue is if this is permitted (in a winding-up by the court or a creditors' voluntary winding-up, by the committee of inspection or, if there is no committee, by the creditors; in a members' voluntary winding-up, by the members in general meeting).[140] Even if the directors' powers are allowed to continue, nothing they do can take precedence over or supplant any action of the liquidator.[141]

When a winding-up order has been made in relation to a company no action or proceeding may be proceeded with or commenced against the company except by leave of the court. The same is true when a provisional liquidator has been appointed or a resolution for voluntary winding-up

---

[137] See *Re JD Brian Ltd (No 1)* Unreported, Supreme Court, Laffoy J, 9 July 2015.

[138] Companies Act 2014, s 677(1). While not quite carrying on the business for the beneficial winding up of the company, *Fitzpatrick v Cuirt Monard Management Company Ltd* [2014] IEHC 136 (White J, 21 January 2014) shows the liquidator having to continue to operate and maintain a sewage treatment plant, when his application was to disclaim this obligation as an onerous one. The liquidator was ordered to continue to maintain the plant as, in the circumstances, it was a statutory requirement to do so.

[139] Companies Act 2014, s 677(2).

[140] *ibid*, s 677(3).

[141] *ibid*, s 677(4).

has been passed.[142] This rule, however, does not apply to the taking of proceedings before the Employment Appeals Tribunal.[143] In *Re Hibernian Therapeutics Global Ltd*[144] Finlay Geoghegan J stated that this rule involves a restriction on a potential plaintiff's right of access to the courts and should therefore be strictly construed. The aim of the rule is to protect creditors and where they will not be affected the court will usually grant leave to proceed.

If the winding-up has not concluded within 12 months after the date of its commencement the liquidator must send a statement containing updates on the liquidation to the CRO (using the CRO's Form E4). The E4 must be sent on the date of the first anniversary of the commencement of the winding-up, and then at intervals of six months.[145]

Completion of Winding-Up

In a winding-up by the court the court may order the liquidator to apply to court for the dissolution of the company.[146] The company will be dissolved from the date of the order which confirms its dissolution and the order must be forwarded within 21 days by the liquidator to the CRO.[147]

As soon as the affairs of the company are completely wound-up in a members' voluntary winding-up, the liquidator must prepare an account of the winding-up showing how it has been conducted and how the property of the company has been disposed of.[148] Once this is done, the liquidator should call a general meeting of the company so he can lay before it his account. The Registrar of the CRO must be sent a copy of the

---

[142] *ibid*, s 678(1).

[143] *ibid*, s 678(2).

[144] [2014] IEHC 41 (Finlay Geoghegan J, 24 January 2014); see also *Re MJBCH* [2013] IEHC 256; for a UK case, see *Re Colliers International UK plc* [2012] EWHC 2942 (Ch). For a case which involved consideration of s 6 of the Irish Bank Resolution Corporation Act 2013 (which required analysis of s 678 – or s 222 of Companies Act 1963 as it then was) see *Wright-Morris v IBRC Ltd* [2013] IEHC 385 (Laffoy J, 15 August 2013).

[145] Companies Act 2014, s 681(2) and (3); failure to do so is a category 3 offence, but the court can order that this requirement is not necessary, per subsection (4); Section 680 outlines the liquidator's duty to call an annual meeting in the case of a members' voluntary winding up; the CRO's Form E3 should be used.

[146] Companies Act 2014, s 704(1) and (3).

[147] *ibid*, s 704(4).

[148] *ibid*, s 705(1).

account and a statement saying that the general meeting was held. When these are received in the CRO they are registered, and once three months have passed the company is deemed to be dissolved.[149]

The procedure at the end of a creditors' voluntary winding-up is the same as that of a members' voluntary winding-up.[150] The liquidator prepares an account of the winding up. He calls a general meeting of the creditors, laying before them his account. He sends the CRO a copy of the account and a statement that the general meeting has taken place. When these are registered, the clock starts ticking and the company will be dissolved within three months. Importantly, if in a court-supervised winding-up the court does not order the liquidator to apply to have the company dissolved, the company will be dissolved by following the steps set out in s 706, as if the winding-up was a creditors' voluntary winding-up[151]: this is another example of the paring back of the role of the court and the saving of costs. In the case of a voluntary winding-up, the liquidation is deemed to have concluded on the date on which the company is deemed to be dissolved. The only time when this is not the case, is if any funds or assets of the company remain unclaimed or undistributed in the hands or under the control of the liquidator on the date of dissolution: in that case, the winding-up is not deemed to be concluded until those funds or assets have either been distributed or paid into the Companies Liquidation Account.[152]

No matter what kind of liquidation it was, the liquidator must retain the company's seal, books and papers for at least six years after the dissolution of the company.[153] For two years after the dissolution of the company the court has the power to declare the dissolution void.[154] Such a declaration would enable proceedings to be taken which might have been taken if the company had not been dissolved.

---

[149] *ibid*, s 705(7).

[150] *ibid*, s 706.

[151] *ibid*, s 704(2).

[152] *ibid*, s 707(5); that account is defined in s 623. If the money is not claimed within seven years the money is paid into the Exchequer.

[153] Companies Act 2014, s 707(2); it is a category 4 offence not to. The CRO eventually — after 20 years — sends all the documents filed in connection with the company to the National Archives (s 709).

[154] Companies Act 2014, s 708(1); application to be taken by the liquidator of the company or by any other person who appears to the court to be interested.

The Insolvency Regulation

The Insolvency Regulation in question is the EU Insolvency Regulation 1346/2000 which came into force in Ireland in 2002.[155] The Regulation provides for recognition in Ireland of all liquidation procedures opened in EU Member States[156] (with the exception of Denmark). It means that foreign liquidators will be recognised by the Irish courts and they will have no difficulties in collecting a debt by way of litigation in Ireland. The Regulation does not apply to receiverships or to members' voluntary windings-up.

The Regulation applies "to collective insolvency proceedings which entail the partial or total divestment of a debtor and the appointment of a liquidator".[157] In the case of a company, the place of the registered office is presumed to be the centre of its main interests in the absence of proof to the contrary. Article 3 of the Regulation states:

> "the courts of the Member State within the territory of which the centre of a debtor's main interests is situated shall have jurisdiction to open insolvency proceedings".

Those will be known as the main insolvency proceedings. Secondary proceedings can be opened in any other Member State if the debtor "possesses an establishment within the territory of that other Member State".[158] The law applicable to the insolvency proceedings is that of the Member State in which they are opened.[159] Any judgment opening insolvency proceedings in Ireland must be recognised in the other Member States.[160] The judgment opening the proceedings in Ireland produces the same effects in any other Member State as it would under Irish law, with

---

[155] In the European Communities (Corporate Insolvency) Regulations 2002 (SI No 333 of2002). The drive towards international harmonisation is represented by the UNCITRAL Model Law on Cross-Border Insolvencies. This is something Ireland has not yet adopted. For an Irish Supreme Court discussion of the principles which apply to cross-border insolvencies which are outside the EU, see *Re Flightlease Ltd* [2012] 1 IR 722.

[156] After 31 May 2002.

[157] Art 1.1.

[158] Art 3.2; for an Irish example, see *Rathville Ltd v The McArthur Group Ltd* [2014] IEHC 355. (Charleton J, 8 July 2014).

[159] Art 4.1.

[160] Art 16.

no further formalities needing to be taken.[161] One of the key concepts of the Regulation is the "centre of main interests" ("COMI").

Article 3(1) of the Insolvency Regulation describes the international jurisdiction as follows:

> "The courts of the Member State within the territory of which the centre of a debtor's main interests is situated shall have jurisdiction to open insolvency proceedings. In the case of a company or legal persons, the place of the registered office shall be presumed to be the centre of its main interest in the absence of proof to the contrary."[162]

In *Re Harley Medical Group (Ireland) Ltd*[163] Laffoy J acceded to a petition to wind up a branch of a non-EU company on the basis that its COMI was in Ireland. Laffoy J stated that Article 3 of the Regulation provided a presumption that the company's COMI was its place of registration (in this case, the British Virgin Islands), but that presumption was open to rebuttal by evidence before the court (which it was, because *inter alia*, the company's "actual centre of management and supervision and of the management of its interests is located"[164]).

---

[161] Art 17.

[162] Lynch-Fannon points to Art 13 as somewhat altering "the apparent strength" of the presumption in favour of the registered office: see Lynch-Fannon & Murphy, *Corporate Insolvency and Rescue*, (2nd Bloomsbury Professional, 2012) at para 1.50. The authors note that at its core, the two possible versions of COMI represent the differences in the "Anglo-Saxon" understanding of this area of the law, as against the Continental understanding.

[163] [2013] 2 IR 596; [2013] IEHC 219 (Laffoy J, 16 May 2013), citing *BRAC Rent-A-Car International, Inc.* [2003] EWHC 128, [2003] 1 WLR 1421, where an administration order was made in respect of a company incorporated in Delaware, because the key issue is COMI (which was the UK in *BRAC*), and not place of incorporation.

[164] [2013] 2 IR 596 at 614.

Realisation of Assets

Introduction

When a winding-up is imminent, the interests of the creditors intrude. Once directors are aware that the company is insolvent, or is headed in that direction, they have a duty to the creditors to preserve the assets (it is sometimes stated as a duty not to dissipate the assets).[1] If they continue to trade with creditors on the basis that the company is in good health, they are trading fraudulently. Where insolvency is looming, directors can be tempted to clear certain debts and leave others outstanding. The law says that if this happens it is a "preference" and it is an unfair one.[2] A liquidator may apply to the court to have the transaction reversed. There are two different categories in this area: unfair preferences and fraudulent dispositions.

Unfair Preferences

Section 604 of Companies Act 2014[3] states that an act done:

> "with a view to giving the creditor[4]…a preference over the other creditors of the company shall be deemed an unfair preference of its creditors and be invalid accordingly if:
>
> (a) a winding up of the company commences within 6 months after the date of the doing of the act, and
> (b) the company is, at the time of the commencement of the winding up, unable to pay its debts (taking into account the contingent and prospective liabilities)."[5]

The six month time period is extended to two years before the commencement of the winding-up of the company where the preference

---

[1] *Per* Street CJ in *Kinsela v Russell Kinsela Pty. (in liquidation)* [1986] 4 N.S.W.L.R. 722 at 730; approved by the Irish Supreme Court in *Re Frederick Inns Ltd* [1994] 1 ILRM 387 and again in *Jones v Gunn* [1997] 3 IR 1 (see Chapter 6); *McLaughlin v Lannen (Re Swanpool Limited)* [2005] IEHC 341 at 3.1.

[2] Companies Act 2014 has replaced "fraudulent preference" with "unfair preference".

[3] Previously s 286(1) of Companies Act 1963, as amended by s 135 of Companies Act 1990

[4] Or any surety or guarantor for the debt due to such creditor.

[5] Companies Act 2014, s 604(2).

is made in favour of a connected person: it will be deemed to be invalid unless it is shown that the preference was not one caught by s 604(2).[6]

Establishing Subjective Intent

The use of the phrase "with a view" is very important: it signifies that the company's *intention* to grant an unfair preference must be established (to establish the company's intention the courts ask what the directors' intention was and deem this to be the intention of the company).[7] In this regard the courts have sought, on these applications, to establish what the "dominant intention" was at the time of the making of the alleged preference.

> "[T]he approach is to seek out the state of mind of the officer or officers of the company making the disposition judged from the circumstances as a whole and drawing such inferences as are appropriate."[8]

This has always been the Achilles' heel of this section because it is very difficult to prove subjective intent. For example, in *Re O'Connor's Nenagh Shopping Centre Ltd*[9] it was accepted by all parties that the *effect* of a mortgage given to the bank within six months of liquidation was that the bank was preferred over other creditors, but Gilligan J found that the charge was entered into by the directors "in order to keep the business going and hopefully succeed with a restructuring plan",[10] i.e. not with an intention to give the bank an unfair preference.

Surprisingly, even if a liquidator proves to the courts' satisfaction that the directors' dominant intention was to give an unfair preference to one creditor, s 604 might nevertheless fail to capture the transaction, if the directors can prove that they did not give the preference of their own free

---

[6] See *Re Cityspan* [2007] 2 BCLC 522 at 525-526 for a particularly implausible argument by a connected person; for a completely different situation, where the person in question was an entirely reliable and truthful witness with a clear recollection of relevant events, who gave her evidence in a straightforward and impressive manner, all the more so as she has been very seriously ill", see *Re Stealth Construction Ltd; Green v Ireland* [2012] 1 BCLC 297.

[7] In *Re Cityspan Ltd; Brown v Clark* [2007] 2 BCLC 522 the directors repaid themselves loans they had made to the company. This was found to be a fraudulent preference, but s 604 cases are rarely as clear-cut.

[8] Per Charleton J, *Kennington (Official Liquidator) v McGinley* [2014] IEHC 356 at 2.

[9] [2011] IEHC 508.

[10] At paras 15, 18 and 19.

will. The argument they would make is that their will was "overborne", i.e., they felt such pressure from this particular creditor that they felt they had no real choice but to make the preference because without free will, the intention to prefer is absent. This was first established in *Re Daly & Co.*[11] The effect of this, as Courtney remarks, is a "perverse" one: the more weak-willed a director the less likely the payment will be regarded as a fraudulent preference.[12] Usher thought it was "absurdly at odds with the aim of achieving an equitable distribution of the assets of an insolvent company".[13] But it has been followed in Ireland, in *Corran Construction Company v Bank of Ireland Finance Ltd*,[14] where a bank official called to the house of a sick director, asking him to remedy a defect in the company's mortgage. McWilliam J stated:

> "I got the impression from the evidence that Mr. O'Neill was trying to avoid their representatives because they had been continually trying to get back the money due to the defendant and that, when they finally caught up with him when he was ill in bed, it was something of a relief to find that they would be satisfied if he would remedy some defect in the mortgage."[15]

In *Parkes & Sons Ltd v Hong Kong and Shanghai Banking Corp*[16] Blayney J found that the dominant motive of a controller of a company in giving the bank a further security, was to save another company, and not to give a preference to the bank. The giving of the mortgage "may have taken some pressure off [his] personal guarantees, [but] it did not relieve him from [them] or reduce his liability on [them]". In that case the controller had been under great pressure from the bank, which had threatened to put in a receiver:

> "At a remove of several years from the time of a transaction, and in the absence of direct evidence, intention may be impossible of direct proof. Instead, circumstantial evidence

---

[11] (1887) 19 LR Ir 83.

[12] Courtney, *Law of Companies* (3rd ed, Bloomsbury, 2012) at para 25.094.

[13] Usher, *Company Law in Ireland* (Sweet & Maxwell, 1986) p 508. See also Keirse, *Object and Effect: The Vexed Question of Intent in Fraudulent Preference Cases* (2005) 12 (7) CLP 182.

[14] [1976] ILRM 175.

[15] *ibid* at 178: It is a very short judgment, and it may be that much of the argument is not recorded in it, but it is respectfully submitted that on the facts of the case, it was equally open to the judge to have found for the liquidator.

[16] [1990] ILRM 241.

allows an inference of intention to be drawn in the appropriate circumstances."[17]

Scope of Section 604

Section 604(2) applies to any conveyance or mortgage or delivery of goods, payment, execution or other act, relating to property made or done by or against a company which is unable to pay its debts as they become due, in favour of: (i) any creditor of the company, or (ii) any person on trust for any such creditor.[18] The provision does not affect the rights of any person making title in good faith and for valuable consideration through or under a creditor of the company.[19]

Several payments may be made, but only some will be found to be unfair preferences. In *Re Oxford Pharmaceuticals*[20] the Court examined a series of payments between parent and subsidiary and found that the first was safe because

> "on the balance of probabilities…the sole influencing factor in making this payment was to regularise the position with the bank, and stabilise the position of both companies, and that [the subsidiary] was not, at that stage, influenced by a desire to better the position of [the parent] in the event of an insolvent liquidation."[21]

At a later point, however, it was "difficult to accept" that the intention of the second and third payments had not been to improve the position of the parent in the event of liquidation.

When a company is being wound-up and an act has been found to contravene s 604, the person preferred is subject to the same liabilities and has the same rights as if he had undertaken to be personally liable as

---

[17] *Per* Charleton J, *Kennington (Official Liquidator) v McGinley* [2014] IEHC 356 at 2 (High Court, 11 July 2014), citing *Station Motors Limited v Allied Irish Banks Ltd* [1985] IR 175. *Station Motors* relied on *Re M Kushler Limited* [1943] 2 All ER 22.
[18] Companies Act 2014, s 604(1).
[19] *ibid*, s 604(5).
[20] [2009] 2 BCLC 485.
[21] *Per* Mark Cawson QC (Sitting as a Judge of the High Court) at [2009] 2 BCLC 485 at 507.

surety for the debt to the extent of the charge on the property or the value of his interest, whichever is the less.[22]

Fraudulent Dispositions

In case an application under s 604 fails, an application under s 608 should always be included in the pleadings as an alternative.[23] Section 608 of Companies Act 2014 is the rule regarding fraudulent dispositions.[24] It is concerned not with the *intention* behind a preference but with the *effect* of the disposition. Despite this, it is a section which "has given rise to only a small number of judgments"[25]).

Section 608 applies where it can be shown to the satisfaction of the court that:

(a) any property of the company of any kind whatsoever was disposed of either by way of conveyance, transfer, mortgage, security, loan, or in any way whatsoever whether by act or omission, direct or indirect, and

(b) the effect of such disposal was to perpetrate a fraud on the company, its creditors or members.

In such cases the court has the power to order any person who appears to have: (a) the use, control or possession of the property concerned; or (b) the proceeds of the sale or development of that property, to deliver it to them, or pay a sum in respect thereof, to the liquidator on such terms or conditions as the court thinks fit. The court will make the order "if it deems it just and equitable to do so".[26] In deciding whether it is just and equitable to make an order, the court must have regard to the rights of persons who have *bona fide* and for value acquired an interest in the property the subject of the application.[27] The courts will exclude sums of money paid to employees of the company, where the employees worked

---

[22] Companies Act 2014, s 605(1).

[23] s 608 does not apply to any conveyance, mortgage, delivery of goods, payment, execution or other act relating to property made or done by or against a company to which s 604 applies.

[24] Previously it was s 139 of Companies Act 1990.

[25] *Per* Finlay Geoghegan J, *Kirby v Petrolo Limited and Stokes* [2014] IEHC 279, at para 19, echoing Laffoy J, in *Devey Enterprises Ltd. v Devey* [2012] 1 IR 127.

[26] Companies Act 2014, s 608(2).

[27] *ibid*, s 608(4); see *Clasper Group Services Ltd* [1989] BCLC 143.

for the benefit of the company in the run-up to the liquidation: such payments will not be fraudulent dispositions. Payments to suppliers for the purpose of continued trading may also be excluded from the fraudulent disposition category, on the just and equitable grounds.[28] There must be impropriety before the provisions of s 608 will be triggered. Hunt J noted recently[29] that the Irish courts have found the following behaviours to be examples of fraudulent dispositions:

(a) Entry on to company premises and the taking of possession of a cash sum and the entire stock of an insolvent company in lieu of rent owed (*Le Chatelaine Thudichum Ltd v Conway*[30]). Here it was held that "the fraud criterion in the section "merely requires that the company, its creditors or members be deprived of something to which it is, or to which they are, lawfully entitled"[31];

(b) Personal expenditure by company directors which had been recorded as business expenditure on behalf of the company (*Devey Enterprises Ltd. v Devey*[32]);

(c) Payment of the proceeds of company sales at a restaurant to a related company (*Kirby v Petrolo Limited and Stokes*[33]);

(d) The use of company funds to settle the private debts of a company director (*Kirby v Muldowney*[34]).

The Interaction of Sections 604 and 608

The interaction of s 604 and s 608 is best seen in *Le Chatelaine Thudichum Ltd v Conway*.[35] The company was wound-up on a day in September and the liquidator applied for a declaration that a certain transaction was an unfair preference, or, failing that, a fraudulent disposition. The transaction in question took place on a day in April. It consisted of the taking by Mr Conway of the cash that was on the premises of a convenience store

---

[28] *Kirby v Petrolo Limited and Stokes* [2014] IEHC 279 at para 30.
[29] *Tucon Process Installations Ltd v Bank of Ireland* [2015] IEHC 312.
[30] [2010] 1 IR 529. See also *Re Leo Getz Ltd* [2014] IEHC 356.
[31] *Per* Murphy J [2010] 1 IR 529 at 539.
[32] [2012] 1 IR 127.
[33] [2014] IEHC 279.
[34] [2014] IEHC 318.
[35] [2010] 1 IR 529.

(€9,500) and the stock (valued at €112,080) in satisfaction of the debts owed to him. The intention to prefer cannot be inferred from hindsight.

Mr Thudicum, who was director of the company which ran the shop, gave evidence. Letting Mr Conway have the money and stock was, in Mr Thudichum's mind, "only…a prelude to their equitable division among the company's creditors". He thought that he and Conway would

> "arrive at a compromise arrangement with the other creditors such that no individual would be left unduly exposed to an unfair share of uncompensated loss in the form of bad debts owed by the company."[36]

Murphy J accepted this: no intention was established. The application under s 604 failed but the application under s 608 succeeded because the effect of Mr Conway's receipt of the cash and stock was to diminish the pool of assets available in the liquidation.

Where the Preference Extinguishes a Director's Personal Liability

In *Re Kerr Aluminium Ltd; Boylan v Bank of Ireland*[37] the crucial date was 26 May, when two important meetings were held: the first an EGM of the company, proposing its own voluntary winding-up, and the second a meeting of the creditors who confirmed the liquidator. The company had a bank account with Bank of Ireland. The overdraft facility was just over €110,000 and this was personally guaranteed by one of the directors, Anthony Kerr. Lodgements amounting to €254,988 were made to the company's bank account between 8 April and 26 May. Were these payments made so that the personal exposure of Mr Kerr would be extinguished? If they were, they were recoverable by the liquidator.

The situation was bleak in April. The company, which provided and fitted aluminium windows, was insolvent. This had been quite clear from the previous September, when the directors signed off on the Audit Report. The company was operating from a premises that it rented from Mr Kerr and it had been defaulting on its rent payments. Between September and

---

[36] *ibid* at 534.
[37] [2012] IEHC 386.

January sixteen employees were made redundant and the company couldn't meet the redundancy payments owed them. One creditor brought proceedings in the Circuit Court to recover €8,797. Another creditor brought proceedings in the High Court to recover €59,810. There was no sign of fresh investment. Mr Kerr was wondering whether or not to apply for examinership or to liquidate. At the beginning of April the company's overdraft was overdrawn to the tune of €106,155. Yet, between April and the winding-up commencement in late May, lodgements amounting to €254,988 were made to the company's bank account. The liquidator said that this conferred a "significant personal benefit" on Mr Kerr because it reduced his personal liability.[38]

The onus of proof lies on the liquidator to prove the dominant intention to prefer. That is well settled law. If it can be shown that there were reasonable reasons why transfers of money took place, it may bring a party over the line. In this case, Mr Kerr was not a party to the application. It was the bank which was contesting the liquidator's claims and advancing evidence. One piece of evidence it advanced, which was hugely important, was a letter from Mr Kerr to the liquidator, written the previous October (when the liquidator was not yet acting as liquidator, but as a financial advisor to the company). In it Mr Kerr explained the company's policy of lodging cheques in its bank account without delay. This was done because "for security...reasons cheques and cash are not to be held at the company premises" and "as a result of the on-going deterioration in general economic conditions there were concerns that cheques may bounce". This was "a plausible explanation" in Laffoy J's view as to why the company "continued to lodge all receipts into the current account promptly".[39] Laffoy J reviewed the fluctuations of the company account and found that no deviation from the *modus vivendi* that had been outlined the previous October had occurred, and that "the totality of the evidence" did "not give rise to the inference that Mr. Kerr made the lodgements...with the dominant intention of preferring" the bank.

---

[38] There was still, for reasons that are not explained in the judgment, €32,663 overdrawn on the account.

[39] [2012] IEHC 386 at 21.

In the course of her judgment Laffoy J reviewed two important decisions, *Re M Kushler Ltd*[40] and *Station Motors Ltd v AIB Ltd*,[41] where the opposite was the case. In *Kushler* the director had personally guaranteed a sum to the bank and, over the course of nine days after the board was advised that the company ought to be wound-up lodgements were made by the company to its account which had the effect of extinguishing Morris Kushler's liability. The bank had never pressed for a reduction of the overdraft: other creditors had sought payment, but had been asked by Mr Kushler to wait. The bank wasn't given notice of the creditors' meeting and at the meeting Mr Kushler stated there was a guarantor but that it was not him. Was there an intention to prefer? Making inferences which involve dishonesty is not something a court will do lightly, but if the court perceives "a taint of dishonesty" and feels there are "solid grounds" it will do so. Lord Greene MR memorably said that "a state of mind is as much a fact as a state of digestion and the method of ascertaining it is by evidence and inference", and was clear that where there was "a strong element of private advantage resulting from payment of the debt", as there was in circumstances such as these, the court would be more inclined to infer an intention to prefer.[42]

Station Motors Ltd was similar. A husband and wife had guaranteed company borrowings in the sum of £75,000 in June. The company was shortly in dire difficulty. An EGM was called in mid-September, and between then and 3 October, when the company went into liquidation, lodgements were made with the intention of preferring the bank and reducing the exposure to the personal guarantees. It was important that "only six cheques were paid out of the company's account on and after 15 September and then only as a result of special representations made by Mr. Murphy," Carroll J found.[43] Because these special pleadings were necessary, the inference to be drawn was that the account was not being operated normally. Carroll J found it impossible not to draw the inference that "the intention to prefer the bank was coupled with an intention to prefer the guarantors" and the payments were therefore unfair preferences.[44]

---

[40] [1943] Ch 248.
[41] [1985] IR 756.
[42] All the quotations above are taken from the speech of Lord Greene MR at [1943] Ch 248 at 251–252.
[43] [1985] IR 756 at 762.
[44] *ibid* at 763.

Custody of the Company's Property

When the liquidator is appointed to a company, he takes the seal, the books and the records of the company into his custody or control, as well as all the property to which the company "is or appears to be entitled".[45] Anyone who, without lawful entitlement, has anything belonging to the company in their possession, must immediately surrender whatever it is to the liquidator.[46]

Circumstances in which Floating Charge is Invalid

In certain circumstances, floating charges will be found invalid. This is where they have been created within 12 months before the date of commencement of the winding-up "unless it is proved that the company immediately after the creation of the charge was solvent".[47] This rule does not apply if the holder of the floating charge can show that the company actually received money in consideration of the charge "at the time of or subsequently to" its creation.[48] The holder of the charge may be able to show that the company received the actual price or value of goods or services sold or supplied at the time, and the way of deciding this is by asking whether the goods or services

> "could reasonably have been expected to be obtained… in the ordinary course of business and on the same terms… as those on which they were sold or supplied to the company".[49]

In the case of connected persons, the 12 month time period is extended to two years.[50] Further to this, s 598 of Companies Act 2014 states that where:

(a) a company is being wound up,
(b) the company was, within 12 months before the date of commencement of the winding up, indebted to any officer[51] of the company or a connected person,

---

[45] Companies Act 2014, s 596(1).

[46] *ibid*, s 596(2).

[47] *ibid*, s 597(1); this rule was previously s 288 of Companies Act 1963. It has not been changed. See Chapter 16 "Floating Charge Granted Before Liquidation".

[48] Companies Act 2014, s 597(2)

[49] *ibid*, s 597(3); see *Re Fairway Magazines Ltd, Fairbairn v Hartigan* and *Re Orleans Motor Co Ltd* (Chapter 15).

[50] Companies Act 2014, s 597(4).

[51] "Officer" here includes a spouse, civil partner, child or nominee of an officer.

(c)   such indebtedness was discharged whether wholly or partly by the company or by any other person, and

(d)   the company created a floating charge on any of its assets or property within 12 months before the date of commencement of the winding-up in favour of the officer or connected person to whom such company was indebted,

then…such charge shall be invalid to the extent of the repayment referred to in paragraph (c) unless it is proved that the company immediately after the creation of the charge was solvent.[52]

Related Companies and the Pooling of Assets

The court may order that

"any company that is or has been related to the company being wound up shall pay to the liquidator of that company an amount equivalent to the whole or part of all or any of the debts provable in that winding up."[53]

This will only be done if the court is satisfied that it is just and equitable to do so; that will depend on: (a) the extent to which the related company took part in the management of the company being wound-up; (b) the conduct of the related company towards the creditors of the company being wound-up; and (c) the effect which such order would be likely to have on the creditors of the related company concerned.[54] The circumstances that gave rise to the winding-up of the company must be attributable to the acts or omissions of the related company, otherwise the court will make no such order.[55] The mere fact that the companies are related is not grounds for making a pooling of the assets order: it is no argument for creditors of the company being wound-up to say that they had relied on the fact that a related company was or had been related to the first-mentioned company.[56] The application may be made by the

---

[52] Companies Act 2014, s 598(1); this was previously s 289 of Companies Act 1963. It has not changed.
[53] Companies Act 2014, s 599(2).
[54] *ibid*, s 599(4).
[55] *ibid*, s 599(5).
[56] *ibid*, s 599(6)(a) and (b).

liquidator or any creditor[57] or contributory of a company that is being wound up. If two or more companies are being wound up by the court the court may order that the companies be wound-up together as if they were one company.[58]

Section 602 of Companies Act 2014: Post-Commencement Dispositions

Any disposition of the property of the company, any transfer of shares in the company, or any alteration in the status of the members of the company, made after the commencement of the winding-up will be void unless the court otherwise orders[59] and unless the act was done with the sanction of the liquidator or a director who has retained the power to act (i.e. where the court or committee of inspection permit the continuance of certain of the directors' powers in a creditors' voluntary winding up, or if in a members' voluntary winding-up, the members in general meeting sanction the continuance of those powers).[60] The idea is the same as usual. Whatever assets there are, which aren't subject to charges, should be available for division between all unsecured creditors equally.[61] Two things should be noted from the outset. The first is that a winding-up begins *when the petition is presented* to the Central Office of the High Court (not, for example, from the date of the liquidator's appointment). The second is that the word "disposition" covers almost anything.[62]

A person who causes any disposition of the property of the company, any transfer of shares in the company, or any alteration in the status of the members of the company to be made will not be personally liable for the act unless the person had actual notice that the company was being wound-up.[63] If the company is being wound-up and it requests of someone

---

[57] "Creditor" means a creditor, by assignment or otherwise, to whom the company is indebted in a sum exceeding €10,000 or two or more creditors, by assignment or otherwise, to whom in aggregate the company is indebted in a sum exceeding €20,000.

[58] Companies Act 2014, s 600.

[59] *ibid*, s 602; this was previously s 218 of Companies Act 1963.

[60] By virtue of s 677(3).

[61] See *Re Gray's Inns Construction* [1980] 1 WLR 711.

[62] Conveyances, transfers, assignments, deliveries, payments, etc.

[63] Companies Act 2014, s 602(3).

that they do cause such an act to be performed the company and any officer of it who is in default shall be guilty of a category 2 offence.[64]

Breadth of Term "Disposition"

The term "disposition" is a very broad one. Case law provides the following three examples of its application.

If money in lodged in a company's overdrawn bank account, the effect will be to reduce its indebtedness to the bank: this is a disposition, and as such, may be recovered by a liquidator.[65]

If the company's bank account is in credit and there continues to be activity on the account after the winding-up has begun, it is settled law in Ireland that such payments were "dispositions" *to the bank.*[66] The argument that the bank was only an intermediary had not benefitted from the transactions in question was rejected n *Re Industrial Services Company (Dublin) Ltd.*[67] Kearns J (as he then was) emphasised the wider element at play. Banks "have a very special role of responsibility in winding up situations," he said. One of these responsibilities was "vigilance". The banks "serve a wider commercial interest" than their own narrow interest because they insure "greater protection for the general body of the creditors". He stated:

> "The Oireachtas by providing for the advertisement of a petition must be seen, it seems to me, as wishing to impose an obligation on institutional creditors in particular, not only to have regard to such advertisements, but to control the operation of company accounts in a particular way after it becomes clear that the company is in financial difficulty. This may appear harsh insofar as the bank is concerned. However, that cannot be a valid reason for construing the section in a

---

[64] *ibid*, s 602(4).

[65] *Re Gray's Inns Construction* [1980] 1 WLR 711, approved in Ireland in *Re Pat Ruth Ltd* [1981] ILRM 51, a two and a half page judgment that starts without giving any background — as if you know about the payments made into the company's bank accounts — and then doesn't proceed to set out the specifics relating to the money in question.

[66] *Re Industrial Services Company (Dublin) Ltd* [2001] 2 IR 118; this is not the case in the UK, see *Hollicourt (Contracts) Ltd v Bank of Ireland* [2001] 2 WLR 290.

[67] [2001] 2 IR 118.

way which banks might regard as more satisfactory from their own commercial point of view."[68]

In conclusion he cited Murphy J in *PMPA Coaches Ltd v Primor plc*[69]:

> "...all payments made subsequent to the presentation of the petition are void unless and to the extent that the same are validated by an express order of the Court. The hardship which flows from this express statutory provision could not be of itself a ground for validating a payment. Such a principle would constitute an effective repeal of the statutory provision."[70]

In *Re Worldport Ireland Ltd*[71] Clarke J squared this circle by suggesting that rather than choosing to nominate either the bank or the ultimate recipient as the sole disponee, the courts might consider them to be "dual disponees".

If a cheque is lodged to an account on Monday but not credited to the account until Friday, and the company is wound-up on Wednesday, when does the disposition occur? In *Re Ashmark Ltd (No 2)*[72] Blayney J stated that the drawing of a cheque did not of itself operate as a disposition of the funds in the company's account: the disposition occurred when the cheque was paid, and so the payment in this case was made *after* the winding-up began and was therefore void unless the court ordered otherwise. The court would not order otherwise as to do so would be unfair on the other unsecured creditors.

The Court Can Validate Post-Commencement Dispositions

Section 602 of Companies Act 2014 states that post-commencement dispositions will be void "unless the Court otherwise orders". The court will never validate a post-commencement disposition unless it is for the

---

[68] *ibid*, at 129.

[69] Unreported, High Court, 15 June 1993.

[70] *PMPA Coaches Ltd*, Unreported, High Court, 15 June 1993 at 6.

[71] [2005] IEHC 189; Clarke J stated: "If, as Kearns J. pointed out, the Bank has a dual role, then, following Industrial Services, it seems to me that I must regard this case as being one where there are dual disponees."

[72] [1990] ILRM 455. Judgment of 8 December 1989, not to be confused with O'Hanlon J's judgment of 9 June 1989, at [1990] 2 IR 10.

benefit of the company, or if it can be argued that by doing so the unsecured creditors would be in a better situation (see Murphy J in *Re McBirney and Co Ltd*[73]). A good example of a disposition which was for the benefit of the creditors is *Re A.I. Levy (Holdings) Ltd.*[74] If a company goes into liquidation, it is likely that any lease it holds will be forfeited. In *Re A.I. Levy* the tenant was being wound-up and two dispositions were made: the lease was sold at market value and the outstanding rent was paid to the landlord. By selling the lease and obtaining market value the creditors were in a better position than if the lease had been forfeited, rendering it valueless. The outstanding rent had to be paid because otherwise the landlord would not consent to the lease being assigned. As a matter of logic, if a post-commencement transaction is carried out at full value the court will validate it because no ill-effects have been visited on the creditors.[75]

---

[73] Unreported, High Court, 2 July 1992.

[74] [1963] 2 All ER 556.

[75] See also *Denney v John Hudson and Co Ltd* [1992] BCLC 901, where the dispositions were necessary to allow the company to continue to trade.

EXAMINERSHIP

Introduction

Two pieces of emergency legislation tell the tale of modern Ireland, the bank guarantee of 2008 and the Companies (Amendment) Act 1990. In 2008 the debts of certain banks were of "systemic importance": in 1990 the imminent collapse of a group of beef companies was about to blow a hole in the government's Programme for National Recovery. *The Irish Times* reported at the time:

> "Amid allegations of fraud, misuse of public funds and foolish and greedy investment by the Goodman group of companies, emergency legislation was rushed though the Dail last night to stave off a catastrophic collapse of the Irish beef industry, arising out of the difficulties of the group, which has control of 40% of a trade worth £1.2 billion."[1]

Such were the beginnings of the examinership process in Ireland. At times it may still be used to "stave off a catastrophic collapse" (see *Re Eircom Ltd*[2]), but it is also a feature of far less dramatic rescue operations. Its purpose is to provide a protected period for a company in trouble, if protection will help it to survive. Examinership is the essential corporate rescue tool in Ireland and the Companies Act 2014 alters very little in the regime.

This chapter is divided into three parts. If you are asked to advise on whether a company should apply for examinership you need to know the following:

1. What are the steps involved in bringing a petition to have an examiner appointed to the company?
2. What factors will influence the petition's success or failure?
3. If an examiner is appointed, what are the consequences for the company and for its creditors?

---

[1] "£700m needed to save beef trade", *The Irish Times*, 29 August 1990.
[2] *Re Eircom Ltd* [2012] IEHC 107, Unreported, Kelly J, 30 March 2012.

PART I

Criteria for Appointment of Examiner

The court only has power to appoint an examiner to a company where

> "it is satisfied that there is a reasonable prospect of the survival of the company and the whole or any part of its undertaking as a going concern."[3]

Three further criteria must be met: (a) the company is, or is likely to be, unable to pay its debts (i.e. it is unable to pay its debts as they fall due[4]); (b) no resolution subsists for the winding-up of the company; and (c) no order has been made for the winding-up of the company.[5] The court may consider whether the company has sought significant extensions of time for the payment of its debts from its creditors, a fact from which it could "reasonably be inferred" that the company was likely to be unable to pay its debts.[6] If a company has any assets which are in NAMA then NAMA must be on notice and a representative of NAMA must be heard in the course of the application.[7] The court has power to appoint an examiner to related companies and the same criteria — likelihood of survival of the company or the related criteria in whole or in part — applies.[8]

Jurisdiction of Circuit Court

Traditionally companies could only petition for the appointment of an examiner in the High Court. The Companies Act 2014 gave the Circuit Court jurisdiction to hear examinership applications for small and medium companies[9] (small companies are ones which have an annual turnover of not more than €8.8m and employ not more than 50 people; medium companies are ones which have an annual turnover of not more

---

[3] Companies Act 2014, s 509(2).
[4] See s 509(3) for the three ways of determining inability to pay debts. Inability to pay debts *as they fall due* is the most common.
[5] Companies Act 2014, s 509(1).
[6] *ibid*, s 509(4).
[7] *ibid*, s 509(5).
[8] *ibid*, s 517; the court does not have to appoint an examiner to each company in a group. In *Re Kilashee Schools Company Ltd* [2014] IEHC 275 Charleton J declined to admit of 1 out of 4 petitioning companies into examinership.
[9] Companies Act 2014, s 509(7).

than €20m and employ not more than 250 people).[10] All the powers granted to the High Court by Part 10 of Companies Act 2014 are granted to the Circuit Court, with one exception: the Circuit Court has no jurisdiction to hear a petition for the winding-up of, or to wind-up, a company.[11] Circuit Court applications should be made in the circuit where the company has its registered office or principal place of business (if there is no registered office of the company and its principal place of business is outside the State the application should be made in the Dublin Circuit).[12]

Presentation of the Petition

The examiner's role is to examine the state of the company's affairs and suggest a method of rescue or restructuring (a "scheme of arrangement"). If there are proposals for a compromise or scheme of arrangement they must accompany the petition.[13] A petition to admit a company into examinership may be presented by the company, its directors, a creditor[14] (including an employee) or shareholders, as long as they hold a minimum of one-tenth of the paid up share capital on the day of the presentation.[15] It can be presented by any of those parties individually, or all together. In practice, it is usually the directors who present the petition in the name of the company.

The petition must nominate a person as examiner, who must consent to his or her appointment.[16] The petition must be accompanied by an independent expert's report (previously referred to as an "independent accountant's report"): the independent expert must either be the company's statutory auditor or a person who is qualified to act as examiner.[17] A person is not qualified to be appointed or act as an examiner

---

[10] For the full criteria, see Companies Act 2014, s 350.

[11] Companies Act 2014, s 509(9).

[12] *ibid*, s 509(10).

[13] *ibid*, s 512(2)(b).

[14] The court shall not give a hearing to a petition presented by a contingent or prospective creditor until such security for costs has been given as the court thinks reasonable, per s 512(3).

[15] Companies Act 2014, s 510(1)(a) to (d); if the company is the holding company of an insurer or a credit institution only the Central Bank may present the petition. See also s 510(3).

[16] Companies Act 2014, s 512(2)(a).

[17] *ibid*, s 511(1).

of a company unless he would be qualified to act as its liquidator.[18] Acting as examiner of a company when not qualified is a category 2 offence.[19]

The statute lists twelve pieces of information that must be included in the independent report and then adds that the expert should also include "such other matters as he thinks relevant".[20] The necessary information ranges from basic matters, such as the names and addresses of the company's officers[21] and creditors, the names of other companies which the directors are directors of, a statement of affairs which gives details of the company's assets and liabilities, to the crucial opinion as to whether the company would have a reasonable prospect of survival as a going concern if it were admitted to examinership. He must state what conditions he thinks are essential to ensure survival. He must state whether he thinks a scheme of arrangement would help. He must tell the court whether he thinks there are grounds for initiating reckless trading proceedings against the directors. He must recommend whether he thinks that certain liabilities incurred before the petition should be paid.[22] It may be that the situation is too dire, and the pressure too great, to allow for all of these steps to be completed. If that is the case the court can give interim protection, lasting no more than ten days, to allow the independent accountant to prepare his report.[23] That way the company is protected immediately and the court will still be able to make its decision with the benefit of the full report. Often interim protection is extended to full protection on the second outing.[24] The independent expert must supply a copy of his report to any interested party on written application being made in this regard.[25] The independent expert may apply to court for permission to redact certain parts of his report before supplying it to interested parties: the question at the heart of such an application is whether the inclusion of certain information "would be likely to prejudice the survival of the company or the whole or any part of its undertaking as a going concern".[26]

[18] ibid, s 519(1); see s 633 of Companies Act 2014 for the criteria.
[19] Companies Act 2014, s 519(2).
[20] ibid, s 511(3).
[21] Including, if the expert is able, the name and address of any shadow director.
[22] Companies Act 2014, s 511(3)(k).
[23] ibid, s 513.
[24] ibid, s 512(6) for the court's powers.
[25] Companies Act 2014, s 516(1).
[26] ibid, s 516(2) and (3).

Good Faith

The petitioner and the independent expert have a duty to act in good faith.[27] If it appears to the court over the course of the hearing of the petition that either of them, in preparing and presenting either the petition or the report, have failed to disclose information available to them which has a bearing on the application, or have failed "in any other way…to exercise utmost good faith" then the court may decline to hear, or to continue hearing, a petition.[28] The need for good faith was first outlined by Costello J in *Re Wogan's (Drogheda) Ltd (No 2)*,[29] at a time when no statutory duty of good faith existed.[30] The reason good faith is needed, he explained, is because the Court is dependent on "the truth of what it is told" and because of the "potential injustice" of protecting a company when the proper thing to do would be to wind it up.[31] If this were applied to the men who occupied the upper echelons of Anglo Irish Bank in 2008 they would have calamitously failed the utmost good faith test. In a situation analogous to a company seeking the protection of the court, Anglo sought the protection of the government. The bank's head of capital markets and acting director of treasury, John Bowe, explained the bank's devious strategy to Peter Fitzgerald, head of the bank's retail funding, in a telephone conversation at the time. The bank was telling the government that it needed €7bn to keep afloat in September 2008, but Bowe confided to Fitzgerald that he had picked the figure "out of my arse", because if the government

> "saw the enormity (*sic*) of it up front they might decide, they might decide they have a choice. You know what I mean? They might say the cost to the taxpayer is too high. But… if it doesn't look too big at the outset… if it looks big, big enough to be important but not too big that it kind of spoils everything…"[32]

---

[27] *ibid*, s 518.

[28] See *Re Belohn Ltd; In Re Merrow Ltd* [2013] IEHC 157 (Hogan J); see also *The Irish Times*, 15 April 2013, "Accountants too cosy with the companies they audit".

[29] Unreported, High Court, 7 May 1992.

[30] It was first inserted by s 13 of Companies (Amendment) (No 2) Act 1999 and has been carried over by Companies Act 2014, s 518.

[31] See also *Re Selukwe Ltd*, Unreported, High Court, 20 December 1991, where despite a lack of good faith Costello J granted protection because of the thirty jobs at stake.

[32] Simon Carswell, "Brass neck and sneers as Anglo tried to hookwink State" *The Irish Times*, 25 June 2013.

The prospect of abusing the State guarantee made David Drumm, the chief executive of the bank at the time, laugh; he said "[w]e won't do anything blatant, but... we have to get the money in... get the f***in' money in, get it in".[33] There was no statutory framework for the bail-out and so there was no legal obligation to seek the protection of the State with good faith and so there was no punishment for anyone who acted in bad faith.[34]

In *Irish Car Rentals Ltd*[35] Clarke J stated that the courts had to take a proportional approach, balancing wrongdoing potentially disclosed in the examiner's report and the risk to jobs which follows a failed examinership application. In *JD Transpeed Express Portlaois Ltd*[36] Barrett J dismissed certain failures of disclosure as arising from "flawed human processes". In *O'Flynn Construction v Carbon Finance Ltd*[37] Irvine J stated

> "[i]t is not a defence to a failure to exercise the utmost good faith to say that the companies are suitable for the examinership process in any event. Suitability for examinership is a separate issue to the standard of disclosure required both by the nature of an order granted ex parte and the specific statutory requirements [of good faith]".[38]

Importantly, "over-optimism" is not something that is considered bad faith.[39] In *Re Vantive Holdings*[40] Denham J said that it was "an abuse of the court's process" to withhold key, allegedly sensitive, information, when presenting a petition, only to then, upon the refusal of the petition, seek the protection of the court a second time, and on this second occasion set the full facts before the court. Such "deliberate strategic decisions" are not allowed.

---

[33] Stephen Collins, Colm Keena, "Drumm was happy to abuse State guarantee", *The Irish Times*, 25 June 2013.

[34] In fact Bowe and Fitzgerald were rewarded. When Anglo Irish Bank became IBRC Fitzgerald was made head of corporate affairs, a PR role, and Bowe, who would later tout his "crisis management skills", became director of corporate development.

[35] [2010] IEHC 235, at para 3.5.

[36] [2014] IEHC 544.

[37] [2014] IEHC 458.

[38] See also *Re Step One Permanent Solutions Ltd* [2015] IEHC 284 (Baker J).

[39] *Per* McCracken J, *Re Tuskar Resources plc* [2001] 1 IR 668 at 677.

[40] [2010] 2 IR 118 at 143.

PART II

Factors Influencing the Petition's Success or Failure

Originally, to be admitted to examinership, companies had to show that they had *"some* prospect of survival".[41] A substantial amount of amendments were made to the law in 1999[42] and a higher test was introduced. These have all been carried over in Companies Act 2014. Since 1999, the test has been that a company must show it has "a *reasonable prospect* of survival…as a going concern". The new test first came before the courts in *Re Tuskar Resources plc*[43]: the comments of McCracken J are a touchstone for all decisions since, and have been cited with approval by Fennelly J in *Re Gallium Ltd*[44] and Murray CJ in *Re Vantive Holdings*.[45] McCracken J said in *Tuskar* that the onus of proof was on the petitioner to satisfy the Court of the reasonable prospect of survival, and failing this, the order could not be made. In *Re Gallium* Fennelly J said that even where the petitioner gets over that threshold, he will not necessarily be granted the order, because the section conferred a wide discretion on the court, and the court takes all the circumstances into account. "The establishment of a reasonable prospect of the survival merely triggers the power, which remains discretionary," said Fennelly J.

> "The entire purpose of examinership is to make it possible to rescue companies in difficulty. The protection period is there to facilitate examination of the prospects of rescue. However, that protection may prejudice the interests of some creditors. The court will weigh the existence and degree of any such prejudice in the balance."[46]

Another paramount consideration is the saving of jobs. Thus, the court may even admit to examinership a "borderline case".[47] As Clarke J stated in *Re Traffic Group Ltd*:

---

[41] See *Re Atlantic Magnetics* [1993] 2 IR 561 and C(A)A 1990 before its amendment in 1999.
[42] The Companies (Amendment) (No 2) Act 1999.
[43] [2001] 1 IR 668.
[44] [2009] 2 ILRM 11.
[45] [2010] 2 IR 118.
[46] [2009] 2 ILRM 11 para 46.
[47] See *Re Star Elm Frames Ltd* [2013] IESC 57 (*per* Laffoy J).

> "It is clear that the principal focus of the legislation is to enable, in an appropriate case, an enterprise to continue in existence for the benefit of the economy as a whole and, of equal, or indeed greater, importance to enable as many as possible of the jobs which may be at stake in such enterprise to be maintained for the benefit of the community in which the relevant employment is located. It is important both for the court and, indeed, for examiners, to keep in mind that such is the focus of the legislation. It is not designed to help shareholders whose investment has proved to be unsuccessful. It is to seek to save the enterprise and jobs."[48]

This consideration does not trump all others. In *Re One Step Permanent Solutions Ltd*[49] a number of the permanent employees were present in court for the hearing of the petition but their "obvious concern and distress" could not outweigh the reasons for declining the petition (substantial Revenue debts, Revenue opposition, poor stewardship of the company, the company's finance provider was secured fully against the book debts of the company and was not likely to suffer any loss on an examinership or on a liquidation and even in examinership the positions of the sixteen permanent employees were vulnerable). Where the evidence before the court is "vague and nebulous"[50] this will often be fatal to the petition. The independent expert's report is of crucial importance. In *Vantive Holdings* it boiled down to mere "management speak"[51]: the projections relied on were "lacking in reality"[52] and Kelly J said of the valuations in question that they were "out of date and can hardly be described as truly independent". The amount of jobs at stake had been puffed up in the petition.[53] There was "something artificial" about the petition and it seemed that a protection period was "designed to help shareholders whose investment has proved to be unsuccessful".[54] The petition was rejected by the High Court and the appeal to the Supreme

---

[48] [2008] 3 IR 253 at 260; see also *Re Seluwke Ltd* (High Court, 20 December 1991) where Costello J felt that the prospects of saving jobs outweighed the lack of candour in the petition.

[49] [2015] IEHC 284 (Baker J, 6 May 2015).

[50] *Per* McGovern J, in the High Court, dismissing the petition in *Re Gallium*

[51] [2010] 2 IR 108 at 113, *per* Kelly J.

[52] *ibid, per* Kelly J.

[53] It stated 650 jobs were at stake; in fact, only 100 people were directly employed. The figure of 650 was largely made up of subcontractors.

[54] [2010] 2 IR 108 at 117, *per* Kelly J.

Court was dismissed, Murray CJ speaking of the need for "sufficient evidence or material" to allow the Court to

> "arrive at such a conclusion on the basis of an objective appraisal of that evidence or material. Mere assertions on behalf of a petitioner that a company has a reasonable prospect of survival as a going concern cannot be given significant weight unless it is supported by an objective appraisal of the circumstances of the company concerned and an objective rationale as to the manner in which the company can be reasonably expected to overcome the insolvency in which it finds itself and survive as a going concern."[55]

While the court would give "due weight" to the opinion of the independent accountant, the weight had to "depend on the degree and extent to which he supports that opinion by his or her own objective reasoning and the appraisal of material or factors relied upon for reaching his or her conclusions".[56] According to Finlay Geoghegan J in *Re Mr. Binman & Ors,*[57] "the proper approach" for the court is to consider what has caused the insolvency and then look to see if there is evidence of an objective nature which would allow it to conclude that the companies have a reasonable prospect of survival.[58]

The business which survives must be "a going concern". The meaning of this phrase was argued in *Re Tivway,*[59] where Denham J stated that "an examinership is not a process for sale"[60] and approved Costello J in *Re Clare Textiles,*[61] where he said

> "a scheme of arrangement…can only arise after the examiner has reached the conclusion…that (a) the company and (b) the whole or any part of its undertaking are capable of survival."[62]

---

[55] [2009] IESC 1 at 20 (11 August 2009); as opposed to the reported Supreme Court decision of 14 October 2009, at [2010] 2 IR 118.
[56] *ibid.*
[57] [2011] IEHC 401, where the examinership bid failed.
[58] In *Re Mr. Binman & Ors* [2011] IEHC 401 at para 30.
[59] [2010] 3 IR 49.
[60] At para 61/ at 68.
[61] [1993] 2 IR 213.
[62] *ibid* at 221.

Looking behind the jargon in the expert's report, Denham J stated that, in essence, the plan was that "the active part of the company is to be sold. It will no longer be within the company. The remaining undertaking is moribund — as a consequence of the property crash"[63] — and this simply could not be said to be the survival of the company as a going concern. It was argued for the companies that the receipt of rental income and the maintenance of a property amounted to a going concern, but the court held that this could only be regarded as low-level business activity which was "essentially passive".[64]

PART III

Consequences for Creditors

The final part of this chapter deals with the consequences for the company's creditors when an examiner is appointed. The consequences are drastic. Courtney says that the provisions are

> "so wide that, with minor exceptions, it may be considered to place a total embargo on creditors or other aggrieved persons taking any steps which would affect the protected company's assets."[65]

Creditors do get a look-in — they must be heard[66] — but their remedies are frozen. They simply cannot enforce their securities or claims against the company for seventy days (and this may be extended by a further thirty days).[67] The classic judicial expression of concern for the position of creditors was enunciated by Keane J in *Re Butlers Engineering Ltd*,[68] where the learned judge pointed out the "drastic abridgement" of their rights, and said it was something the Court "must never lose sight of": "in particular," he said,

> "it should be borne in mind that even the comparatively short breathing space…given by the appointment may have serious consequences for the creditors, given the fact that their nominal

---

[63] *ibid.*
[64] [2010] 3 IR 49 at 72.
[65] Courtney, *Law of Companies* (3rd ed, Bloomsbury, 2012) at p 1407, para 22.060.
[66] Companies Act 2014, s 515.
[67] *ibid*, s 520.
[68] *Re Butlers Engineering Ltd*, Unreported, High Court, 1 March 1996.

remedies remain in abeyance, while the control of the company remains in the hands of those who, in some cases at least, have contributed to its insolvency."[69]

In *Re Gallium*[70] Fennelly J stated:

"The entire purpose of examinership is to make it possible to rescue companies in difficulty. The protection period is there to facilitate examination of the prospects of rescue. However, that protection may prejudice the interests of some creditors. The court will weigh the existence and degree of any such prejudice in the balance. It will have regard to the report of the independent accountant."

Protection begins from the date of the petition. No winding-up or s 212 proceedings may be commenced and no receiver may be appointed.[71] Except by leave of the court no other proceedings in relation to the company may be commenced.[72]

The examiner will be faced with debts that have been incurred just before the company entered examinership (employees' wages, electricity bills, various debts that are incurred in the normal course of trade). Will he pay them? Section 521 of Companies Act 2014 states that none of these debts may be paid unless the independent expert's report recommended they, or part of them, should be, or unless the court authorises the payment. If there is no such recommendation in the report, the examiner or any interested party may apply to the court for the discharge of all or part of a given debt. If a failure to pay would reduce the company's prospects of survival the court will approve it.[73]

The Position of Receivers and Provisional Liquidators

If a receiver has stood appointed for more than three days then the court cannot hear the application.[74] This means that the company only has a small window to present an examinership petition after a receiver has

---

[69] *ibid* at 10.
[70] [2009] IESC 8, [2009] 2 ILRM 11 at para 47.
[71] For the full list of frozen remedies see s 520(4).
[72] Companies Act 2014, s 520(5).
[73] *ibid*, s 521(2).
[74] *ibid*, s 512(4).

been appointed. Once protection is given, no receiver may be appointed. If a receiver stands appointed to the company or any part of it for less than three days the court can order that he cease to act entirely, or that he act only in respect of certain assets. He can be ordered to deliver all books and information he has acquired and used to the examiner, and to give the examiner full particulars of all his dealings with the business or asset of the company. Where a receiver stands appointed to the whole or any part of the property or undertaking of that company at the date of the presentation of a petition, the court may make "such order as it thinks fit", including an order as to any or all of the following matters:

(a) That the receiver shall cease to act as such from a date specified by the court;

(b) That the receiver shall, from a date specified by the court, act as such only in respect of certain assets specified by the court;

(c) Directing the receiver to deliver all books, papers and other records, which relate to the property or undertaking of the company (or any part of it) and are in his or her possession or control, to the examiner within a period to be specified by the court;

(d) Directing the receiver to give the examiner full particulars of all his or her dealings with the property or undertaking of the company.

The court will only make any of the above orders if it is satisfied that there is a reasonable prospect of the survival of the company as a going concern.[75] Section 440 of Companies Act 2014 states that preferential payments (as they would be called in a winding-up) may be paid out of any assets coming to the hands of the receiver in priority to any claim for principal or interest in respect of the debentures: s 523 of Companies Act 2014 allows the court, on the application of the examiner, to disapply s 440.

Where, at the date of the presentation of a petition in relation to a company, a provisional liquidator stands appointed to the company, the court may make "such order as it thinks fit", including similar orders to the ones outlined above.[76] If he stands appointed the court may appoint him as examiner, may order him to cease to act, may ask him, as it can ask a receiver, to deliver up all books, records and so on, to the examiner. The court has the

---

[75] ibid, s 522(3).
[76] ibid, s 522(2).

power to make any ancillary orders that it thinks are necessary to ensure the aims above are met.[77] Where a petition is presented in respect of a company at a date subsequent to the presentation of a petition for the winding-up of that company, but before a provisional liquidator has been appointed or an order made for its winding-up, both petitions shall be heard together.[78]

The Position of a Charge on Book Debts

If a bank has a fixed charge on a company's book debts can it take any action to realise the whole or any part of its security? As a matter of common sense, considering the aims of examinership, and the need to put every asset and advantage towards the survival of the company, it would make no sense to allow one sum of money, or one asset, to be boxed off, and inaccessible to the examiner. He must have all the company's available assets at his disposal when trying to come up with a way to save the company as a going concern. In *Re Holidair*[79] the Supreme Court held that such an attempt, without the examiner's consent, was void.[80] If a floating charge crystallized because a receiver was appointed, it will decrystallise when the examiner is appointed: the asset, brought briefly down to earth, begins to float again. The examiner has the power to certify fresh borrowings during the examinership while the secured creditor looks on distraught, because the fresh borrowings will rank ahead of their secured claim as a cost and expense in the examinership.[81]

Powers of the Examiner

Any powers or rights which a statutory auditor has under the Companies Act 2014 (i.e. rights regarding the supplying of information, a duty on officers to co-operate[82]) apply to an examiner.[83] Where the court has appointed an examiner to a company no person is entitled to withhold from the examiner possession of any deed, instrument, or other document belonging to the company, or any accounting records, receipts, bills,

---

[77] *ibid*, s 522(4).

[78] *ibid*, s 522(5).

[79] [1994] 1 IR 416.

[80] The same is true if the bank tries to exercise a sale of a secured property. See also *Re Exchange Travel (Holdings) Ltd* [1991] BCLC 130.

[81] In general, see O'Donnell, "Appointing an Examiner: Learning to Live with the Culture of Corporate Rescue" (1997) *Bar Review* 246.

[82] See also s 526.

[83] Companies Act 2014, s 524(1).

invoices, or other papers of that nature relating to the accounts or trade, dealings or business of the company, or claim any lien on any aforementioned document or paper.[84]

The examiner has power to convene, set the agenda for, and preside at meetings of the board and general meetings and to propose motions or resolutions and to give reports to such meetings.[85] The examiner is entitled to reasonable notice[86] of, to attend and be heard at, all meetings of the board of directors of and all general meetings.[87] The examiner has a very broad power to "take whatever steps are necessary" to "halt, prevent or rectify" acts or omissions which in his opinion would likely be detrimental to the company.[88] The examiner can apply to court to determine or clarify any of his powers[89] and can "ascertain and agree claims against the company" if directed to by the court.[90] Usually the board of directors remains in situ for the course of the examinership[91] but the examiner can apply to court for an order allowing him to supplant the directors in any or all of their functions.[92]

The examiner has a limited right to repudiate a contract that has been entered into by the company to which he has been appointed prior to the period during which the company is under the protection of the court.[93] Any provision of an agreement entered into by the company that provides that the company shall not:

(a) Borrow moneys or otherwise obtain credit from any person other than that person or those persons; or

(b) Create or permit to subsist any mortgage, charge, lien or other encumbrance or any pledge over the whole or any part of the property or undertaking of the company

---

[84] *ibid*, s 527(1).

[85] *ibid*, s 524(2).

[86] "Reasonable notice" also means that the examiner must be given a description of the business to be transacted at any such meeting, in advance of the meeting, per s 524(4).

[87] Companies Act 2014, s 524(3).

[88] *ibid*, s 524(5) and (6).

[89] *ibid*, s 524(7).

[90] *ibid*, s 524(8).

[91] See the comments of Murphy J in *Re Edenpark Construction Ltd* [1994] 3 IR 126, at 136-7.

[92] Companies Act 2014, s 528.

[93] *ibid*, s 525(1).

shall not be binding on the company if:

(1) The examiner is of the opinion that the provision, were it to be enforced, would be likely to prejudice the survival of the company or the whole or any part of its undertaking as a going concern; and

(2) The examiner serves a notice on the other party or parties to the agreement in which the provision is contained informing the party or parties of that opinion.

If the conditions (1) and (2) above are satisfied then the kinds of provisions at (a) and (b) will not be binding, from the moment the examiner serves notice to this effect and this will last for the duration of the court protection.[94] The company under protection may apply to court for permission to repudiate certain contracts,[95] for example, to repudiate the lease of land.[96] Any such applications must be made by motion on notice to the examiner, to the other contracting party, and to any person who suffers loss or damage as a result of the repudiation.[97]

Examiner's Report

The examiner must formulate proposals for a compromise or scheme of arrangement in relation to the company "as soon as practicable after he or she is appointed".[98] This should be done within 35 days of his appointment: in practice, this is a tight time period, and the Act allows for an extension of time by the court.[99] One of the factors which makes the time period tight is that a meeting of members or creditors must take place, to consider proposals.[100] The examiner is allowed to dispense with the usual notice period for these kinds of meetings, but must give not less than three days notice.[101] In addition to the 70 days of court protection which comes with admission to examinership, the examiner can apply *ex parte* for a further

---

[94] *ibid*, s 525(2), (3), and (4).
[95] *ibid*, s 537.
[96] *Re Linen Supply of Ireland Ltd*, Unreported, Supreme Court, Murray CJ, 10 December 2009.
[97] RSC, Ord 75A, r 19.
[98] Companies Act 2014, s 534(1)(a).
[99] *ibid*, s 534(2)(b).
[100] *ibid*, s 540.
[101] *ibid*, s 534(2).

30 days[102]: this is particularly relevant where the examiner feels that he will be unable to deliver his report to the court within the 70 day period. Any party affected by the extension, may on notice of motion to the Examiner apply to the court to set the said order aside upon grounds to be specified and verified in an affidavit and on such application, the court may make such orders as it thinks fit.[103] When the examiner has prepared his report he must deliver it to the court by way of an *ex parte* application.[104] It must contain a full account of each meeting convened by the examiner, the proposals put before each meeting (which should be attached in an appendix).[105]

Confirmation of Proposals

As soon as the examiner's report is delivered to the court, the court will set a date for the consideration of the proposals and their possible confirmation.[106] This is a hearing at which a number of interested parties may be heard, including the directors of the company, and importantly, any creditor or member whose claim or interest would be impaired if the proposals were implemented. This hearing might be quite soon, or it might be delayed somewhat, where, for example, there is significant creditor opposition to the scheme of arrangement, one of the complaints of the creditors being that they have too little time to consider the scheme.[107] The court cannot confirm any proposals unless:

(a) At least one class of creditors whose interests or claims would be impaired by implementation of the proposals has accepted the proposals; and

(b) The court is satisfied that: (i) the proposals are fair and equitable in relation to any class of members or creditors that has not accepted the proposals and whose interests or claims would be impaired by

---

[102] *ibid*, s 534(3); Rules of the Superior Courts, Ord 75A, r 16 (SI No 255 of 2015 came into operation on 1 July 2015).

[103] Rules of the Superior Courts, Ord 75A, r 16.

[104] *ibid*, Ord 75A, r 17(1).

[105] *ibid*, Ord 75A, r 17(2).

[106] Companies Act 2014, s 541.

[107] This was the case in *Re Laragan Developments Ltd* [2009] IEHC 390 (Clarke J); the report was presented to Court on 26 June. Clarke J fixed 7 July for the proposed confirmation hearing and called this "an unusually long period." Objections to the report were to be submitted to the solicitors for the examiner by 2 July.

implementation; and (ii) the proposals are not unfairly prejudicial to the interests of any interested party.

It will not confirm any proposals if the sole or primary purpose of them is the avoidance of payment of tax due.[108] It will not confirm proposals in relation to a related company if they would impair the interests of the creditors of the company "in such a manner as to unfairly favour the interests of the creditors or members of any company to which it is related".[109] When the court does confirm proposals, they are binding on all the members or class or classes of members, and on all creditors or classes of creditors, who are affected, and binding on the company.[110] The court has the power to modify the proposals, rather than refuse them outright.[111]

Meaning of "Impairment"

A creditor's claim against a company is impaired if the creditor receives less in payment of his claim than the full amount due in respect of the claim at the date of presentation of the petition for the appointment of the examiner.[112] The interest of a member of a company in the company is impaired if: (a) the nominal value of his or her shareholding in the company is reduced; or (b) where the member is entitled to a fixed dividend in respect of his or her shareholding in the company, the amount of that dividend is reduced; or (c) the member is deprived of all or any part of the rights accruing to him or her by virtue of his or her shareholding in the company; or (d) the percentage of his or her interest in the total issued share capital of the company is reduced; or (e) the member is deprived of his or her shareholding in the company.[113] It is for the examiner to prove to the court that the proposals are fair and equitable.[114] Even if a creditor can show that he would do better in a winding-up, this will not

---

[108] Companies Act 2014, s 541(4).

[109] ibid, s 541(5).

[110] ibid, s 541(6).

[111] See, for example, *Selukwe Limited,* Unreported, High Court, 20 December, 1991, where Costello J rejected the part of the proposal which freed the directors from personal guarantees they had given to the bank. See also *Re Camden Street Investments Ltd* [2014] IEHC 86 (Finlay Geoghegan J, 28 February 2014).

[112] Companies Act 2014, s 539(5).

[113] ibid, s 539(6).

[114] *Re Eylewood Ltd* [2011] 1 ILRM 5.

necessarily incline the court to reject the proposals.[115] Fennelly J, in *Re SIAC Construction*,[116] stated: "[t]he court will need to assess any claim of a creditor to be unfairly prejudiced by proposals from all angles". O'Donnell J stated in *Re McInerney Homes Ltd*,[117] that it would not be "wise" to have in place a comprehensive definition of the circumstances of when a proposal would be unfair, and not necessary, because the Companies Act

> "appears to invite a Court to exercise its general sense of whether, in the round, any particular proposal is unfair or unfairly prejudicial to any interested party".

The court will look for a "credible basis" in any opposition.[118] In *Re Pelko Holdings Ltd*[119] the creditor, a financial institution, opposed the petition on the basis that it was "premature", despite the fact that the company was insolvent; this was an illogical argument which only sought to mask what Hogan J found to be the true reason: a simple "general dislike of the [examinership] process".

Costs of the Examinership

The court may from time to time make such orders as it thinks proper for payment of the remuneration and costs of, and reasonable expenses properly incurred by, an examiner.[120] These applications are made *ex parte*, supported by an affidavit which describes the work done by the examiner: his account should be thoroughly particularized.[121] The High Court has stated:

> "it is clear that the court must be astute to ensure that the examiner is remunerated only for work which falls properly

---

[115] In *Re Traffic Group* [2008] 3 IR 253 the Revenue argued that on a winding up there may have been more funds available to meet their entitlements as preferential creditor. Clarke J stated, at 264, "if there were an extreme and disproportionate disparity between the position of a creditor on a winding up and under the scheme proposed compared with the position of other creditors under both alternatives, same might be a factor to be properly taken into account in ruling against confirmation of the scheme."

[116] [2014] IESC 25, at para 72. See also *Re Antigen Holdings Ltd* [2001] 4 IR 600.

[117] *Re McInerney Homes Ltd* [2011] IESC 31.

[118] *Re McInerney Homes Ltd* [2010] IEHC 4 (Clarke J).

[119] [2014] IEHC 226 (High Court, Hogan J, 28 April 2014).

[120] Companies Act 2014, s 554.

[121] Rules of the Superior Courts, Ord 75A, r 22.

within his remit. If he does work in excess of that he cannot be remunerated for it."[122]

The court is very conscious of the costs of the examinership. In *Re Sharmane Ltd*[123] Finlay Geoghegan J stated that the total charge out costs computed from the hours spent and relevant hourly rates for the examiner and those working with him were only one factor to be considered and that the court "must also have regard to the nature of the work carried out, the complexity of the work and the importance or value of the work to the client".[124] In *Re Missford*[125] Kelly J reduced the hourly charge out rate of all personnel involved in the examination by 16%.[126] In *Re Marino Ltd*[127] Clarke J rejected the argument that there should be a fixed hourly rate charged by all insolvency practitioners, and allowed €375 per hour for partners in the case, €300 for associate directors and €80 for trainees. The question of the level of examiner's fees is something that usually only comes up in cases of a failed examinership.[128] In practice, an examiner will often have to negotiate his fee downwards to ensure a potentially viable scheme of arrangement (a reduction of 10% in overall fees is not unusual in successful examinerships). If the examinership fails, the company will usually go into either receivership or liquidation, in which case the costs of the examinership will ultimately be visited on the company's creditors.

Usually, the examiner is entitled to be indemnified in respect of his pay, his costs and his expenses out of the revenue of the business of the company to which he has been appointed, or the proceeds of realisation of the assets (including investments).[129] The costs and expenses which are sanctioned by the court are paid in full and in priority to any other claim, secured or unsecured.[130] They rank ahead of any debts arising out of any compromise or scheme of arrangement or in any receivership or winding-up of the company.

---

[122] *Re Missford* [2010] 3 IR 756 at 761.

[123] [2009] 4 IR 285.

[124] *ibid* at 297

[125] [2010] 3 IR 756.

[126] Kelly J followed *Re Coombe Importers Ltd*, Unreported, High Court, Hamilton CJ, 22 June 1995; In *Missford*, the interim examiner, a person of 25 years of insolvency experience, charged an hourly rate of €425. He was assisted by a supervisor, senior, semi-senior and junior. Their respective hourly rates were €210, €185, €150 and €100.

[127] [2010] IEHC 394.

[128] *Per* Clarke J, at para 3.2.

[129] Companies Act 2014, s 554(2).

[130] *ibid*, s 554(3).

STUDY GUIDE FOR STUDENTS

What follows is a guide for students, undergraduate and FE1, who wish to read the chapters in a way that focuses on examinable topics.

Chapter 1 – Introduction

Chapter 1 is introductory material, unlikely to form the basis of an exam question, but fundamental to an understanding of the different corporate structures available in Ireland.

Chapter 2 – Separate Legal Personality

One of the fundamental ideas in company law is this: You are a legal personality and if you incorporate a company it will have a *separate* legal personality. This idea began in *Salomon v Salomon & Co Ltd*. That is a case you should understand, but you would rarely need to go into the facts of the case in an exam (that might look like "padding"!). What is most important is that you can give illustrations of when the principle has applied. Chapter 2 gives you these. The next thing you need to know is when the principle will be disregarded. Be able to know the four circumstance for this, and be able to answer a question on all four as well as a question which focuses only on the single economic entity cases (know, too, that the concept of SEE has gone out of fashion).

Chapter 3 – Corporate Authority and Capacity

Most of the first part of this chapter focuses on the concept of "ostensible authority". There may be situations where directors or officers of the company enter contracts without being empowered to do so. The question of this chapter is "what happens in such cases?" Who loses out, the outsider company or the company the person who exceeded their authority belongs to? Whenever this is considered the test outlined by Lord Justice Diplock in *Freeman & Lockyer* must be applied. You need to know it and be able to cite other cases which illustrate what a representation can be (i.e. conduct, and a tacit representation). The chapter shows how this must be done, and gives particular attention to the first step in the test — the nature of a representation — because it is often the subject of confusion. Part II considers the doctrine of *ultra vires*, its origins, modification and the reasons for its abolition for the LTD (it has been retained for DACs).

Chapter 4, 5, and 6 – Directors

Together with corporate borrowing, "directors" is the most voluminous area of your company law course. It is an area of the course that you cannot do without and when it comes to exams it sometimes appears twice on one paper, in different guises. Scenarios involving directors often require you to combine your knowledge of their duties with other areas of this course, for example, the law on substantial property transactions between companies and directors (Chapter 6), the law on winding-up on just and equitable grounds (Chapter 16) and on oppression (Chapter 12), so you won't be fully ready to deal with those aspects until you have read those chapters.

Be ready to deal with the following problem type scenarios:

You may be presented with a scenario which will ask you to outline the common law duties of directors (you will very often need to do this at the outset) and go through the case law on conflicting business opportunities (sometimes there will be a substantial property transaction element thrown in). There is a large body of case law on conflicting business opportunities, but there are two or three essential cases, around which the rest orbit, and are useful to cite simply because they are more recent restatements of the rule. Sometimes a feature of the scenario will be that a director's wife has incorporated her own company, which rivals her husband's (but in reality, he is in collusion with her) (see *Stiefel Laboratories*).

A second kind of problem scenario may ask you to advise shareholders who have not received their dividend in the post. Can they require a director to declare a dividend? Is the company not "their company"? You will have to explain what powers the directors have to run the company and when their powers as shareholders come to the fore again. You will have to refer to directors' statutory duties (previously known as their common law duties); discuss the powers of the directors to manage the day-to-day business of the company; know case law on shareholders trying to usurp the day-to-day management of the company by the directors and to case law (e.g. *Flitcroft's case*) and statute on directors wrongly declaring dividends (e.g. s 122 of Companies Act 2014, dealt with in Chapter 10).

In a third scenario which requires you to begin with a discussion of directors' duties at common law and then go on to consider whether a transaction or arrangement would fall foul of ss 238 or 239 of Companies Act 2014 or require disclosure under s 231 of Companies Act 2014. You need to know what a "connected person" is. If someone connected to a director is carrying on a very similar business, what is the effect of that? What if one of the directors has set up a rival business which is ostensibly run by his wife? You may be told that the two directors in question are 50:50 shareholders in the company. This should trigger your knowledge of s 569(e) of Companies Act 2014 (see Chapter 16).

That leads us to essay questions. Here are the most common kinds of essay.

You may be asked to discuss whether you think s 158 of Companies Act 2014 is the cornerstone of corporate governance (this is the section that confers day-to-day powers of management on the directors: answer, yes it is).

Second, it is important to know who directors owe duties too. Traditionally it is to the company only, but a question sometimes appears which asks you whether this clear rule has been eroded over the course of the twentieth century (answer: the rule still holds good, but over the decades the courts have recognised a duty to creditors — when the company is headed toward insolvency — and statute has granted a useless, wishy-washy duty on directors to "have regard" to the company's employees. There is no duty owed by directors to shareholders in Ireland or the UK).

Third, you need to know how a person can become a director and what his duties and liabilities are as a director. There are three ways a person can become a director. The first is by appointment. The other two are when the court finds that the person in question played a significant role in the management of the company, either by calling the shots from a shadowy sideline (a "shadow director"), or by acting as a director in everything but name (a "*de facto* director").

Chapter 7 – Restriction and Disqualification

Questions on restriction are universally well-liked by exam candidates because they are easy. You need to know the five point test set out in *La Moselle* and approved in *Re Squash* and you need to have a case or two which bolsters each point. You must know the statutory language — that the onus is on the director to prove he acted honestly and responsibly. Most of the case law turns on questions of responsible or irresponsible behaviour. Findings of dishonesty are rare. For questions on disqualification, they key is to know your statute and be able to point to seven or eight cases which show varying degrees of bad corporate conduct. This will enable you to judge whether a person's behaviour would merit a two or a seven or a 12 year disqualification period.

Chapter 8 – Directors' Personal Liability on Insolvency

There are times when directors, or other officers of the company, will be obliged to pick up the tab for losses incurred as a result of their decisions, or will be forced to pay back money that they should not have received. There are very few cases on reckless and fraudulent trading so you should know your statute well and know *Hefferon Kearns* (1993), *PSK Construction Ltd* (2009) and *Hunting Lodges* (1986) well. You should know examples of the kind of conduct that the courts will deem fraudulent. A second area in the chapter is the failure to keep proper books of account: know, for starters, *Re Mantruck Services Ltd* (1997) and *Re Dev Oil and Gas Ltd* (2008). Misfeasance is rarely invoked but the chapter gives you two important Irish cases on it.

Chapter 9 – Meetings

Two kinds of question usually arise out of this material. The first asks you to describe the three ways in which members may make decisions (in general meeting by resolution, by using the written procedure, by informal agreement — called the *Buchanan* or *Duomatic* Principle). The second kind of question asks you to contract the meetings of members with those of directors (answer, the meetings of members are subject to a huge number of rules — pay particular attention to what is necessary for a meeting to be properly called, e.g. notice and quorum — and the meetings of directors are very informal).

Chapter 10 – Shares and Membership

This chapter and the previous one may be called "general knowledge" chapters. They are not often the subject of specific questions in exams, but you need to be aware of the material because it is basic to the fabric of company law and runs through the other areas of the course. There are features like the register of members, the rights and duties of shareholders (right to vote, to a dividend, to transfer shares, etc), the fact that directors have to declare their interest in shares, how to define a share, and the circumstances surrounding the declaration of dividends, which is fertile ground for problem questions. You should be able to define a share in terms of the rights it gives and the obligations it confers.

Chapter 11 – Transfer of Shares

There are two strands to this chapter: the right of directors to refuse to register a transfer of shares, and a treatment of pre-emption clauses. Sometimes students are asked to take an examiner through this area of the law step-by-step in an essay question. More often, students will be faced with a problem question. A classic share transfer scenario would ask you to advise two directors as to the entitlement of the wife/spouse of the deceased third director, whom they don't like, to be registered and her right to a dividend and attend the AGM (short answer, the rights of the directors are the same as if the deceased member were alive and making a share transfer). A variation on this is where one shareholder has transferred his/her shares to an "outsider", the outsider comes to the directors looking to be registered and they are "horrified" because they are afraid that this spells the end of their closely held company, and turn to you for advice. Another scenario might run as follows: A man incorporates a business and wants to give a shareholding to an employee who had been pressing for some time to become a partner. He's afraid that, at some point, this person will sell them on to whomever he feels like, so you have to advise him on directors' rights of refusal and pre-emption clauses. The director will want to know what happens if the other person dies. If there is a death in the question, you will be taking about "transmission" of shares (i.e. it happens by operation of law). In all other cases, you are dealing with "transfer" of shares. The key to directors successfully refusing a transfer of shares is that they must act bona fide and in the interests of the company.

Chapter 12 – Protection of Minorities

Shareholders' interests may be disregarded, or they may be oppressed by the way directors are exercising their powers, or by the manner in which the company's affairs are being conducted. If this occurs the party complaining of the wrong may apply to court for relief under s 212 of Companies Act 2014. If the court is of the opinion that any of the above are happening it has power to make "such order as it thinks fit...for regulating the conduct of the company's affairs in future...with a view to bringing to an end the matters complained of". The court is given a broad power. It can direct or prohibit any act. It can cancel or vary any transaction. It can order that the shares of any party be bought, either by other members or the company itself. If the court has altered the company's memorandum or articles the company may not change them back after the proceedings are done: in fact, any change in this way made by the court has the same effect as if it were made by a resolution of the company, and a copy of the order must be delivered to the CRO within twenty-one days of it being made. Thus, s 212 is a powerful remedy for oppressed shareholders. When the topic comes up in exams there are three common essay questions. The first asks you to simply discuss s 212, arguing whether or not it is an effective protection against oppression. The second will ask you to contrast s 212 with the rule in *Foss v Harbottle*, an old common law rule that is alive and well but rarely invoked with success. The third might ask you to discuss s 212 generally, noting any limitations it has (answer: it is only available to members and mismanagement of the company will not constitute oppression). When the topic comes up as a problem question, the classic scenario is as follows: A director and minority shareholder is being excluded from the day-to-day running of the business by the other two directors. The other two tell him not to bother opposing them because they are able to outvote him. They may say things that can have the air of a threat, such as "we can remove you as a director because we have the majority shareholding". They may have transferred an asset of the company — perhaps at market value, in which case he's simply being excluded from the running of the business, but perhaps to another company which they control, and at an undervalue, in which case they are perpetrating a fraud on the company and disregarding his interests. The oppressed director/shareholder will come to you for advice and you have to tell him about s 212 and possibly the exceptions to the rule in *Foss v Harbottle*. Another scenario could involve a pair of siblings or friends or directors who have fallen out. Up until their falling out they each ran a distinct part of the business. Now each may be behaving in a way that harms the other person's side of the business (be able to discuss winding up for just and equitable reasons, s 569(e), Chapter 16). A variation on this may require you to discuss directors' duties and the provisions that deal with substantial property transactions involving directors and the prohibition of loans to directors and connected persons (covered in chapter 6).

Chapter 13 – Capital Maintenance

Capital maintenance is the most technical area of your company law course. The rules are set out in statute and unlike, perhaps, topics such as directors' duties, receivers, winding-up, or disregarding corporate personality, the area doesn't lend itself to being understood intuitively. It will help to focus your mind when reading the chapter if you if you consider throughout the most popular forms of question that arise out of the area. The first is an essay question, something like this: "The purpose behind capital maintenance is the protection of a company's creditors. Discuss". The second kind of question is a problem question. It requires you almost exclusively to focus on s 82 of Companies Act 2014, and to advise clients of the steps they must take to successfully complete the Summary Approval Procedure, and the consequences of failing to do so.

In addition to this you should know the statute which prohibits companies from paying dividends to shareholders other than out of their distributable reserves, the general rule which prohibits companies from reducing their share capital and the rule which allows companies to issue and buy back redeemable shares.

Chapter 14 – Company Borrowing: Charges

The importance of this area cannot be overstated. *Together with the material on "directors", this is the largest chapter in the book.* It can be split into three parts, though there is significant overlap: (1) you should be able to define what a floating charge is in contrast to a fixed charge (using case law such as *Yorkshire Woolcombers*, *Illingworth*, the *Cosslett* case, *Re JD Brian*); (2) you should know the two kinds of procedure for the registration of charges, the consequences for failing to register a charge and the possibility of asking the court to register a charge late; (3) you should know the four types of retention of title clauses, illustrating each with at one or two cases, knowing which two types must be registered and which two types do not need to be registered. Know the kind of language used in charges (such as the retention of "equitable and beneficial ownership" in *Bond Worth* and the "irreversibly mixed" comments in *Borden (UK)*).

Chapter 15 – Receivers

With this chapter, we enter into the insolvency part of the course. When a bank has a charge on a property, and the borrower defaults on repayments, the bank can appoint a person known as a receiver to the property, or to the company, depending on the terms of the agreement. It is his job to sell the charged assets with a view to satisfying the debt. The topic lends itself to problem questions. Often they will be divided into three parts. You need to know: (1) about the unique agency of receivers and what the law says with regard to obtaining the best possible price for the assets they are selling, and what duties receivers owe to the company; (2) what duties receivers owe to guarantors of the company's debt; and (3) what duties receivers owe to unsecured creditors.

Chapter 16 – Liquidators and Liquidations

The first half of this chapter deals with things that should be in your general knowledge: how is a liquidator appointed? What kinds of liquidator are there? What powers does the liquidator have? Can a members' voluntary liquidation be converted to a creditors' voluntary liquidation? Can a voluntary liquidation be converted to a court-supervised ("official") liquidation? And so on.

The second half of the chapter deals with the grounds under which the court will wind up a company. Two in particular are important — winding-up for inability to pay debts and winding up for just and equitable reasons. You should know a lot of case law on each area as they lend themselves to problem questions.

The chapter then discusses the different kinds of voluntary liquidations (members' and creditors'), the committee of inspection, and so on. It discusses the order of priority in a liquidation (i.e. who gets paid by the liquidator and in what order). The chapter ends with two more "general knowledge" sections: how a winding up is completed and information about the insolvency regulation (neither of which is usually exam material).

Chapter 17 – Realisation of Assets

When a liquidator arrives on the scene he may find that some of the company's money or assets have been spirited away shortly before his appointment. If this were allowed to stand, the creditors would lose out. To prevent it from happening with impunity, the legislature enacted a number of provisions that allow liquidators to obtain court orders for the return of the missing assets. There are four relevant sections in Companies Act 2014 – ss 604 and 608 (unfair preferences and fraudulent dispositions), s 602 (post-commencement dispositions), and s 597 (circumstances in which a floating charge will be deemed to be invalid). Know that s 604 has a weakness: it requires subjective intent to be proven. An application under s 604 should always be taken with an application under s 608, which concerns itself with the *effect* of the transaction. For s 602, know a number of cases which illustrate the breadth of the term "disposition".

Chapter 18 – Examinership

Examinership is a process which did not exist in Ireland before 1990. It was introduced to provide help for companies which were in danger of failing. If a company can satisfy the court of the necessary proofs the court will grant it a period of protection, during which it can regroup, make proposals to restructure or write down debts, and during which it will be shielded from all efforts by creditors to commence proceedings against it or to enforce securities. Problem questions often come in three parts. You should know: (1) the law in relation to "getting over the line" to appoint an examiner; (2) cases which throw light on the factors that influence the court when it considers whether the company is suitable; and (3) what the effect of examinership is on the company and its creditors, on receivers, and on provisional liquidators.

Index

M

N

O